I0421760

Jane K. Marshall

Bearing Witness
in the
Time of Trump

Bearing Witness in the Time of Trump
by
Jane K. Marshall

© 2019 by Jane K. Marshall.

All rights reserved. In accordance with the U. S. Copyright Act of 1976, the scanning, uploading and electronic sharing of any part of this book without the written permission of the author/publisher is unlawful piracy or theft of the author's intellectual property. If you would like to use material from this book (other than for review purposes), prior written permission must be obtained by contacting the author. Thank you for your support of the author's rights.

Marshall, Jane K.
Bearing Witness in the Time of Trump

Summary: Bearing Witness: One Woman's Observations in the Time of Trump

ISBN: 978-1070631974

Cape Cod Publishing
Cape Cod, MA 02632

Published in the United States of America

The cover design was created especially for this book by Alison Victoria Sullivan, Illustrator, Cape Cod, MA.

Over the past three years or so, reading the "manuscript of the day" evolved into a ritual of sorts. I would read the day's essay aloud in the comfort of our living room while Bill and Lily (the cat) listened carefully. Bill was very encouraging and often supported the work with valuable suggestions. Lily, not so much... However, Bill was of the opinion that Lily enjoyed the sound of my voice, while he looked forward to whatever it was that I had conjured on a particular day. "It's fun," he said. Well, it was that for me as well.

Alison Sullivan, whose husband remains the best teacher of my memory, radiated unwavering excitement as to the project. Like Bill, she provided sage suggestions and a teacher's encouragement. Alison also provided the wonderful art of the cover and inside title page. And, it must be said, art often illuminates in a way that surpasses even words.

Michael Halloran, a man of infinite patience and kindness, "saved the day" on several occasions with his computer expertise. Once even making an unscheduled "house call" at 9 PM!

Thank you Bill, Alison, Mike, and many others, those who read bits and pieces of the manuscript in progress. For me, writing is the beginning of conversation. I am so grateful to those who listened, commented, and generally supported the belief that a citizen's voice might just matter.

Many thanks, too, for Sharon D. Anderson of the Cape Cod Writer's Studio. Her invaluable knowledge couched in kindness saw me through the process of publishing.

To Bill Munroe

Who listened...and listened...and listened...
And cared.

Author's Note

"The American people believe..." This arrogant pronouncement, often utilized by particularly self-serving politicians, undermines the will of the electorate. Far from illustrating truth as to public sentiment, this faux and manipulative statement attempts to corral public thought. The practitioners of this form of marketing most readily engage in Washington power-games, cavalierly excluding their constituents by way of limited public discourse. To be sure, "town halls" happen occasionally; however, these gatherings sometimes amount to publicity stunts - planned after the waters have been carefully tested. How then can voters telegraph actual beliefs and thoughts? Though letters to editors of print newspapers offer a voice for the voiceless, the brevity of these opinion pieces denies a substantial understanding of the experience and ideas of those governed.

The impetus for writing *Bearing Witness*, giving a voice to the governed, drives the narrative of my book. In this time of societal and intellectual enclave, the need for a "speaking out" - in order to provide a platform for the concerns of citizens - proves particularly urgent and necessary. Though my ideas reflect a particular stance regarding the rise of Donald Trump, the audience I envision for this work is broad. Agree or not with arguments presented, *Bearing Witness*, above all, represents a call for respect for those who are not in positions of power. Moreover, the outsider placement of a typical citizen may indeed provide an objective and therefore unbiased view - a view worth noting.

We ought to consider world history at times such as these. Also, I believe we must vigilantly review "near history" - those details of our individual memory as they relate to political events. This was the premise of my project: the notion that emotional as well as intellectual processes be expressed, shared and saved.

Bearing Witness: One Woman's Observations in the Time of Trump (an alternate title) presents a diary of sorts, that is, it was written episodically as I endeavored to respond to what I was witnessing during Trump's candidacy, the transition, the early days of Trump's presidency and beyond. Some of the entries are brief, especially in the candidacy section. Others tender full-blown essays. Satirical poetry and a fiction section, based on George Orwell's *Animal Farm,* are included as well.

Bearing Witness offers an honest and realistic history of my and, most likely, others' reactions to unprecedented American political-maneuvering, that which precipitated an essential incredulity. The mood of the work is fluid, reflecting both unfolding developments and a way of coping with these events. (Humor is sometimes evident amid detailed accounts of serious concerns.)

While some might argue journalistic history inevitably provides details of behavior just as soon not revisited, I believe it is incumbent on citizens to remember vividly, for contemplating, even near history, enables a more comprehensive assessment of our nation's standing - presumably leading to improvement.

Contents

Preface

Part One: Donald J. Trump's Destructive Candidacy

Part Two: The Transition

Part Three: The Early Days of Trump's Presidency

Part Four: Fiction Addendum (*Animal Farm* Revisited)

Part Five: Parting Shots

How to Read/What to Expect from this Book

Written over the course of a three-year period, *Bearing Witness* imparts particular reactions to on-going events. Therefore, the impetus for each of its five sections varies.

Part One makes the case for voting against Trump amid unfolding developments.

Part Two illustrates an essential incredulity as to Trump's ascendancy, necessarily coupled with expressed emotion, a mirroring of an "age of anxiety" precipitated by the president-elect's erratic verbiage and behavior. Part Two is perhaps the least circumspect of the sections. Yet, because it memorializes an honest response reflective of many a citizen, an important story is told, one that should not be overlooked.

Part Three offers excruciating detail as to the early days of Trump's presidency with the president's and his surrogates' frenetic behaviors carefully monitored. This section offers, by far, the most exacting coverage of day-to-day developments. Part Three relied on the gargantuan effort of the fourth estate in its coverage of a frenzy of activity.

Part Four seeks to illustrate where we find ourselves, by way of political fiction based on George Orwell's *Animal Farm*. Part Four also offers a respite from the unprecedented pace of developing news and events deliberately choreographed by the Trump administration.

Part Five reflects the firmly entrenched ethos and mind-set of Trump's administration and offers response by way of intellectual analysis. Throughout the book, but especially in Part Five, I have endeavored to understand and convey understanding through analogy, memory of past experience and by way of recalled literature/history. The duration of the writing of this book and the episodic nature of its structure has resulted in a varied tone and uneven quality. However, each section serves a purpose and each illustrates the reality of an unprecedented time in our history.

Preface

As I see it now, I was essentially driven; bearing witness to the unfolding events of the past three years or so seemed urgently necessary, for I was (and remain) astounded and dismayed by what I see as the hood-winking of America.

Never before have we seen antithetical reality consumed so eagerly. Never before have we witnessed a relentless and extensive coarsening of discourse - a discourse that would ultimately preclude thought in favor of blind rage. One man, enamored with the practice of manipulation, demanded attention and held court thereby halting rational debate and the dissemination of vital information and thoughtful ideas.

Who enabled such a debacle? I suspect we will look back and note the culpability of many including cable-news producers, who gleefully gave Trump a platform for foolery, as well as various power-holders. However, in the long-term, we must address our very culture: our acceptance of the palaver of reality-shows, our winner/loser mentality as well as our penchant for tribalism, sometimes precipitated by profound feelings of alienation. In the end, America accepted "divide and conquer" - did not manage "heal and find common ground."

Part One: Donald J. Trump's Destructive Candidacy

T-Rump

Like T-Rex, a horrifying dinosaur fascinating to young children, T-Rump pillages our landscape. But this is no fantasy. Trump is single-handedly undermining a country of decent values and ideas with talk that damages our standing in the world and, perhaps even more important, our psyche, for the language of hatred is particularly corrosive.

Trump does this with supreme arrogance. He has gleefully stated something on the order of: "I could shoot someone on Fifth Avenue and get away with it." In fact, he has "gotten away with murder" - spewing vile and egregious statements - seemingly with impunity. Slanderous statements, such as those that insinuate that our sitting president is somehow in cahoots with ISIS and now a double-down statement that declares that both President Obama and Secretary Clinton are "founders of ISIS" result in hand-wringing but no real consequences for T-Rump. It has been this way throughout his candidacy. Trump's rhetoric has exponentially escalated with each hate-filled lie. "Just how far can I go?" he must ask himself. The answer appears to be dangerously far.

I am reminded of a very frightening book, *Lord of the Flies*, that depicts murderous children who lost all of their inherent decency by succumbing to fear (our current fear has to do with changing demographics and economic conditions). It all started with name-calling. But in the end, "Piggy" was dead; the children had forfeited their humanity and any hope of peace.

I truly believe that we, the citizens of the United States, will not reprise *Lord of the Flies*. That we have come this far, though, is cause for concern. We must redress the wrongs of Donald Trump - and ask ourselves "How have we come to this?"

When Politics and Entertainment Merge

Well, knock me down with a feather, hardly... Former governor Rick Perry is to appear on "Dancing with the Stars." Surprise, surprise. Perhaps Donald Trump will follow him next season. One can only hope... My point? A line has. been crossed. A confluence of politics and entertainment has occurred thereby endangering our democracy. Too many potential candidates for President of the United States view the job as a venue for attention or accolades, and competition, the game, is played for its own sake only. Needless to say, Trump is a prime example of a reality-TV presidential candidate. Fantasy has become reality. We are viewing a vast video-game of "I'm a winner." Especially flagrant this election season, in truth, such madness has been brewing for some time now.

Remember Sarah Palin? How could you forget? She's made a name for herself in the reality-show context. Why, oh why, did John McCain choose her as a running mate back in 2008? I suspect he chose her because she was perceived as physically attractive, a beauty-queen candidate. McCain did not choose her for her vast experience as a legislator or political leader. I doubt very much that he would have considered a Golda Meir look-alike. We noted McCain's priority, the precursor to his ultimate defeat; few could countenance the notion of Palin as a standby-president. Fortunately, the public was not as enamored with superficial competition as McCain had thought.

We have much to do in order to understand truly the role of media in presenting candidates to the public. Certainly, the visual presentation of a candidate influences a visceral reaction. For example, those who merely heard the Nixon/Kennedy debate concluded that Nixon had won while TV viewers, when offered a choice between the cool, attractive candidate and his perspiring, mundane counterpart, concluded otherwise. Exactly what did this mean? We ought to ask.

Well, we've come a long way from 1960s politics, in any event. Now the entertainment factor rules supreme. News outlets are owned by entertainment corporations. These same news outlets often appeal to the superficial need of the electorate in order to garner a profit. The hard work of actually listening to the specific ideas of candidates has been usurped by name-calling and unsubstantiated innuendo - the creation of emotionally-wrought dysfunction - Carol Burnett's "Mama's Family" recreated in a political race. Not funny at all, when one considers the consequences of deciding a vote via such entertainment...

Expediency and Politics

We are quite used to promises made by politicians - promises geared to particular audiences during the throes of a campaign. Politicians are often wedded to the notion of pleasing all of the people all of the time, though not all at the same time. It comes with the territory. To be fair, it makes sense to address issues of interest to particular groups or segments of society - preferable to ignoring important issues.

And it's true that knowing one's audience is essential when offering a stump speech. If one momentarily forgets audience, or veers off audience-driven needs, one is apt to cause oneself a metaphorical injury. When Hillary Clinton spoke of closing coal mines in coal country, she was met with derision - even though she spoke of the need to replace mining jobs with other energy jobs. I guess it was the insensitive way she put her proposal, to the very specific crowd, that

5

did her in. Certainly, Hillary evinced an honesty during her speech, for at some point coal will have to go. Cleaner options simply make sense. However, honesty is not always the best policy in the optics of a campaign, unfortunately. A misstep in the name of verisimilitude may prove lethal.

Recently, the other side of the coin, the pandering to audience, was illustrated in a remarkably ludicrous way. In the space of hours, Donald Trump presented radically different visions of his immigration policy. In Mexico, along-side the president of Mexico, he evinced a conciliatory, measured stance. A few hours later in Arizona he was back to bombast and a hardline position - this as he faced his base. Thereafter, Trump stated: "I'm softening. I'm hardening. I'm softening..." Sort of reminded me of the classic Daffy Duck cartoon: you remember, when Daffy went from "wabbit season" to "duck season" in the space of a few minutes with less than pleasing results. In Donald's case, the public and media were left scratching their heads. No problem for Donald, for he was still generating news coverage while the pundits attempted to dance on the point of a pin. Unbelievable.

Obviously, the views of American citizens are not monolithic but are based on divergent experience. Too often politicians take on a "Music Man" stance (Remember that musical?) - that of an outsider who professes to understand the fears and realities of particular communities. Better to educate oneself as to the underlying feelings and concerns of variant constituencies. Such an education would require listening to the voices of individuals directly. I would welcome the idea of "citizen summits" - meetings arranged to enable honest conversations. Too often, candidates make assumptions as to experience based on outside punditry and their own limited, personal participation.

A place to start might be conversations with authors of diverse background, authors who have created pictures of American life in various communities, people who have witnessed and lived involvements that speak to the needs of actual human beings. For examples, candidates might sit down with J.D. Vance (*Hillbilly Elegy*) in order to glimpse the truth of "rust belt" life. Jacqueline Woodson (*Another Brooklyn*) has spoken eloquently of a particular urban-reality. Thus, a conversation with her would undoubtedly prove enlightening.

The Office of the Presidency requires a listening and a learning. Less ego. Fewer assumptions. More compassion.

Thoughts on Immigration

It seems to me that the subject of immigration is a particularly thorny one. On the one hand, I realize that there are many in the world who are being persecuted and killed. I wish to save the innocent children of Aleppo who deserve a chance at life, for example. ("Give me your tired, your poor..." - The Statue of Liberty). Yet, I am also reminded of a conversation I had with the wife of the minister of a church in New Haven. Her husband is European, so they visit family there frequently. She spoke movingly of a clash of cultures: Jewish people there, for example, are loath to speak up against the minority culture as practiced by Muslim immigrants, for fear that hatred, so well understood by victims of the Holocaust, would be unleashed. Certainly, it is intolerable to expect those of the original, majority culture to witness the slaughter of animals on balconies (for example) in the name of religious tolerance. There must be a rapprochement or a two-way understanding of belief and custom. Respect is paramount, and sensitivity to the beliefs of all parties must be practiced.

I'm also aware that the radicalization of immigrants often occurs not in the first generation of immigration but in the second and third. One must ask why this is so. I suspect that the children of immigrants have witnessed disrespect and worse. Having no memorable knowledge of conditions in their originating countries, they lash out against the practiced prejudice of the new culture.

We have witnessed such prejudice in our own culture with every wave of immigration. I became particularly aware of this phenomenon when living in Washington Heights (Manhattan). The neighborhood had a history of intolerance and upheaval. First, Jewish families faced difficulties - to be followed by a wave of Irish immigrants who dealt with disrespect as well. Later, Puerto Ricans moved in who would ultimately be displaced by Dominicans. There was no melting-pot mentality evident, but rather the existence of enclaves inhabited by those who would hunker down and hope for a way forward.

I think that suspicion and fear of the other is especially rife in anonymous cities. In smaller communities, perhaps there exists the possibility for one-to-one human interaction. I do know that when the New Haven high school of my teaching experience was small, there was very little difficulty as to differences of religion, ethnicity or, for that matter, sexual orientation - the latter especially note-worthy considering the adolescent population. However, I do realize that the aforementioned may be impossibly naive. Smaller communities have indeed experienced upheavals having to do with unfairness and clashes of cultures.

Yet, I believe that a nation built on immigration (US) must find a way to practice fair immigration. I don't believe in isolationism. I do believe in mutual respect and empathy. Immigration presents a very complex conundrum, to be sure, but not necessarily an impossible one. Perhaps we can learn from history. Perhaps we or our children will consciously work to find a tolerable and tolerant way. To do otherwise is to negate the very premise of our country.

And They've Said We're Emotional?

Women have often been maligned as too emotional. That's rich. Given that Trump's base is comprised largely of white, working-class men who support his entirely emotion-driven campaign, one has to question that old saw. Think about it. Please. Where are the intellectual ideas in Trump's verbiage? What specifics has he offered aside from a wall - an appeal to jingoistic fear - or a banning of Muslims - ditto.

As to Trump's rhetoric? Pure emotion. Measured speech by others, including President Obama, is erroneously viewed by some as merely "politically correct." Yet, language matters. In the larger world, one should not spew incendiary remarks willy-nilly, for every utterance is scrutinized by friend and foe alike. One does not mouth off with impunity. In fact, incendiary words may be reused as weapons to our detriment. It is not good enough to be required to state again and again: "What I meant was..."

Then there is the notion of audience. Emotional speech is meant to manipulate an audience - not to think, but to feel only. The intent of such speech is self-serving. Conversely, the rhetoric of the intellect attempts to explain plans - ideas that should be unpacked carefully. Measured speech recognizes complexity. Trump's simplistic, off-the-cuff talk is essentially empty of intellect, the measure of an unqualified hysteria-monger. Let us trump Trump with (gasp) thought.

Strength Through Civility

For months, we have been subjected to the invective of Donald Trump. At first, I thought: Let's not join him in displays of name-calling and immature behavior. Let's stick to the issues and call him on every simplistic, seemingly off-the-cuff idea that he espouses. Build a wall? Really? Such an idea smacks of the gated-community culture and jingoistic isolationism. Deport all undocumented immigrants? An impossible task - not to mention the moral and economic implications of such a policy. Sit down with the North Korean dictator and give ultimatums to NATO? Donald, do you understand the meaning of the word, ally? Prohibit all Muslims from entering the country? Use surveillance in Muslim communities, existent in our country? These ideas undermine the very fabric of our multi-cultural, immigrant-built society. Not to put too fine a point on it, Donald, you don't know what you're talking about.

You have equaled any reality-show I can think of for vulgar, idiotic language and puerile innuendo. The media is fascinated with you. Their mistake, in my opinion. But we live in an entertainment-driven culture. Kind of like the old Roman Empire days when unfortunates at the Coliseum were fed to the lions. And we all know what happened to the Roman Empire... Well, perhaps you don't, Donald. Let's just say, it wasn't pretty.

Now your Republican party-members are calling on you to get serious. "Quit the name-calling and focus on issues," they say. Well, I am of the opinion that it's too late for such a tactic. You have unleashed an incivility that will soon come back to bite you. For example, perhaps someone will print out "Trump's a Rump!" bumper-stickers by the millions and distribute them via social media. Might prove to be a lucrative enterprise... Pithy little slogan, isn't it? And while all of this school-yard tit-for-tat ensues, "Rome burns." Disgraceful.

Leadership in a thriving democracy promotes strength through civility and unity. Weakness resides in name-calling nonsense, the precursor to division and an ultimate undermining of our very identity.

One final point: Incivility, more often than not, is employed as a cover for broad-based ignorance.

Fear and "Super-Man" Trump

Fear: a reaction to perceived threat, an emotion easily manipulated by those who hope to attain power - well-used by demagogues.

The rhetoric of fear is bombastic and manipulative, its premise based on understanding that those who succumb to base fear welcome "saviors." The demagogue/ "Super-Man" speaks: "I will make it right. I will provide jobs for all. I will crush our enemies." No plans are provided. No thoughtful response is required. The populace is not encouraged to become part of the solution. Rhetorical fear-mongering fosters juvenile regression and/or the impotence of intellect overrun by emotion.

Roosevelt was correct when he said: "The only thing we have to fear is fear itself." If the populace succumbs to fear and demagoguery, we will have morphed into unthinking children, easily swayed and manipulated. We will have sacrificed our value. We are our own worst enemies when we fail to think for ourselves, when we relinquish our adult roles.

Promises and platitudes will not solve our problems. Demand more from those who profess to lead. Take the lead as well, for the intellect of the electorate matters. We know that "Super-Man" doesn't really exist... but, we do.

Trump=Demise of Respect=Un-American

Trump's rhetoric is fundamentally un-American. This isn't fun and games anymore. Forget "It's not personal. It's just business." When a candidate for the highest office in the land smears a duly-elected, sitting president with outrageous slander, he should be held accountable. Evidently, the Donald appears to be incapable of subtle thought processes. Whatever drifts into his mind drifts out. However, to suggest that President Obama may know too well the machinations of ISIS is akin to yelling "Fire!" in a crowded theatre.

Trump respects no one. Not immigrants nor women nor, indeed, the very premise of these United States. He foments hatred by way of instilling fear in the electorate. He lives in an animal world of fight or flight. He wants us to live there as well. But we are not animals; rather, we are rational, thinking human beings. We shall not be cowed by fear. We shall instead unite by way of rational discernment. Our disagreements must be sorted out with respect and cogent behavior. For if we succumb to base fear, we shall destroy ourselves from within. We are Americans - presumably united in our strength and our will to ensure "justice for all."

It has been said: "Where there is no vision, the people perish. Where there is division, there is strife. Where there is unity, strength." Trump's vision is bogus, built on the sound-bites of hubris. He seeks to divide in order to conquer, this for his own gratification only. Yet, his vitriol will not be rewarded, for this country, these United States, "the home of the brave," will not be cowed by disrespect and resultant unrest.

Especially now, we must denounce fear and embrace civility in our discourse, presumably a discourse that transcends entertainment-value and lives in a wiser place. Then "We shall overcome..." - the dark days of Trump as well as hatred in all of its manifestations.

On Experience and in Praise of "Useless" Degrees

I got to thinking about the experience necessary for the Office of President of the United States. Perhaps government experience affords a practical necessity. Hillary Clinton knows the landscape and has worked her way through it, not always with success, but acquiring a learning and, in the process, accepting the reality of having to depart from old ideas on occasion. Moreover, her general experience includes an attitude of working respectfully with people, with purpose beyond self, transcending the mere business of self-enhancement, I think. Donald Trump, on the other hand, literally knows business only, and he has dealt with people solely on his terms throughout. He rarely listens or questions.

Which leads me to my essential question and point: How does one assess necessary experience? Are large life-experiences and diverse educational experiences prerequisites for the "top" job?

As an aside, I was hired once for a position based on my "useless" English degree along with my experience as a volunteer in the Child Life Center of a large New York hospital. My title? Recreational Therapist. I had no hospital credentials nor a degree in occupational therapy. To be sure, the hirer had witnessed my interactions with hospitalized children. Yet, I'll always remember that she noted as well:

13

"Anyone who studied literature must have an interest and an affinity for the emotional workings of others' minds." So much for denigrating a "useless" English degree. Later on, I would become a teacher of literature but, interestingly enough, my hospital experience served me well as I considered and realized the humanitarian scope of the work of a high school English teacher. My point? Broad-based humanities-study and experience matter.

In fact, temperament based on humanitarian awareness is essential - especially for the job of president. For example, operating as the President of the United States demands an understanding of the workings of diplomacy - considering diverse opinions and viewpoints. Nothing good is accomplished without a listening of variant expression. Moreover, the presidency requires an understanding of others that goes beyond the con-man assessment of weaknesses to be used via manipulation. Quite simply, others must be acknowledged and respected. Though we rarely speak of the necessity of broad-based humanities-education and/or experience as a background requisite for the office, perhaps we should.

Arguably, Abraham Lincoln was the finest president to ever serve this country. Think for a moment of the temperament and the interests of this paragon of a president. First, and perhaps foremost, he was a humble man. He was also a man of continuing self-development, as he frequently questioned himself and engaged in self-education, including the study of literature. And Lincoln wrote speeches that transcended politics - speeches that healed a nation, as he considered the vanquished as well as the victorious. He was a humanist precisely because he lived beyond self - intellectually and emotionally. In a sense he still lives, for his example serves as a model for what the presidency can be honest, hopeful, unifying and, in the end, even transformational.

In the future, perhaps we will once again revere a humanities-based, educational system that crosses divides through study of human philosophy and expression, lately lacking with education's mere information-driven focus. Perhaps, one day, we will produce another Lincoln.

As to today's Republican Party and its professed ownership of "the party of Lincoln", one cannot imagine a GOP leader of current manifestation (Trump, Ryan, McConnell) uttering the following words:

"With malice toward none; with charity for all, with firmness in the right; as God gives us to see right, let us strive to finish the work we are in; to bind up the nation's wounds; to care for him who shall have borne the battle, and for his widow and his orphan - to do all which may achieve and cherish a just, and a lasting peace, among ourselves, and with all nations."

- from Lincoln's Second Inaugural Address

Republican Presidential Quiz

Instructions: Match quotations with speakers. (A=Abraham Lincoln; B=Dwight Eisenhower; C=Donald Trump.)

1. "America will never be destroyed from the outside. If we falter, and lose our freedoms, it will be because we have destroyed ourselves."

2. "This world of ours...must avoid becoming a community of dreadful fear and hate, and be, instead, a proud confederation of mutual trust and respect."

3. "When someone challenges you, fight back, be brutal, be tough."

4. "You don't lead by hitting people over the head - that's assault, not leadership."

5. "There's nobody bigger and better at the military than I am."

6. "I hate war, as only a soldier who has lived it can, only as one who has seen its brutality and stupidity."

7. "Military glory - the attractive rainbow, that rises in showers of blood."

8. "If you can get good ratings, they'll cover you even if you have nothing to say."

9. "'Tis better to be silent and be thought a fool than to speak and remove all doubt."

Answers: 1. A (Lincoln) 2. B (Eisenhower) 3. C (Trump) 4. B (Eisenhower) 5. C (Trump) 6. B (Eisenhower) 7. A (Lincoln) 8. C (Trump) 9. A (Lincoln)

I ask you: Which quotations connote strength, experience, character and wisdom - characteristics required for the Office of President of the United States?

The Danger of Entitlement

When one is born into a state of entitlement, danger looms. I know that this sounds counterintuitive. Obviously, one's material needs are met; however, the process of self-development with regard to learning empathy and fairness may be undermined in fundamental ways. When one is given a million dollars as a young adult, one bypasses the notion of working up from the bottom. One never has to put up with an unpleasant boss, for example, nor know the experience of financial distress. To some extent, the development of empathy requires a visceral awareness of the experience of hardship.

Entitlement, in effect, implies that the recipient is deserving, not by the merit of his own sweat and tears but because he is magically pedigreed, worthy for ancestral reasons. Perhaps, such an individual comes to believe he is remarkable. He may even spend much of his time proclaiming his "exceptional quality" to the world by displaying his name on buildings, aircraft and products.

This need for recognition, I believe, comes ironically from a place of self-doubt; a resultant quest for power ensues, a power the individual may believe proves worthiness. In extreme misunderstanding of the use of power, this same individual may conclude that he can say anything, do anything with impunity.

17

Those who are comfortable in their own skin do not feel the need to lord it over others. Those who have not experienced entitlement are more apt to see themselves as part of a whole - able and willing to understand experience from varying perspectives. Perhaps because they are not segregated in elite circumstances and experience a broader spectrum of society generally, these individuals may have better access to situations that require the thoughtful development of empathy and fairness.

Of course, not all who experience privilege lack a moral code. Many are raised to know the fortuitousness of their circumstances. Many are urged to "give back" in ways that demand that they develop the intellect and the soul. These individuals spend their lives helping others. They are, for examples, doctors, teachers, scientists - leaders of many persuasions. They need not proclaim their existence in bold name placement. They are known for their deeds among those that matter - the recipients of their empathy. And with this realization, they are "rich," indeed.

Response to Trump

If I were the nominee of the Democratic Party, this is how I would respond to Trump's shenanigans:

I do not respect or give credence to your rhetoric, for your calculated speech serves only as a distraction from important issues. Occasionally, you voice random policy ideas, but these proclamations are dangerous in their simplicity.

I believe your rise in the Republican Party has much to do with disappointment and fear as experienced by our electorate. It is human

18

nature to wish for someone to proclaim infinite power to change what needs changing. But simplistic bombast will not put to right all of the complexity of trouble in our world.

Simplistic idea #1

Deport all illegal immigrants. Not only is this idea unfeasible, it fails to address the particular instances of families, migrant workers, whole segments of society that we have up until now regarded with a semblance of compassion and respect.

Simplistic idea # 2

Build a great wall that will seal off Mexico from the United States. An insulting gesture that connotes isolationism and jingoistic thought. Why not build a wall around the whole country? We could become one big gated-community imprisoned by our own making.

Simplistic idea #3

Ban all Muslims from entering the United States thereby alienating and disrespecting our own Muslim citizenry.

Simplistic idea #4

Defeat ISIS by "bombing the hell out of them." Never mind collateral murder. Never mind the outcome of further disintegration of countries and culture. Live for today only - and the notion that we are all-mighty, if not all knowing.

And now I have sent a cannon-ball across your bow, Mr. Trump. Please respond to these concerns with serious ideas as to the defense of your positions, if possible. Cogent plans as to the future of this nation would be welcome as well.

Vetting

The latest Trump idea has to do with vetting would-be immigrants. First of all, the idea is not new. Evidently those who seek asylum are already scrutinized - the process taking up to two years to accomplish. Such a process must entail more than "giving a test," for why would an aspiring terrorist admit to believing in Sharia Law, for example?

Yet, the idea of vetting is an interesting one. Are presidential candidates adequately vetted?

Certainly, Hillary Clinton has been questioned repeatedly about everything and anything. But then, she actually has government experience to consider. She has also turned over material having to do with personal tax returns as well as documents pertaining to the Clinton Foundation. Any whiff of malfeasance while in office has been investigated thoroughly. The outcome each time indicated that Clinton had not committed an actionable offense, nor has she committed perjury. Some might argue that she has misled the public. She herself has admitted to "short-circuitry." She has also admitted to being wrong about the use of a private email-server.

Donald Trump, with absolutely no government experience, cannot be faulted with governing mistakes. However, as his campaign has touted his vast business experience, it would seem his behavior in that arena warrants a careful look. It has been said that he has routinely "stiffed" vendors. His Trump University venture is under scrutiny for possible fraud. Moreover, he has not released tax information that would enlighten the electorate as to his business practices as well as his commitment to support his country.

There is something inherently wrong with this picture. How is it that having no political experience is actually a plus when running for office? How is it that a world-wide charitable foundation becomes a liability? When was having to declare bankruptcy accepted as a mere business practice? How is it possible that the electorate would consider a candidate with no record of governance and a sketchy record of business practices?

Yes, we need the idea of vetting, Mr. Trump. Let's put you at the top of the list. We could begin with your tax returns.

Atticus Finch v. Daffy Duck

I see President Obama as an Atticus Finch-type character, as portrayed in *To Kill a Mockingbird* only: measured, elegant of speech, an intelligent man capable of empathy and respect for others - including his opponents. Trump? Well, an evil Daffy Duck comes to mind: hysterical, vulgar of speech, a self-absorbed entity capable of "vicious," verbal vindictiveness toward others - especially those who question his ideas.

Language matters. Behavior matters. Ability matters. The President of the United States reflects our very nature to the world. Atticus Finch must not be followed by an anti-social Daffy Duck.

The leader of the free world ought to represent the best of us. We need an open-minded listener, thoughtful planner, unselfish doer. Furthermore, the job requires vision beyond self-aggrandizement. We need a leader who seeks the position for the right reason: service to others.

As to foreign adversaries, it is more than likely that an enemy Bugs Bunny is waiting in the wings relishing the possibility of making mince-meat out of Daffy Duck.

To: Women Who Are Considering Voting for Trump

All mothers should give their daughters the following advice as to potential relationships with men (and all relationships, for that matter): Avoid those who are unable or unwilling to apologize ever and run as fast as you can from a person who claims he always gets what he wants. Red flags, indeed, for the attributes implied by such behavior and language include selfishness, hubris and potential abuse of power. These same red flags also prove useful when considering the character of a potential President of the United States, man or woman.

To be sure, it takes a bit of ego to even consider the position. But I'm talking about pathology here. The sort of person who will never back down from a perceived slight. The kind of person who relishes cruelty of words toward opponents. In short, a person who sees the world as his domain only. Such a personality is incapable of reflection or self-assessment. Caught in a child-like sphere of "I want," he bumbles from baby-gate to baby-gate in a fruitless quest for autonomy. You see, the behavior is a veneer, a smoke screen of machismo that attempts to hide a terrible case of arrested emotional-development.

Symbolically, at least, an elected president becomes the head of the American family, a position that requires allegiance to all who make up the fabric of the United States. He or she also telegraphs to the

22

world our beliefs and values. In a sense, we are dependent upon the psychological makeup of the leader of our country. As with a potential life-partner, the stakes are great. I counsel all women to consider Trump as they would potential husbands/partners. Is he capable of compromise? Is he kind? Is he capable of emotional growth? - for presumably we continue to grow throughout our lives. Is he unselfish? Is he reflective as to self - and ideas generally? Would you trust him to honor and care for you? Is he intellectually ready to take on great responsibility?

Clearly, Trump does not meet these very basic criteria. Rather, he is unkind, unyielding, unaware and uninterested, but not unselfish. Go figure.

Donald, It's Time to Take Your Ball and Go Home

"Double-down Donald" clearly does not understand an oft-quoted definition of insanity: doing the same thing over and over again and expecting different results. Donald will never apologize for the offensively egregious remarks he has made during the course of his entire debacle of a candidacy. He cannot bring himself to believe that he is human - capable of error. Instead he rephrases and lashes out in accusations that assert others, not he, are waging "vicious" attacks. Add double-speak to double-down.

It's time to take your ball and go home, Donald. The game is over. You were never a team-player. You were in it for your own personal glory - spiking the ball beyond the foul line - assuming that no one noticed your un-sportsman-like behavior. You see, Donald, there are basic rules in place, human decency among them. No, you cannot say or do whatever you want with impunity. Sooner or later, you will be kicked out of the game.

From your perspective, I think it would be better to refuse to play anymore. Go ahead and cry "foul" or "rigged" or any other face-saving excuse you can conjure. Just go home.

The Mentality of the Game

Ever wonder why millionaires are prompted to become billionaires? After all, there is only so much one can do with wealth: buy stuff, ensure well-being of family, perhaps, in a moment of altruism, give to charitable or educational organizations. Exactly what drives a person in the quest for much more? I suspect that money-makers enjoy the on-going game of making money. The need to win becomes a kind of drug - a way to define a living - or enhance the notion of self. Yet, such behavior is not practiced by would-be billionaires solely. In many ways, game-playing defines our culture.

Competition forms the heart of all game-playing, and at the heart of competition is the need for validation. Sociologically and psychologically we accept the idea of superlatives: the wealthiest, the brightest, the toughest, the prettiest...and on and on. Our country is touted as exceptional, the best, and therefore, by proxy, we are the best individuals in our own minds.

Perhaps the notion of competition is wired into our human nature with regard to the primal antecedent of survival of the fittest. Yet, the symbolism of winning permeates the entire mind-set of this culture - be it in the use of language or in the very structure of the ways in which we conduct our lives. We "beat" diseases. We score the most medals in the Olympics. Our team "trounces" the opponent. We win the spelling bee. Our university is bigger and better than other institutions. Our children are stars. Our stars, those we revere, are larger than life: wealthier, brighter - inherently more powerful than we will ever be. However, we continue to imagine ourselves as stars in our own right.

We practice game-playing seriously, when we compete for positions in education, and later, in the work-force. In our spare time, we continue playing games: of sport, with cards and internet-video-games; even in our dreams, we compete with and/or defeat individuals or situations.

My point? Game-playing has become a crescendo, especially dominating the latest presidential election-cycle, increasing in intensity even as we face the final "home stretch." Game-playing as we have never seen it before, in the political context, in the race for arguably the most powerful position in the world. The presidency reduced to a game...

Once Bernie Sanders exited the field, the tenor of the race changed dramatically. Though some may disagree fundamentally with the ideas Sanders put forth, all must note that his campaign was idea-driven. Bernie's primary focus? Progressive (as in seeking progress) throughout. Most important, his operation valued substance over strategy. Hillary's campaign, on the other hand, employed both substance and strategy equally; often she was pulled into substance largely due to the stances put forth by Sanders. And lately, Hillary's campaign has largely embraced strategy over substance. Trump? For him, it was a game from day one - strategy the only viable focus.

Above all, Trump enjoys the roar of the crowd. He envisions himself as the ultimate winner - not the lone president who will bear the burdens of office, isolated from adulation. I truly wonder if Trump has contemplated what would surely follow a win. Does he really think he can bluster and insult his way through a governing position? Does he really think he will govern on his own, like a king, demanding and getting the subservience of his countrymen? His language seems to indicate that he believes so: "I know more than the generals." "I will make America great again!" Needless to say, his belief is mired in the "I" not the "we." In Trump's mind, he is the champ, the star, all-knowing, invincible.

Winning is paramount in Trump's mind. What he would do with a win is anyone's guess ... including his own. What we have done - in accepting the notion of game-playing to the extent that we have - is troubling.

Antithetical Reality

Donald Trump has been caught (and caught up) in many lies. Yet, it is his method of mendacity that merits special notice. Beyond engaging in "I know you are, but what am I" non-arguments, Trump has often accused his opponents of the very behavior he exhibits - even before the inevitable criticism of punditry and the public ensued.

"Lyin' Ted" covered for Trump's own lies. "Crooked Hillary" deflects from his own questionable business dealings, most notably Trump University. Hillary is the bigot - not Trump who has called Mexicans "rapists, drug-dealers." And on and on. The repetition of these bogus accusations ensures a branding on the public consciousness. Moreover, the outrageous nature of Trump's shtick garners media attention daily. Trump has managed to direct the process of an election and/or con us all with lies.

Engaging in a kind of Orwellian double-speak comes naturally to Trump. Like the pigs in *Animal Farm*, Trump is audacious and relentless. Underlying fear provides the bulwark of support for his intellectually absurd pronouncements. Add conspiracy theories to the mix, and he's off to the races.

Many have labeled Trump a fool, ignorant of speech and lacking basic understanding of world challenges. Such a conclusion misses an important point. Trump is Machiavellian by nature - crafty by way of manipulation. He holds court and causes metaphorical heart-burn among the intelligentsia. Yes, Trump is sly, unethical and uncouth - but totally stupid? I'm afraid not.

Trump's antithetical reality did not originate with him. Lesser proponents of this game had sullied the political landscape previously. Remember the cry of "You're inciting class warfare" as a response to working people's apt criticism of the shenanigans of the one percent? Eventually, the privileged backed down from their double-speak pronouncement, preferring dignity to demagoguery. After all, they had a class-standing to maintain. Trump doesn't care about that. He happily embraces coarseness and/or crude behavior in his quest for ultimate validation, power. Presumably of the fleeting kind, one can only hope... Hope and speak up!

Update (3/4/2017) Trump has labeled Obama "sick." Time to worry.

Update #2 (5/19/17) We learn that Trump told Russian officials during a private meeting in the Oval Office: (newly- fired) "Comey is a nut job." Trump will eventually learn that the reign of antithetical reality is fleeting.

President of the Class

I must admit that I once momentarily wondered if perhaps Trump's candidacy was an incredible ruse to help Hillary win. I mean, it

27

seemed so obvious that Donald wasn't really interested in the job. He even seemed to not understand what the job entailed, nor did he do anything to educate or enlighten himself, as to particulars. He just went about "being Trump" - albeit a cartoonish Trump. Was it all a joke? To what purpose?

I now believe that Donald is incapable of this sort of joke or an elaborate subterfuge. He is merely a high school (or junior high school) boy running for the president of his class. Like many boys in that position, he seeks not to actually do anything substantive to improve the well-being of his classmates. No. He is primarily engaging in a popularity contest. He wants to feel important. He needs to feel important. Or more to the point, he needs constant attention.

As a former teacher, I've seen like characters in action - the children who disrupt classes in order to call attention to themselves. I well remember a boy who valued such interaction above all else - craving positive or negative attention. It seemed not to matter which. Of course, there are usually background reasons for such behavior. Whenever possible, the empathetic teacher tries to encourage positive behavior and then reinforce such behavior with praise. Whenever possible, this same teacher tries to ignore the negative pleas to be noticed - occasionally a near impossible task.

Sometimes it is even necessary to remove a negative-attention-seeking student from the classroom temporarily, so as to deny the response he seeks while at the same time ensuring the needs of his classmates. Frankly, such an emotionally needy child causes angst to himself, his peers and the adults in his sphere, for usually the attention-seeking scenario plays out on numerous occasions. However, with patience and empathy in play, more often than not, the child eventually learns to cope with the idea of appropriate connections with others. He grows up. He won't be 13 forever.

Unfortunately, in Trump's case, negative behavior has been rewarded with the constant notice of mass media. He has garnered millions of dollars of free advertising with obnoxious and puerile language. And while this was going on, the rest of the "class" was put on hold. (Would that a Bernie Sanders had been allowed such a platform.)

The teacher in me wishes to deal constructively with Donald Trump - saving him from himself while ensuring that those around him are saved from his singular dominance of the landscape. Let's face it, Trump has managed to hold court - creating the tenor of this entire election cycle. So, while my empathetic side envisions treating Donald Trump humanely and without rancor, I do not condone ignoring the pressing problems that affect us all in so doing. Therefore, as insulting as it may seem, let me speak directly to Donald: "Grow up! If this doesn't happen, you must leave the class."

Having said all of that, this former teacher, of course, realizes that Donald Trump is not running for president of his class. He is running for the Office of the President of the United States. He certainly must be denied the position. There can be no question about that.

Note: A friend, upon reading this piece, raised the question of stake-holders in the episode of an unruly student: Where is the principal or guidance counselor? More important, why do other students leave it to the teacher rather than speaking up: "Hey, Trump kid, we want to learn. Stop your foolishness or get out!"?

In the larger context: Why, indeed?!

Rump Roast

Former sages/leaders are turning over in their graves. However, their words live on, thankfully. The imagined roast of Donald J. Trump ensues - remarkably aided, in part, by his voluminous, vitriolic rhetoric.

Part One: Awards Segment (Based on beauty pageants. Appropriate, no?)

Mr. Sexism Award

"It's certainly not ground-breaking news that early victories by the women of 'The Apprentice' were, to a very large extent, dependent on their sex appeal." -- Trump

Susan B. Anthony rebuttal: "I do not demand equal pay for any women save those who do equal work in value. Scorn to be coddled by your employers; make them understand that you are in their service as workers, not women."

Mr. Autocrat Award

"I will make America great again!" -- Trump

John F. Kennedy: "Ask not what your country can do for you; ask what you can do for your country."

Mr. Fear Award

"It's going to get worse. We're going to have more World Trade Centers." -- Trump

Franklin Delano Roosevelt: "The only thing we have to fear is fear itself."

Mr. Bigotry Award

"They're rapists (Mexican immigrants); they're bringing drugs, they're bringing crime..." "There should be a complete shut-down of Muslims entering the United States." -- Trump

Trump also stated he would consider creating a data-base of Muslim-Americans and require them to carry special ID cards. Sound familiar?

Eleanor Roosevelt: "Pit race against race, religion against religion, prejudice against prejudice. Divide and conquer! We must not let that happen here."

Mr. Isolationism Award

"I will build a wall to keep Mexicans out." "We'll call it the 'Great Wall of Trump.'"

Barack Obama: "Even if we wanted to, we can't seal ourselves off from the rest of the world. Today a nation ringed by walls would only imprison itself."

Mr. Ignorance Award

"This very expensive global-warming bull---- has got to stop. Our planet is freezing, record lows (it being winter), and our global-warming scientists are stuck in ice." -- Trump

Carl Sagan: "It is far better to grasp the universe as it really is than to persist in delusion, however satisfying and reassuring."

Mr. Bravado Award

"I love war, in a certain way, but only when we win." -- Trump

Dwight D. Eisenhower: "I hate war as only a soldier who has lived it can, only as the one who has seen its brutality, its futility, its stupidity."

Mr. Missing the Point Award

"Too many people don't care about winning today...I call them losers." -- Trump

Abraham Lincoln: "I am not bound to win, but I am bound to be true. I am not bound to succeed, but I am bound to live up to what light I have."

Part Two: Special Guest Appearance -- Bozo the Clown

Bozo's advice to Donald: "Get a new look. Mine. More natural and a better fit."

Experience

Let's set aside notions of Trump's mendacity and idiocy for now...
The last time I applied for a job, I was required to provide would-be employers with my educational resume as well as pertinent work experience. Within the context of such situations, admittedly the chicken or the egg precursor-scenario comes to mind. How does one obtain experience if experience is a prerequisite? Putting that little conundrum aside for a moment, I pose the question: Does experience not matter when running for the Presidency of the United States?

Only four presidents have served without the prior experience of elective office. Three of these four, however, served in the military - presumably garnering leadership-experience within the context of a government agency. The fourth had served previously as secretary of commerce.

Donald Trump, on the other hand, has no government experience whatsoever. His experience lies solely in the business world. Some are enamored with this outsider status. Those folks feel that government experience necessarily implies cronyism and corruption. This is a short-sighted view, in my opinion, illustrative of "throwing the baby out with the bath water..."

At the very least, voters should have extensive access to Trump's less pertinent experience in order to make informed decisions as to his capabilities and character. To be sure, Trump has provided some sort of financial disclosure. However, the disclosure is brief and incomplete. Presumably his tax returns would indicate his penchants as well as his experience. Then there is the question of Trump University...

Trump has also provided entertainment credentials - as a reality-TV star. Not a plus, as far as I am concerned. Having said that, Ronald Reagan started out as a movie star, but he went on to gain experience as Governor of California. Though many at the time recoiled from his Hollywood history, Reagan was given a pass, for he had moved on, after all.

What is wrong with the Trump picture? Everything. No government experience, less than transparent views of business history. Really nothing on show but statements of grandiosity. Yes, I am cognizant of the notion of on-the-job training, but on-the-job training for the Presidency of the United States? Absurd.

Teamwork

Donald Trump has once again reorganized his campaign team. Yet another advisor has been removed from a position of prominence. Why? Could it be that Trump eschews the idea of teamwork? Is he able to listen to the counsel of others - learn new ways of approaching problems and situations? Or is he bent on listening to himself only? It would appear, the latter. The problem is, to quote John Donne (and the Bible), "No man is an island unto himself." While Trump may believe that he can exist solely in his own sphere, with his own thoughts supreme, the Office of the Presidency demands an understanding of the whole - to include others' viewpoints, experiences and, yes, dreams.

I sometimes think that Mr. Trump is woefully ignorant of our very history. Does he not understand that the President of the United States cannot govern "by divine rule?" We broke away from King George III at the outset of our democracy. Our government provides checks and balances meant to preclude the rule of one person. Mr. Trump

34

would be working with Congress, after all. He would need to give allegiance to the idea of a Supreme Court. His word would not automatically be law, thankfully.

Does Mr. Trump not understand the complexity and the enormity of the problems he will face? Would he be able to work with Cabinet-members, for example? When they advised him, would he listen? Or would he attempt to micro-manage all aspects of decision-making, an impossible task? Conversely, would Trump serve as a figure-head only, yet feeling the need to make occasional pronouncements? Would he simply fire those who had the temerity to question his pronouncements? Would constructive criticism result in a Trumpian fit of pique?

With regard to his campaign team, either Trump made poor choices in the first place - or he actually doesn't want a team at all. His latest CEO seems to be a mirror image of Donald J. Trump - a no-holds-barred sort of communicator with bloviating tendencies. Trump likes people who are like Trump, providing they like him - a big proviso...

Trump would be wise to emulate King Lear by hiring a fool who wasn't really a fool, someone who would tactfully point out his fatal flaws. But then he'd have to listen to his fool - or not as was the case with King Lear - that is until it was too late to matter...

The Purpose of Debate

Way back when, high school debates were governed by rules such as; no name calling, no appeals to emotion, no interrupting, no yelling "unfair" and, on a positive note, cogent ideation of the argument at hand - basic civility, in other words. The Republican primary-presidential-debates broke many of these rules. Donald Trump sees debates as entertainment or a platform for his antithetical reality - accusing others of lying to cover his own lies, for example. He's good at this. He often makes preemptive strikes, though he maintains he is just hitting back when others are "unfair." He is the student in the classroom who disrupts and gets attention with outlandish behavior. He prevents others from learning.

What is the purpose of a presidential debate? Trump thinks it is all about winning. I maintain that debates are meant to inform the public of detailed policy-positions. The electorate relies on debates for information and candidate-stances. Yes; we need fact-checkers. Otherwise candidates are able to obfuscate and mislead. So, don't tell me that a moderator is unnecessary.

I'm not interested in who is louder or better at put-downs. Nor am I interested in the "winner" mentality. Especially, I do not want to view attention-seeking disrupters. This is serious, and I wish to learn.

An Aside

Following the first Clinton/Trump presidential debate a pundit passed off an interesting take on the state of discourse in our country. He maintained that times have changed with regard to codes of conduct. To be more precise, we no longer revere good manners, politeness - basic civility. It's true that popular culture has revealed a coarsening of behavior. Watch many television programs, and note conversation based on disrespect. I remember a particular sit-com of 1988 that seemed to hint at a shift in what was then thought to be acceptable behavior - a TV family that conversed in put-downs and one-liners - a language of disdain. I also watched a classroom of children begin to emulate this phenomenon, much to my dismay.

When discussing codes of class conduct, necessary for maintaining a semblance of order and respect for all participants in the classroom, I often spoke of the message behind polite discourse, an acknowledgment of another beyond self, a respect that enhances both the giver and the recipient. Good manners are not the affectations of a particular strata of society, but rather are indications of altruism. Polite language results in a kind of peace that negates a war of words. This is not to say that differing positions are diluted; rather, mature discussion is based on listening to the other side intently so as to understand better a point of view.

There are those who will dismiss basic civility with the label of "political correctness" - often with a sneer. In reacting this way, those folks have proven my point. When did respect for others become a weak position? In fact, it is a strength. Most parents guide their children through the process of impulse control and thinking beyond self. Many believe that the hard work of diplomacy produces strong families, communities and countries. The practice of respect, above all, enables a learning, an expansion of intellect and emotion.

Therefore, I do not accept the pundit's acquiescence as to coarse language and behavior. We may be viewing rancor every day in entertainment and elsewhere, but that does not mean that we need to accept and practice this childish, self-absorbed stance.

As to Donald Trump's discourse, many have lauded his authenticity. However, it must be noted: Authenticity and impulsivity are not one and the same.

Update, written some 19 months later:

The television show referenced above, *Roseanne*, has resurfaced to the delight of many citizens. All of the main characters have returned, older but no wiser - as to the necessity for productive and/or civil discourse. Millions will cheer examples of disdainful put-downs. They will feel better momentarily. But nothing will change. Ironically, impotent ranting is employed by both a demoralized, disenfranchised electorate and a bloated, self-serving billionaire-president. That Trump would attempt to align himself with those who have not enjoyed the privilege of his life - through language, pretending to be at one with the masses - is perhaps the unkindest cut of all. He is not just an unseemly president; he is a shameless imposter.

Conspiracy Theories

Let's face it, we live in an age of anxiety. And with anxiety comes run-away imagination. The complexity of the 21st century world is daunting, to say the least. A simple understanding of the way government or power works, an impossibility. Faced with the nagging conclusion that our world is out of control, or at least out of our control, we attempt to find culprits - those who are promoting evil agendas behind the scenes. Now don't get me wrong; I firmly believe that we must question the motives of those who govern. Power creates strange bed-fellows or singular, mutually beneficial alliances - often to the detriment of those governed. Yet, I would caution against believing outrageous conspiracy theories that are meant to make us feel smart, or at least less hood-winked, while simplifying complex issues by offering the dreaded-monster scenario.

Donald Trump especially enjoys conspiracy theories. He has stated, for examples: President Obama was born in Kenya, and this "fact" was covered up. President Obama and Secretary Clinton are "founders of ISIS." Elections are rigged. Ted Cruz's father was connected to the assassination of President Kennedy. And on and on... Imagination run wild, indeed. Yet, there is calculation at work here. By muddying the waters, by stoking the burning embers of distrust in government, Trump gains traction among those who desperately seek someone to blame for the many inequities that trouble our nation.

It is tempting to entertain conspiracy theories, for they explain away the complexity of our world. However, without cogent evidence to support such theories, we must conclude that they ultimately serve to hood-wink us in the broadest sense. They are also insulting with regard to our perceived ability to sort through information in a quest for true understanding. Conspiracy theorists assume that we think as children think, wary of imagined monsters, clamoring for a father-figure who will slay our foes.

Bottom line: We must unpack conspiracy theories and demand evidence of claims. Above all, we must know that we possess the intellect and the common sense to see a complex landscape clearly. We ought to question the motives of others; yet, we ought to question our own as well. To be sure, we crave simple answers and, on occasion, culprits to dispatch. But let's face it, easy answers are not usually viable or true.

We should imagine our ability to listen carefully, to steadfastly weigh all possibilities - to think honestly. Once again, I quote John Donne: "Therefore, send not to know, for whom the bell tolls; it tolls for thee." In other words, each and every one of us must retain the power of thought, so as to forge our own destinies.

An Admittedly Outlandish Conspiracy Theory

Ever so slowly the American public is being brainwashed via entertainment. The industry seeks to foster regression into childhood states of being. Ads appear on television every five minutes or so in order to diminish the capacity of the human attention-span. Programming features puerile appeals to emotion: rage, name-calling and "I know you are, but what am I" non-argument. Vulgarity rules. Simplistic language replaces sophisticated vocabulary and sentence structure. Why? (You might ask.) Just maybe, someone wants to undermine the public's ability to reason.

"Good one!" the audience yells when Honey Boo-Boo utters an ignorant quip. "Right on!" follows "Duck Dynasty" philosophy. "The Real Housewives of Wherever" model atrocious, juvenile behavior. "Let's sell them more stuff on the Home Shopping Network. 'Don't think, buy!' is our motto," opines some nameless entity in a back room somewhere.

Meanwhile, television news is co-opted as well with its focus on appeals to emotion and characters of arrested development. We watch Trump, the school-yard bully, insult everyone in his path. We watch Giuliani pitch a screaming fit amidst outrageous accusations. We watch mealy-mouthed legislators sit on the sidelines, wringing their hands in dismay, but not abandoning their party's nominee. But we don't watch those folks too much, as they are eclipsed by the loud-mouths. It's all one big, reality-show...

Just in case television brain-washing proves ineffective, the usage of drugs is made easier (read as metaphorical as well as real chaos). It's all about money, see? If marginalized people are reduced to dependent beings, well, that means fewer folks clamoring for a reinstatement of the American dream.

Perhaps some multi-national group of oligarchs, bent on creating a 21st century version of feudal society, does not really exist, and thus is not behind such manipulation, but you could have fooled me... Talk about globalization.

The aforementioned is an outlandish conspiracy theory, as they usually are. Perhaps, just read between the lines?

A Nightmare: Trump's Cabinet

Nightmares are inevitably frightening, outlandish - and indicative of subconscious fears. Sometimes they are symbolic in nature. Sometimes they simply exaggerate existing realities.

My nightmare came in two distinct parts. In part one, Trump has won the election. He is President of the United States. The White House has been encased in gold. The inauguration ceremonies included a fly-over of Trump's jet followed by a phalanx of Trump helicopters. A three-dollar bill was issued with Trump's likeness to commemorate accession. Male babies born on that fateful day were all named Donald. I nearly woke up screaming...

But part two inevitably followed - the announcement of Trump's Cabinet. Spoiler alert: Part two did result in hyperventilating and blood-curdling howls. A list of Trump's "dream" Cabinet ensues. Note: The Trumpster gleefully announced beforehand that all appointees would be "outsiders." (Someone ought to acquaint Donald with the notion of multiple definitions...) Additional note: Quotes are Donald's.

Secretary of State: Steve Bannon

Apt to be a cushy job as foreign nations have already indicated they want nothing to do with him.

Secretary of the Treasury: John Paulson

Vast experience as a hedge fund manager. Made over 4 billion dollars with credit default swaps. "Think what his brilliance will do to this country!"

Secretary of Defense: Sarah Palin

Because she can see Russia from her house. By the way, still considered an outsider as her tenure as governor was truncated.

Attorney General: Rudy Giuliani

"He yells and talks tough; I like that."

Secretary of the Interior: Trump Golf and Casino CEOS

"Let's put that land to good use, and help the Indians as well."

Secretary of Agriculture: Monsanto Agriculture Empire - Biotech Developer

"I'm all in favor of developing stuff."

Secretary of Commerce: Paul Manafort

Provides an expertise in trade deals, especially with regard to Russia and Ukraine.

Secretary of Labor: Roger Ailes

"Knows labor. Does he ever!"

Secretary of Health and Human Services: Dr. Drew Pinsky

Clearly an outstanding diagnostician. He doesn't need to see a patient in order to offer his expertise, as shown with his assessment of Hillary Clinton.

Secretary of Housing and Urban Development: Eric Trump

Remarkable resume as to urban development - for the 1%.

Secretary of Transportation: Trump National Transportation Service CEO

"See my 'tricked-out' Trump jet as well as transport at Mar-a-Lago Club, Need I say more?"

Secretary of Energy: Coal and Oil CEOS

"Drill Baby, Drill!" "Down with Wind Turbines! They Kill Hundreds of Eagles Each Year!" "Coal will be King Again!"

Secretary of Education: School Privatization Crowd

"Everything's a business."

Secretary of Veterans Affairs: Donald Trump, Jr.

"Though my boy never served in the military, he understands sacrifice, as do I."

Secretary of Homeland Security: The Incredible Hulk

"He'll get the job done!"

Of course, the above is all a bit of hooey or falderal. However, given Trump's disdain for existing government officials, do you not wonder just how he would fill these positions? Also, who would deign to work with him?

May the travesty of Trump's candidacy, in the end, seem like a very bad dream. Moreover, may we learn something in its wake.

Update (11/17/2016): Horrors! It's barely satire!

Trump et Alia This Past Year

It is as though a large segment of the population lives in junior high school mode. Trump behaves like a j.d. (juvenile delinquent, that is, certainly not a J.D., Juris Doctor). Juvenile delinquent: one who garners attention simply by being obnoxious. I am angry with news outlets that report on Trump's every childish action or comment. But then, evidently the public is amused by his antics. Unfortunately, news outlets often pander to the public by embracing the notion of "entertainment." And it must be acknowledged, many viewers vicariously enjoy "sticking their fingers in the eyes" of others - a way of venting frustration. Their only recourse to a government that has disappointed them (they think) involves hurling an insult or causing or witnessing an assault of some kind. It is difficult for me to accept this impotent, child-like behavior.

Though I did not watch the State of the Union Address in its entirety, I did read the text of President Obama's speech online. I appreciate its tone. Certainly, this president has never been bombastic or spoken ever other than in a civil and thoughtful manner. It is truly shameful that he has been treated with disdain and disrespect by many. It scares me - the nastiness of comments, the thinly-veiled racism. And why does bluster and a "he-man" persona trump (pun intended) intelligence, reflection and, yes, common sense? In fact, it does not. I have to believe Americans will walk away from crass spectacle, ultimately. In the meantime, I wonder how the rest of the world views our culture.

Update: The British Parliament has discussed whether or not to ban Trump from entering the U.K. I rest my case...

Fast forward a month or so... It's too late. The rest of the world must view our country as the land of incivility, the land of emotional outbursts - our values demeaned in an on-going reality-show of incessant vulgarity. We are living in a place of pure reaction rather than reasoned reflection. Ideas of policy have given way to discussions of "man-parts," after all. I find this devolution unimaginable on some level, and yet it has happened. I am embarrassed for us all. Tolstoy, I believe, viewed the role of leadership as a reflection of society rather than adhering to the "great man" theory of government where an individual saves the day with rarified insight. If this be the case, then surely our culture, our very make-up, has reached a new low.

Citizens are rightfully frustrated with the status quo. And many government participants need to acknowledge their culpability in this sorry state of affairs. Nearly eight years have passed with an accomplish-nothing Congress and obstructionism played out arrogantly, blatantly. The current leader (Obama) was not prevented from reaching the highest position in the club, but sore losers would not accept his ascendency; rather, they just refused "to play with him"

45

- to extend the juvenile metaphor. Brinkmanship with regard to shutting down the government played out with nary a thought as to the effects on citizenry. Foolish discussions as to the leader's birthplace deflected discussion on the real issues of a decaying infrastructure, rampant underemployment or unemployment, inequality in many guises. Finger-pointing reached an essential absurdity when the current president was portrayed as responsible for the Great Recession. "Let's rewrite history to our own advantage," they crowed in back rooms.

Amidst all of this, bogus discussions of the Constitution and citizens' rights occurred. "Your right to bear arms will soon be denied," they exclaimed, rather than engaging in reasonable discourse as to the appropriateness of assault weapons and the amassing of arsenals. Meanwhile, the constitutional right of a president to put forth a candidate for the Supreme Court was stymied with the pig-headed (beyond arrogant) statement: "We will not consider any candidate, Republican or Democrat, suggested by this president." This isn't government; this is war-like maneuvering. We deserve better, or maybe we don't, if one views this behavior as a mirror of our own standards.

Obfuscations and the conflicting realities inherent in our understanding of our country's government result in a sense of unease, which in due course leads to fear, and, I fear, ultimately an undermining of a united people. We watch a juvenile delinquent play "King of the Mountain" - "the shining city on the hill" (perhaps an arrogance in itself) is all but forgotten now.

(**Note to reader:** Feel free to skim the next few pages as the writing is uneven - including a rant whose saving grace is the memorialization of Trump's destructive words. Other entries indicate a temporary impotence of intellect born of incredulity: expressed horror, in other words.

I like to think of myself as essentially kind - a measured sort of individual. Writing prompted me to think more clearly, I believed, and even enabled me to vanquish emotionalism. However, I am in reality, a typical human-being, fully capable of profound disappointment as well as the resultant confusion that stems from experiencing disgust and fear. Though you may not believe the following, I assure you it is true. All along, my "gut" told me that Hillary would not win; intuitively, I could not visualize her as president. Intellectually, I countered such a feeling with logical argument. How could she not win? There was no contest when one considered qualifications such as intellect, experience and temperament. And so, several of the following pieces presume a Hillary victory. As it turned out, I and many others had merely engaged in wishful thinking.**)**

For Those Who Take Their Entertainment Seriously: How I Wish It Had Happened

Pilots for Trash TV Shows:

"Out of Control"

Trump's pitch: "I'd like to punch him in the face."

Deemed too violently provocative. Denied.

****

"Insults for Fun"

Trump's examples: "Little Marco," "Crooked Hillary," "Lyin' Ted," "Rapists...Pigs...etc."

Deemed too juvenile - name-calling. Denied.

****

"Hyperbole Horror Show"

Trump's lame contributions: "Disaster," "Terrible," "They're Trying to Take Your Guns Away."

Again, deemed too juvenile - blatant appeal to emotion. Denied.

****

"Linguistic Limbo Dance: How Low Can You Go?" (Trump's premier idea)

Examples:

"Only Rosie...dog, pig." (Low)

"I like war heroes who are not captured." (Lower)

Mocking a disabled person. (Lower still)

Suggesting President Obama, Secretary Clinton in cahoots with ISIS. (Extremely Low)

"Second Amendment people might be able to do something. I don't know..." (Beyond low/wildly unacceptable)

****

Donald Trump is hereby disqualified as a pitchman for Trash TV.

More to the point, we deem him unsuitable for any and all positions of authority... including dog-catcher.

In a Nutshell (Why Trump is Wrong for the Presidency)

1. He has no experience beyond making money for himself and his heirs.

2. He is vulgar.

3. He is vindictive.

4. He lacks emotional intelligence.

5. He seeks flattery.

6. He has no sense of humor - like Nixon - unlike Kennedy, Obama, Reagan.

7. He is self-absorbed.

8. He is impulsive - eschews reflection.

9. He is ill-educated - doesn't read.

10. He is not curious.

11. He lacks a moral code - as witnessed in his business dealings and myriad examples of his disrespect for others.

12. He is a shell of a man.

All I Know of the (Particularly Difficult) Child I Learned from Donald Trump
(World-view of a Recalcitrant, Five-Year-old Brain)

1. "Teachers are stupid." (as Trump views anyone who disagrees with him)

2. "I hate that nasty doctor who gives me shots, but I like the nurse who gives me lollipops." (why Trump admires Putin)

3. "Yup. I hit him, but he started it." (mantra of Trump's campaign)

4. "Why can't I jump off the garage roof? You're UNFAIR!!" (Trump's view of the media)

5. "I hate reading. Legos are fun!" (Trump refuses to read; a devotee of TV instead)

6. "I only talk to pretty girls." (Trump's distain for women)

7. "I love the three stooges! I want to be a stooge when I grow up." (self-evident)

8. "NO. I did not eat 25 cookies. The Cookie Monster broke in and stole them. I saw him do it." (indicative of Trump's mendacity and belief in antithetical reality)

9. "Fighting is so much fun!" (again, self-evident; general mode of operation)

10. "If I don't get what I want, I'll huff and I'll puff and blow the whole house down." (Trump's penchant for threats under duress)

And perhaps the most puerile thought-process of all: "Johnny threw rotten tomatoes at the bus, too!" (Unfortunately, too many give credence to juvenile deflection.)

Even if Donald Loses, He's Won

To: Cable News Outlets

I can hardly stand it. Day after day of disgusting drivel. The conversation dictated by Donald Trump with every asinine and worse comment that he utters. Donald's Orwellian double-speak at every turn. Outrageous and bigoted statements given full attention. News shows dedicated to parsing statements that don't deserve the dignity of a prolonged response. I'm sick and tired of it.

I don't need to be told that the initial letter Trump's physician wrote was unprofessional. I don't want to see any more attention paid to attention-seeking Donald. Don't you get it? Trump doesn't care whether the attention is positive or negative. He just wants the attention. And you give it to him every day all day long,

Just for a change, spend your news hours explaining what Hillary has done in the past regarding legislation. Give time to her civic-accomplishments - even before she was in the public eye. Talk about suggestions others have made regarding her platform. Discuss her platform in detail. Give us something we can actually ponder. We cannot consider Trump's legislative history for obvious reasons. To be fair, press him on his platform - a platform remarkably thin on specifics thus far. If this fails, forget about giving Donald equal time. He's used up his time quota with insults and bad behavior. In fact, he has driven news cycles from day one in such a manner. If you never mentioned his name again, he'd still be ahead as far as attention and coverage are concerned.

Yes, I fault cable television news. Donald has already won, in one sense, for you've given him an unprecedented platform for foolery. He's loved every minute. You've ignored the needs of thinking, American citizens who figured out his shtick long ago. And all of his nonsense is spewed throughout the world. We have become a laughing-stock. We have been compromised by a clown, a misanthrope, a man without human decency. Please ignore him for a bit. Trust me, he'll react with desperation - a desperation that will be his ultimate undoing. He is bound to metaphorically implode should he lose his audience. Audience is all that exists for Trump.

News is meant to edify the electorate not feed the ego of one snake-oil salesman. Cable Television News: You've been conned big time.

P.S. Had I wished to view reality-TV shows ad nauseum, your broadcasting would have fit the bill.

P.P.S. Honestly, your programs have given me some fodder for previous writing. However, enough is enough. The electorate needs journalism of substance: information, ideas.

Anger Creates Ugly Faces

Please take a moment to peruse old photographs of individuals caught up in moments of anger. For example, view archived images of the crowd as James Meredith integrated "Ole Miss" in 1962. Ugly. Out of control. View as well little Ruby surrounded by jeering faces as she walked to school during the same time period. Witness the faces of some near-apoplectic supporters of Trump when faced by protesters from the other side. Look at the faces of the other side as well. These faces, more frightening than a child's rendition of monsters, are cause for great alarm.

Take a moment to analyze your own facial expression when confronted with a candidate you viscerally abhor. Now ask yourself the question: Have I fallen into the trap of emotional manipulation? Ask yourself as well: Am I able to stand back and calmly assess my feelings? Have I become contaminated by the very emotions I detest in others? Have I, too, become an ugly American?

Self-assessment is never easy. However, to fail to see one's own failings is foolish. In my assessments of Donald Trump, I have often veered into "smug territory." I admit it. I am emotionally affected by what I see as appeals to fear, anger - and the potential for destruction. I cannot ignore the danger of one who, in my view, is inept and proud of it. I see the power of emotional manipulation and fall victim to it myself to the extent that I, too, am angry. The difference between my

53

response and the response of an out-of-control, jeering mob has to do with my awareness of the extent of my feelings and the notion that relinquishing thought in the moment of emotion is tempting, but ultimately self-destructive.

And so, I promise to listen carefully to those of the Trump camp when they coolly and cogently express concerns - even though, given all that has occurred, I presume that I will not ultimately agree with many of their opinions. However, I realize that I am not an all-knowing entity, but rather someone who must consider different perspectives. Having opted for careful listening, I hope to avoid the ugly face of intolerance.

PostScript: Full Disclosure

I must admit that I have difficulty viewing Fox News - though I have tried, on many occasions, in order to understand better a point of view. My difficulty arises not with the ideas put forth exactly, but with the tone of many, not all, I hasten to add, anchors. I do not call them out by name here; I think those who appear to be awash in fury will be recognizable to you, the reader. Though other networks offer an array of personalities - some prone to smugness - by and large, over-the-top anger and emotionalism given free reign is not on full display, and thus they are easier (for me) to watch.

Rapprochement in the Era of Trump

There's hope for a rapprochement, but only if those in power overtly consider citizens who have been ignored and forgotten. The only positive outcome of Trump's candidacy has been the ongoing acknowledgement of the great frustration of some, so that a focus on the overlooked could conceivably become the norm.

One hopes Hillary has the heart and the energy necessary to listen and to act. Presumably she will build on her vast experience. Perhaps we shall come closer to providing the means for the pursuit of dignity for all.

Many were willing to back the offensive Trump solely because he was perceived as an outsider. That seems nonsensical. A billionaire-outsider? A representative of the struggling working-class? No. He just "played" us with his anger and calculated "anti-elitist" shtick (and lack of cogent ideas), primarily for the purpose of self-enhancement.

Time to focus on the future. Imagine a woman in the White House! And a chance for change in the way Congress operates - if gridlock is broken. Perhaps an acknowledgement that Congress has become a "club?"

Working people of all persuasions wish to see government employees working, not merely running for office or engaging in political power-struggles. We reject elitism. We need to see true professionalism. We need to see work done.

Where Do We Go from Here?

Though nothing is certain in life, I do believe that Trump will lose the election. If this be the case, many will be relieved. However, others will feel that the dream of the outsider was simply that, a dream. For some, cynicism will reign. The country may become divided as we have rarely been divided before. I fear that the fall-out of this emotional, often angry, electoral process will continue, and residual frustrations will serve to further weaken our nation. Perhaps, in the eyes of the world, we are compromised, even now. We must get back to American optimism - to believing in "We, the People."

We need to consider our individual dreams and fears. We also need to consider the dreams and fears of others. There must be a rapprochement. There must be a healing.

Primarily, we need to think about what has happened over the course of this past year. For examples: We need to question the very structure of the electoral process. We need to understand the workings of media. We need to consider vetting candidates. In fact, no question or idea should be excluded in this very necessary, post-election analysis. What follows are a series of questions/concerns from my perspective. I realize that other points of view need to be considered as well.

Question #1

Why are we conducting inordinately lengthy campaign seasons? It seems to me that those who govern spend too much time merely becoming elected to the detriment of time allotted to actual governance. Frankly, the campaign process appears to be infinite. Did not Republication leadership state outright in 2008 that their primary goal was to defeat President Obama in 2012? Should term limits be extended to Congress?

Question #2

Should we consider imposing a cap on campaign spending? After all, many millions of dollars are spent on these ventures. From the average citizen's perspective, such treasure is desperately needed elsewhere. How can special interest groups be reigned-in so that the process is inherently more egalitarian?

Question #3

Why is gerrymandering in practice? It seems to be fraught with the possibility of malfeasance. Should the Electoral College premise be revisited or amended in some way? Why do super-delegates exist?

Question #4

What is the essential responsibility of the media as to coverage of all candidates? Many news outlets have become entertainment-driven. Does this not set up a less than serious conversation? Why are all candidates not given equal time?

Question #5

How do we fairly vet a presidential candidate? Should government experience be a prerequisite for the office? Should tax returns and business ventures be scrutinized by law? Should the physical and mental health of a candidate be subject to some sort of screening? Should candidates be required to submit written proposals for their respective agendas? Should debates be required? Should debates be limited in number - thereby presented as important, finite chances to convince the electorate of the candidates' credibility?

I'm quite sure that others could present additional and important ideas and questions. The point is, question we must, for we are strengthened when we question and when we listen to the questions of others. We, the people, need to partake of the process of governance - that is if we are serious about being fairly represented. After all, democracy requires the engagement and commitment of its citizenry.

Then and Now (As I See It)

The kiddie show host exhorted his audience, innocent children to raise their milk glasses

to the image of Ike, a former general

who later described war as an exercise in stupidity and futility And later still, warned of the "military-industrial-complex."

JEK: cut down too soon

Did not promise to make America great again but respecting its citizenry said: "Ask not what your country can do for you; ask what you can do for your country."

LBJ: though often called ruthless, proved a tireless champion for civil rights - throughout - and he was a Southern white boy...

Also, a demander of congressional, "wait for it, " WORK.

Felled by a war of hubris.

Nixon: of China diplomacy, EPA, USSR détente

He enforced desegregation.

Then paranoia, Watergate...

Ultimate humiliation ended it all.

Ford, wishing to heal a nation,

pardoned Nixon and paid for his largesse.

Carter of Camp David, Salt II
Energy crisis
Iranian hostages

Most notably, post-presidency, humanitarian work

- and finally revered.

"Tear down this wall!" Reagan of easy humor
- and an actor's tough stance
"trickle-down economics"

then sad decline.

Bush #1: inherited difficult economy -
focus on foreign policy
Gulf War
Controversy: Clarence Thomas

Clinton: "down-home" personality
improving economy
NAFTA

peacetime
Children's health care

Ignominious personal-behavior

Impeachment

A foundation; world concerns ensue.

Bush #2: 9/11, tax cuts, No Child Left Behind, Katrina

War in Iraq: Mission not Accomplished
Great Recession.

Obama: economic stimulus legislation, Affordable Care Act,
repeal of "Don't Ask, Don't Tell"

Osama bin Laden, no more
Out and then back in Iraq
Iran nuclear agreement

Gun safety and other ideas -

Recalcitrant Congress....

- Obama is dignified throughout.

The Choice:

Hillary Clinton: government and societal experience to the highest
degree. Bright, educated - circumspect - cogent expression and
specific plans offered. And I believe she is a fighter for others, her

motivation. Her sin? She is a woman of expediency - in her personal life, some ascertain. Elsewhere? Does the "glass ceiling" encourage expediency? Is there a place for expediency in governance?

Donald Trump: no legislative experience. Impulsive, called authentic. Divisive, combative alpha-male. Promises to single-handedly make America great again, unfathomable hubris. Ethics of business practices (involving the less fortunate) and personal conduct called into question. Is his primary concern self-aggrandizement? I think so.

Addendum: Our presidents like their constituencies have not been flawless. However, in hindsight, we remember fondly those who were thoughtful and dignified of expression.

And, once again, I recall the history of Lincoln - deemed a humble person, a questioning person, though an astute politician. He evinced equal parts intelligence and compassion - what we desire... what we need.

It's Over, or is It?

Too late to make sense of Donald Trump.
Too tired to care about his pathology.

Yet, I must, for have we not seen his ilk before?
And innocents suffered in unimaginable, vile ways.

His example: fear-mongering, hatred - the lead-in to madness...

The corruption of once life-affirming folk with a calculated tactic of division

- on a scale that confounds.

Some so-called "Christians" support this "demi-god"

This temptation into evil
This antithesis of any "Lord's Prayer"
This supreme denigrator.

Should such corruption metastasize, it would reveal the cancer of the American soul.

And yet,

If Donald Trump is not the manifestation of an irredeemably sickened society, if goodness and intelligence prevail,

then we may look deep into our souls with a true faith - not labeled but felt.

And we shall find the means to legitimate change.

Part Two: The Transition

(Warning: Many of the following entries, written during the transition period, reflect my emotional reaction to the electoral process and its outcome, indicating as they do a rising concern and an angry tone in some instances. However, to delete these thoughts would be dishonest. Such writing tells its own story, the effects of alarm. On a more positive note, now I can say that I understand better the experience of the self-perceived, "marginalized" person, for I have lived the attending emotions - at least to some extent. I imagine many who voted against Trump, the majority of the popular vote, in fact, also grappled with uncomfortable incredulity.)

Postmortem: Note to Friend

Your feelings as expressed in last email speak to the feelings of many of us, I think. And I do believe that because Hillary is a woman, she was not afforded fair treatment. Strong women are not viewed in the same way as strong men. We know this. Though I know you've sworn off the news for a bit (totally understandable) - right now thousands of anti-Trump protesters are on the streets of New York. Many of them women - but not all. I think this may be a moment for a new women's movement. A time to come together as a political force.

For me, other emotions come into play as well: fear, disbelief and sadness. Having lived in the Midwest, Wisconsin way back when, I was aware of the resentment toward the coasts, especially the East, and I note that the current electoral-map demonstrates this divide. (Still knowing full well that the popular vote will probably favor Hillary.)

Trump does not display the intellect nor the interest necessary for governing, so I imagine others will be in charge. And this has happened before. I see Trump's tenure as short in any case; I even fantasized that he would get cold feet when he finally realized what he now faces. (For him life is a game, and the particular competition he so enjoyed is over.) I know, wishful thinking...

May our frustration with those who would dismantle our values - and our sadness as to the frailty (really dearth) of intellect as it is now practiced by much of the electorate - result is a movement for true change. The demonstrations must continue - not limited to the streets - rather, in all sorts of ways.

Political Vocabulary

The presidential election process was especially demoralizing for this former English teacher. First and foremost, it was conducted in a particularly emotional way, as opposed to an intellectual exercise. Also, all of the rules for high school debate class, as well as for general discussion commonly experienced in any humanities course, were broken. As Donald Trump essentially "ran the show" with reality-TV glee, name-calling, appeals to crass emotion, and half-baked conspiracy-theories ruled the day. His very vocabulary was limited to repeated vague words such as "great," and conversely, "disaster."

Other words were given false meaning, Outsider became savior. Elite became a simple pejorative - no longer indicating status based on wealth and power or its other meaning, excellence. As Donald Trump spoke in a "down-home" manner, none accused him of elitism, though he is wealthy and enjoys power. As to excellence, well the jury's out even with regard to his business acumen. Certainly, his rhetoric was not excellent nor were his very vague plans for future "greatness."

Time and again average citizens were accused of stupidity or elitism when presenting anti-Trump arguments. I experienced this myself. Invariably, a carefully constructed argument, presented in an editorial, was met with vitriol rather than counter-argument. But when one individual labeled me an elitist, I had to laugh, momentarily. I'm quite sure he was not referring to excellence. As to wealth and power, I am a retired, public-school teacher, for God's sake, hardly elite.

Letters to the Editor

#1

Last night thousands of angry, anti-Trump protesters were on the streets of New York. They will not be silenced.

Other emotions came into play as well: fear, disbelief and sadness. One hopes both parties will undergo a seismic shift as to how they view the disenfranchised - those who fell for the promise of a man they perceived as a savior - even as they threw away adult- thinking with their embrace of a person of arrested development, as witnessed in his candidacy.

I believe some soul-searching is occurring now - within the Democratic Party especially. How is it that the old party of the working-class has lost so much of its base? May our disgust toward those who would crush our egalitarian values result in a movement for true change.

To those who will dismiss my ideas by calling me a "lamebrain" in the Trumpian way of insult: I am not disheartened, and I shall continue to speak.

#2

In response to "If You Want Change, Do Something Constructive," one must once again confront the use of the buzz words: "socialism" and "political correctness." Would you prefer plutocracy?

The word, socialism, appears to send chills up the spines of some folks. Yet, with practices such as Social Security and Medicare, we have indeed accepted socialistic premises. Would you disband such programs for complete privatization?

When did political correctness become a dirty term? Is it so terrible to countenance varying views and people by way of kindness and respect?

The editorial writer espoused the notion of the right to protest; though very quickly protesters were labeled as "whiners" and "spoiled." Is Donald Trump a whiner as well? We have never known him to pass on an opportunity to yell "unfair" when things seemed not to be going his way.

Will President-elect Trump make a positive difference in the lives of working people? Or will he serve those of prestige and power primarily? So far, many of his Cabinet choices appear to favor the billionaire-class. I sincerely hope that "plutocracy" does not become the buzz word du jour.

Having said that, the author of the original letter to the editor expressed an understandable weariness with respect to the divisiveness of this election cycle. And she's correct in promoting continued self-education as a way forward - leading to constructive change.

We Are Diminished

Some view the outcome of the presidential election as a much-needed "shake up." However, it was not necessary to put the nation (and especially minorities, immigrants, etc.) at risk for four years. I believe that Trump is dangerous. Who knows what he will do and therefore unleash? Better had the electorate perceived egoism masquerading as concern for the underdog. Better had intellect won over pure emotion. To be sure, there has been prior corruption in government; the

Democratic Party, notably, has lost its way, and a dynastic view of potential White House occupants has proved problematic.

I would have welcomed Bernie Sanders - for his integrity. His vision represents a measured revolution of intellect and empathy. Though he promises to hold Trump accountable for horrific stances, the truth is, with the Republican Party holding both the House and the Senate, procedural rules, that which allowed the Republican Party to baulk previously whenever they wished, could simply be invalidated. What recourse would people like Bernie then have?

This is a very frightening time - and not so much for people in my position of age and circumstance - but for those who are especially vulnerable. Though, when basic decency and integrity are maligned, and cynicism and team-mentality take over, all are diminished.

A Particularly Terrible Combination: Self-Absorbed and Stupid

Has Trump ever thought of others in a professional capacity?

Has he engaged in community work? Served in the military or elsewhere? Even his charitable giving (a second-hand help) has been called into question.

Has he ever tried to "see the other side?" There is no evidence to say so. He "doubles down." He is vindictive. He yells "unfair" when things don't go his way. He is not a grownup.

Has Trump produced cogent thought? Is his education broad? Has he ever evinced any thought beyond himself? Not that we've seen.

We must conclude that he is ignorant
- uninterested in a world beyond an egoistic fiefdom. He misunderstood the premise of NATO.

71

Other off-the-cuff statements
- on abortion, trade, immigration inevitably required "re-statements" any number of times. In other words, he cared little - certainly not enough to generate serious thought.

Consider emotional intelligence, or in Trump's case, lack thereof.

For is not emotional intelligence the bedrock of all intelligence?

Thinking beyond oneself piques interest in a great world. And emotional intelligence is prerequisite for ethical behavior.

In one sense, Trump is not strictly stupid. He is sly - absolutely cognizant of others' negative emotions
- all stemming from fear
- of losing all - of being less.

Perhaps Trump is crazy like a fox.

Like the fox, he has lived solely to feed himself and his offspring.

As to the above, I sincerely hope that I am wrong - that I have mischaracterized the man
- or that redemption and growth ultimately will define Donald J. Trump.

This is the world's prayer.

President Chump

A "choron" is headed for the White House. A "choron"? Yes. This is my made-up word. It means: one who chooses to act like a moron. Kin to a "chelfish" charlatan. Chocked full of ego. Known for his

72

cheddar-colored hair. Not to be confused with a merely charismatic choice.

A choron refuses to countenance others' concerns. He does not read or question. He cannot abide criticism. My concern? He will not change - even faced with calamity. A choron sees us as chattel only. However, in so doing he chastises himself as well. Nothing good is born of the chicanery and calumny he often employed on the way to victory. Moreover, he may, in the end, choke under pressure, and many then would be chastened. After all, we all have choices.

Do I choose to be churlish here and now? Cheesy, even? Yes, and this is not to my credit. But I'm contemplating a confused chameleon in the White House. For sure, I'm not chortling. This writing represents brazen bravado and, perhaps, a childish response to what I thought would be a chimerical outcome. President Chump... Who'd have thought it?

When Satire is Not

Over the summer I wrote what I thought was a satirical piece on Trump's "Nightmare Cabinet." As it happened, the essay proved to be more prescient than satiric. I had been concerned about the possibility of a Trump presidency, and the writing served as a warning with regard to Trump's penchant for surrounding himself with loyalists - not that claiming loyalty, in order to accomplish a vision, is necessarily an unreasonable requirement. The problem with Trump is that he sees such loyalty as the only requirement.

I come back to the newly-elected president's vision of the world, a vision that comprises his own need primarily, I believe. He seems not to be interested in representing everyone, though he says that he is. One could easily surmise that this whole endeavor to attain the White

House had much to do with enhancing his own self-image. What Trump fails to understand is that his very image might result in exclusion rather than expansion in the long run; he is thinking small as opposed to large. As an example, a Cabinet of exclusion will telegraph a denial of the need for expansive thinking, intellectual engagement, and ultimate learning - prerequisites for a successful, enduring presidency.

The President of the United States must be prepared to learn. The job is not merely one of power-wielding, of desire for ultimate self-stature. It is arduous; it is humbling. On occasion, it is heart-breaking - provided one understands the great weight of tough decisions. Unfortunately, I do not believe that Mr. Trump understands this, at least not yet. Thus, I am worried.

Thankfully, this country has checks and balances. The Senate will consider, at the least, major appointees by way of a confirmation process. One hopes that even though the Senate is Republican by majority, the body will carefully consider the qualifications and histories of each of Trump's loyalists. It is particularly important that the Senate uphold its promise to represent all of the people, to go beyond party-politics. We need statesmen/stateswomen rather than party-hacks.

The tenure of any politician is finite, as are our individual tenures as human-beings, but the decisions made today will go far beyond our needs and, indeed, beyond our life expectancies. It would behoove Donald Trump and each and every member of the Senate to acknowledge the essential frailty of the human condition - both personally and in the largest possible context - as we move forward.

Self-Promoter-in-Chief: Tales of a Third-Rate Magician

"Pick a card, any card." The public gladly did so. "Nothing up my sleeve." Debatable. Trump is a master at sleight of hand. Oops, there's a headline on an out-of-court settlement as regards Trump University? Something Trump said he'd never do. He must pivot quickly to the *Hamilton* cast: "So rude!"

"Drain the swamp" down the drain with retread party-hacks nominated for Cabinet positions? The president-elect throws a victory party/rally. Arrives in style on the Trump jet; this never fails to impress.

Folks noticing that Cabinet positions are to be occupied primarily by billionaires. Save one thousand jobs at Carrier - glossing over the fact that corporate taxation will be reduced big time. Don't mention that only the little people pay taxes.

The name of the game is self-promotion. Did Obama stage a victory lap when the auto industry was saved? Unfortunately, no. Trump understands very well. that there can be no let-up in self-promotion. So, prepare yourself for an extravaganza at every turn. A phalanx of Trump helicopters when Putin comes to call. Fireworks with the appointment of a Supreme Court Justice with Trump's name emblazoned in the sky.

As to any defeats Trump may suffer, he'll cry him a river, and commission a number one hit to be written: "Unfair!"

The Aftermath: Still Blind Rage

He wrote an editorial

of sincere bewilderment

- a sad, even elegiac, commentary.

It seemed to him that
misogyny had won.

He could not countenance
the vitriol, the contempt for women
- most of all.

He mourned the seemingly lost values
- of kindness and respect
- concerned that his grandchildren would have to endure.

And the readership responded

with sarcasm - belittling words

that indicated essential smallness of spirit.

There was no largesse in winning.

Still blind rage...

In a village in Maine

- 300 strong marched in protest

- with signs urging Love and Compassion.

And the organizer of this event
 received threatening hate-mail

Law enforcement was alerted, for many were frightened.
Still blind rage...

When actors in New York
staged a respectful protest,
the victor responded with wounded pride
- and with disparaging remarks
- his usual way.
Still blind rage...

Even in victory
negative emotion runs rampant,
for when the winner fails to see the ephemeral quality of winning,
he does not know that a fine must be paid

- for not listening - for not hearing
beyond the chants of blind rage.

And should the winner persist in refusing to hear and see others,
he will forever engage in an all-consuming, paranoiac exercise:
the supposed enlargement (merely the protection) of self

- beholden only to blind rage...

(Another Note to Reader on Upcoming Pages:

Though lapses occur in the immediate-following entries, attempts at humor seek to temper outrage. The human comedy. So much of what we are viewing is plainly unnecessary. Also, self-reflection and a bit of humility help to quell residual cynicism born of worry.)

I Got the D.T.s

I got the D.T.s, and I don't even drink - well, not much, anyway.

It's the only way to explain the proper noun D.T.s - how the Donald Trumps. I mean, it must be a hallucinatory experience...

We elected someone who uses the "P" word?! - someone who joked about shooting a person on Fifth Avenue, denigrated Angela Merkel and cozied up to Putin.

- a man who seems to know only two words: "disaster" and "great." (Please, someone give this pol a dictionary for Christmas!)

Perhaps I should increase my alcohol intake. Medical DTs might be preferable to the scourge of D.T. - the teetotaler.

He doesn't smoke; good for him. He doesn't drink; ditto.

But the man is a gobbler - in more ways than one

No, I shall not court the DTs.
I need my wits about me
- now more than ever.

I got the D.T. blues...

Trump and "P" Words (Exclusive of That One)

Donald Trump, a pampered, powerful and portentous would-be potentate, promised to put the proletariat first. His plebeian and sometimes puerile language endeavored to put pomposity in the dustbin of discourse. He also knew that parading a pulchritudinous daughter could only pump up his image.

In his mind, power resided in the pedestrian past-times of an already pugnacious public. He would put forth paltry plans by way of a people's entertainment - an updated version of pitting unfortunates against lions - a perfidious past-time, indeed, reminiscent of a pernicious play, known for paucity of politic points presented, hardly a promotion of peace.

Post-election, Trump still resides in primary-land. Still tweeting petty pronouncements. Still pondering pulverizing punches. And when our eyes are feasting on that pointless pseudo-punditry, a plutocracy is in the making. Puffed-up princes of Wall Street are poised for power.

I'm sure more "P" words will promulgate in the White House come January. For now, I've decided to put Trump on pause. I mean, what's the point?

My fellow plebs, if by chance you believed in the palaver of Trump, (in the future) seek not pity, nor feel petulant, but plan for a more than palliative politician to follow post-Trump, and pray for peace and prosperity for all.

(P.S. Lest you characterize me as an "elitist," I chose to look up some of those "P" words.)

When Pigs Fly

Well, the impossible has happened. Donald Trump is flying high, not merely in his gold-plated jet, but on the world stage. A candidate of no governing experience, sketchy business practices, ludicrous and ever-changing ideas and a penchant for mindless, vindictive twittering has won.

Needless to say, I would have preferred nearly any of the other candidates - on the right or on the left - to the anti-intellectual. Trump. He doesn't read; he doesn't listen. He simply reacts. In fact, Trump gives "reactionary" a whole new meaning. It is the uncertainty that accompanies this man that gives me fits. That and the notion of a great swath of the populace accepting vainglorious grandiosity as truth. Along the way, news became entertainment with alternative, fake stories relished and believed. Truly outlandish (and slanderous) proclamations ensued, for example, President Obama / Secretary Clinton deemed "founders of ISIS." And such statements were cheered, revealing an antithetical reality of unbelievable proportion.

Bottom line: an ignorant child is in charge, perhaps. Or will Trump respond to the flattery of opportunists poised to set a particular agenda? Though I am sick and tired of hearing the word, unprecedented, I concede that the impossible has happened. This is not a nightmare, but reality.

Moreover, hell has frozen over in Aleppo.

These times call for a resurgence of mindful vigilance - a return to intellectualism in response to the unrestrained emotionalism of this past year. Our great libraries exist to provide access to history, philosophy, literature and more. I, for one, plan to eschew mesmerizing, addictive and placating pastimes in order to ponder.

Yes. I shall read the thoughts of those who have witnessed and assessed difficult times. I shall try to understand the genesis of this strange, new world - and speak out lest pigs flying becomes mundane.

Easy for Me

My friends and I are worried. Products of the sixties - a time of hope for fundamental change as to war-mongering, inequality, of working to ensure that hate was overcome by love - we cannot believe that divisive rhetoric appears to have won the presidential election. We are stunned, angry and sad.

I spent my professional life teaching. The greatest lesson learned, as far as I was concerned, was my realization that far from being the arbiter of wisdom, I would become the recipient of the collective wisdom of my students. Eventually, I knew that they had experience to share - that they deserved to be heard. I would learn to listen. My students represented the future, after all.

In time, I believed that conversation had to occur - conversation that would establish respect for point of view and varying dreams. I was happiest, when students pointed out something that I had missed in the analysis of a poem or a painting, for then I knew I was actually teaching. I learned to be a facilitator rather than a lecturer. Of course, I had to become secure enough to leave arrogance at the threshold of the classroom door. That would take some time.

And now I am retired and older. I see life through the lens of one who has weathered triumphs and tragedies - feelings of optimism and joy as well as emotions of self-doubt and despair. Now I have time to sort through experience by way of writing and in conversation with others.

The luxury of time. I can watch Fox News as well as MSNBC. I can tune in the PBS News Hour. I have the opportunity to read various newspapers and write about my reactions to what I see, coming to understand even better what matters. But it wasn't always this way. As a worker, I had little time to keep up with the news of politics. Certainly, no time to listen to divergent views, I was dancing as fast as I could to meet the day-to-day responsibility of providing for myself and my students.

As an admirer of George Orwell's *Animal Farm* - for its honest portrayal of human nature - I often find myself recalling the story. The ruling class of Orwell's short novel, often called a fable of sorts, understood well that the masses, kept busy with relentless labor, would have little time to consider the reality of their governance, for it takes time to carefully listen, question and draw conclusions - time only made available to those who no longer work or work under the most advantageous of circumstances.

In my comfortable retired state, I could not understand the appeal of Donald Trump. Why did the electorate not see his obvious emotional-manipulation, his supreme arrogance masquerading as "regular guy?" Why were his insults tolerated? How is it that his vast inexperience in governance - actually, no experience beyond amassing wealth - was discounted? Why did many admire someone who has never worked as they have? Never had to put up with an unpleasant boss nor had to worry about putting a meal on the table? The answer lies in Trump's visceral appeal - his understanding of the great frustration of those who have been ignored for far too long. And these workers, the bedrock of our society, did not have the luxury of time to fact-check Trump's statements. Their days were spent working, some in more than one job. They had no time to read multiple newspapers or watch varying newscasts, no time to analyze the situation, no time to question even their own motives and feelings.

Just as I had to learn to listen to my students with utmost respect and with the realization that I was as much of a student as they, I have come to the conclusion that I must listen now, not just to like-minded friends of my circumstance and generation, but to those who hold different views, in order to engage in conversation about the hopes and dreams of all, though never to countenance hatred or disrespect!

Now is not the time for rancor - or even anger. Now is the time for conversation, for raising ideas and suggestions that will promote open mindedness. Now is the time to replace emotion with thought, and to finally note that participants in a democracy need time to think. And that is the salient conundrum, for ultimately good government is prerequisite for the luxury of time.

President Obama

He identifies - is identified - as black

Though, in fact, he is a confluence of race

representing America in black and white

- this - a segue to words appearing on a printed page.

This writer-president

whose unfettered intellect

ponders history, philosophy

- finds the road that leads to an ethical stance.

- seeks expansiveness of spirit

- longs for morality.

Though hatred - racism –
played its part,
unbridled emotion
reason's counterpart
hates cool intellect
the potential vanquisher
most of all.

So, base anger has emerged as the winner.

Yet, like a fire,
such rage burns exceedingly hot,
burning those who engage.

And blind rage is finite,
for a fire feeds only upon itself in the end.

We acknowledge that fire is ephemeral

while cool intellect
- like an ever-flowing river –
replenishes the body and the soul.
It is infinite in its character.
It is the reality of wisdom.

Believe this:

Elegant thought will be revered into posterity.

It lives on the page

and in our open hearts
- as the only way forward.

After Word

Too old for hero-worship

- though not so old

that I fail to recognize and appreciate

transcendence of spirit

- over anger, the destructive force.

Sadness

- in its process –

may offer a light
- the hope of redemption.

I will make something
- for solace.

While making something,
I will not be engaged in tearing down.

(Yet Another Note to Reader:

Please brace yourself for additional, passionate reactions of incredulity and frustration. Once again, these are followed by additional attempts at humor, on the way to a renewed vow of vigilance as to Trump's actual presidency.)

Not My President

I'm mightily tired of the call for folks like me to "get over" the election. Many got over the election of George W. Bush, though the first election was mired in the controversy of hanging chads and disregard for the popular vote. Many also accepted the second election. In the end, Bush's presidency resulted in mission not accomplished in Iraq and the Great Recession. This time around we're dealing with a whole new beast, and I do not use the word lightly. Donald J. Trump sees the world through the prism of demagoguery and, more to the point, a self-serving agenda.

Many fear our democracy will be undermined in myriad ways: bloviating tweets rather than reflective meetings with the intelligence community, denigration of the press in the attempt to silence dissenting voices, outlandish "plans" for health care that somehow are never articulated but merely promised, an agenda of divisive legislation to include: a wall, the demonization of American-Muslims. Well, one could go on and on...

Many will continue to stand firm in opposition to Trump. Ratings for the swearing-in of President Trump will be low, this a form of protest. Dissenting voices will be heard with demonstrations far and wide.

This is still America; we get to voice our concerns loud and clear - and will do so as long as we must.

Yet Another Example of "I Know You Are, But What Am I?"

One could set one's watch by Trump's tweeting responses to criticism. Case in point? His response to Meryl Streep's impassioned speech at the Golden Globes Awards show. Though he claims he didn't see/read her remarks, the usual "over-rated" comment was flung Meryl's way soon thereafter. What a joke... First of all, is anyone else wearied by Trump's meager vocabulary? "Over rated, disaster" etc.?

More to the point, once again the Donald has deemed another to be what he is. Over-rated in business, one could easily argue. Beyond over-rated as to potential presidential-material, and this is putting it mildly. Dare I say, over-rated as an adult, a human-being? Yes, I dare.

Even were one to believe his pathetic explanation of mocking a disabled person, one would expect a fully-formed, empathetic adult to apologize for any "misunderstanding" that ensued from his disgusting display of disrespect. Not going to happen...

Would that we could hire the "English Nanny" to straighten out Donald. Would that we could put him in the "time out" chair for the foreseeable future.

KFC: Kellyanne F. Conway

She is clucking her way to the White House. However, she is not a typical, "fowl"-mouthed Trumpian acolyte - much too cool in her use of language to resort to mere name-calling. "No way, Conway," she tells herself, "I prefer a more sophisticated con." Her diversionary tactics, at first glance, seem cogent in comparison to Trump's typically hysterical response to criticism. But look closely; a relaxed demeanor cannot cover for straw-man-type argument. Here's an example: Streep calls out Trump on his disparagement of a disabled reporter. KFC accuses Meryl Streep of callously ignoring the torture of a disabled man in Chicago. This is a neat bit of sleight-of-hand, but it is still a con.

Rarely flummoxed by pointed questions, KFC is a sinister version of the con-man she represents. Because she is impervious to slights, Conway does not wear her ego on her sleeve, and, as a result, she looks like a Rhodes Scholar in comparison with Trump. However, make no mistake, KFC is made of the same cloth; winning is all in Trump world. Imagining KFC playing Lady Macbeth to Trump's Lear, behind the scenes, is apt. Though she will not enjoy the mantle of great power herself, Conway will be part of the realm, and I guess that's good enough as far as she is concerned. The way of the con is exhilarating in its own right, after all.

In writing the above, I have come perilously close to ignorant, Trumpian rhetoric. However, hauling out the talons, while unkind, may cause others to see KFC for what she is. Yes, I feel some shame, for I am not usually called to join others in a disparagement contest. Yet, here I have participated to some degree in a mud-fight. Mea culpa from the mud-hen... But I ask you, who is ultimately to blame for the shameful tenor of current political discourse? I believe you will agree that his name rhymes with an apt slogan, "Dump the Grumpy Rump-Chump!" As he dispatched many in the primary season who refused to follow his brawling lead, perhaps I cannot be faulted for lowering my standards on this occasion?

You should ignore that last bit. I am still feeling sullied with this immature rant.

That's Entertainment (not Art)

We live in an age of the worst of entertainment: insult and tit-for-tat nonsense. Unfortunately, vulgar behavior, the equal of any cheesy reality-show, continues to gain headlines. It is unthinkable (in more ways than one) that the president-elect spends his time responding via twitter to criticism in an inane and childish fashion. Who cares that his little (again, little, in more ways than one) feelings are hurt?

In the broader sense, scurrilous entertainment has mesmerized the public. What happened to art? Why do many partake of juvenilia over adult pastimes? All well and good to enjoy mindless, escapist programming on occasion. Who doesn't? Yet, when it comes to governance/big issues, one must "put away childish things" - mere headline-grabbing, puerile, Trumpian behavior - in favor of adult circumspection.

Remember the Russian statement: "Religion is the opiate of the masses"? Well, scratch that for: "Incessant, childish 'entertainment' drugs up America." While we witness daily tantrums by Trump via twitter, we are not paying attention to the specter of hurried confirmations of Trump's billionaire Cabinet. We are also not questioning his 36-year-old son-in-law's accession to power. Nor are we demanding to understand the intricacies of the business-empire of Trump with regard to foreign entities. More fun to yak about Donald's latest insult, for this requires little in the way of brain-power: reading, thinking, and assessing.

Years ago, I made it very clear to my high-school students that I was not to be viewed as an entertainer. I would do my best to create interesting and provocative lesson plans but "song and dance" was not on the agenda. My point? Education, in all senses of the word, depends on the give and take of mutual responsibility. When one is merely entertained, one is passive. Partaking of the arts, on the other hand, requires thought and the emotional connection of empathy in its broadest meaning. In the end, my students appreciated my stance, for soon, on the best days, they knew that what they thought was important; moreover, they understood that their ideas would be revered. They saw the glimpses of freedom that are afforded those who question and create.

Let's face it, there is no art in *The Art of the Deal* by Donald J. Trump. And the deal always benefits himself. It's time to demand that the president-elect take mature ownership of the position he is about to assume. Self-enhancing business must be put away. Childish "entertainment" must cease. Conversely, the public must own being governed by way of thoughtful and questioning behavior.

I'm No Economist nor Social Scientist, But...

It seems to me that many folks have memory deficits, that is to say, short memories. For example, President Obama did not cause but inherited a Great Recession - born of deregulation run wild and resultant malfeasance: economic "bubbles" that burst upon the scene with terrible results for the average citizen. I provide here a small example compared with what others went through. Our house, bought at the height of the market, is worth considerably less now. Far more important, many others lost their jobs, their homes - their essential dignity - yet, the corruption associated with deregulation was soon forgotten.

That Obama was unable to magically take us back to those halcyon days of absolute full-employment, rising wages and alternative-job creation in a mere eight years is remembered instead, and folks focus on legislation such as The Affordable Care Act (that managed to insure 20 million previously uninsured citizens) as if it were the ultimate cause of their disappointment.

If one revisits past history, other examples come to mind. Many vilify Roosevelt and Johnson for their social-welfare programs. Yet, Roosevelt's plans, for example, were, at least in part, responsible for an extended period of enjoyed prosperity. How many people benefited from Johnson's view on Medicare and Social Security?

To be sure, programs as set up, have shelf-lives. Change occurs and the on-going process is complicated - requiring monitoring, tweaking. But to forget all that has gone before, while focusing on parts of a whole, is to deny history - to willfully forget in the way of blaming those "culprits" to whom we have access. Short-sighted, I'd say.

Trumpster in the Dumpster: A Little Ditty to Keep You (Actually, Me) Sane

Don't worry. Trumpster will be in the dumpster (of history) before you know it.

You see, he will soon realize

that the playground is larger than he ever imagined.

And adulation is spare after victory - when promises are broken - and hype is not ripe.

Many will tell him; "No!" He'll hate that... And a 3 am tweet will only momentarily satisfy; the sentiment will still be "No!"

One can control a fiefdom. - but not, a great, big complicated world. Stuff will happen...

History tells us that blowhards are a flash in the pan. Soon ignored, they   head   for   the   hills
Or live in some sort of alternative reality - of teeming flatterers - who gladly glad-hand while taking over.

Frankly, it's the take-over that should give pause...

But this is meant to convey cheer. Be not Chicken Little of "the sky is falling" fame.

Nor Benjamin, the donkey, in *Animal Farm* who said something like: "Life will go on as usual - badly."

You'll find no self-fulfilling prophecy here: Learn from the past! Plan for the future! Be now!!

The old adage comes to mind - with a tweak: "Living well, admirably and with hope, is the best response."

Therefore, seek not revenge: Promote peace, aspire to a true understanding, and at least attempt to care for those who have behaved badly; to do otherwise is to become them.

After the Turkey Replaced the Eagle

He hit the twitter send-button. Gobble, gobble, gobble. "Over-rated, disaster ... sad!"

Re: Putin

"Great leader ... because he likes me."

Gobble, gobble, gobble.

Re: Conflict of Interest

Gobble, gobble, gobble.
The capons will run the business. "Don't worry; we're in the clear..."

Re: Media

"Unfair!" "I don't recognize you!" Gobble, gobble, gobble.
(But they recognized him.)

Re: FBI, CIA

"I don't like you either!" "You gotta go!" Gobble, gobble, gobble.

(But they didn't go.)

The upshot?

The subsequent president refused to pardon the gobbler.
(All "back taxes" - recompense - paid.)

And the eagle soared once more.

The Three Stooges, Rush Limbaugh, Ann Coulter and (Ta-Da!) Donald Trump

Everyone loves a fool - until maimed by one.

Back in the annals of time, my brother and I spent an afternoon watching "The Three Stooges" on television. We laughed and laughed at the antics of these fools but soon emulation came into play - with predictable results. Once my mother ascertained who had done what to whom and why, quite rightly, "The Three Stooges" met its demise as far as we were concerned.

Many years later on an interminable road-trip to Maine, fatigued by the monotony of an interstate highway and beyond the reach of NPR broadcasting, my fellow-traveler and I tuned in to Rush Limbaugh. I'm ashamed, now, to admit that he made us laugh. Though vehemently opposed to his take on politics and his world view, generally speaking, he evinced a sophomoric humor, especially in his use of mimicry. And a bored driver even found the name of Limbaugh's sidekick, Mr. Snerdly, to be somehow endearing. That "ditto-heads" of little humor called in to espouse similar views soon prompted us to find a golden-oldies channel. Rush's delivery may be funny, but his underlying message and influence is decidedly not, even slightly, amusing.

The problem with humorous shock-hosts is that their genre is soon invaded by dead-serious denigrators. Ann Coulter comes to mind. There is nothing even remotely humorous about Ann - unless one takes great joy in the evisceration of fellow human-beings. Her crocodile smile reminds me of Jack Nicholson's maniacal grin in *The Shining,* you know, when he says: "Here's Johnny." Such a persona gives one the willies - as should Ann Coulter despite her blonde hair and trim figure - though, the stiletto-heels might offer a clue...

My point is: Just as "The Three Stooges" is inappropriate viewing for young children, so, too, is much of the adult entertainment we consume today. The coarsening of communication, as witnessed in countless venues, celebrates denigration, and the notion of revenge is lauded as well - usually in the most sadistic manner possible. That's entertainment?

When Donald Trump burst upon the political scene - actually he insinuated himself rather stealthily into our consciousness, ironically through entertainment - many were amused by his persona and his antics. "He's funny, but he'll never reach his goal. Don't worry." And while I did not worry then, neither did I see him as funny. Well, you know how this story ends... As it turned out, a stooge has become President of the United States. I liken Trump to Moe, the hapless stooge with the distinctive hair-do. And they have even more in common; Moe is forever reacting to Curly's onslaughts - just as Trump cannot help but respond to criticism. Throughout the campaign we witnessed Trump's behavior, the equivalent of Moe's fingers in eyes, slaps on faces and frying pans bashed on heads - linguistic violence, if you will. Where was Mum when we needed her? The television should have been shut off right at that point, for we are not so unlike small children when all is said and done. When bad behavior becomes the norm, all become desensitized to one degree or another.

Back to Moe of "The Three Stooges" - just for a quick point. Invariably Moe became enraged when Curly did something thoughtless, like discarding a banana-peel inappropriately so that Moe slipped on it. In Trump's case, others are not providing hazards to his well-being, but either pointing out the flaws in his argument or responding to Trump-initiated vitriol. That Trump has neither apologized when wrong nor considered counter-argument indicates that we are dealing with a particularly recalcitrant individual. Perhaps such behavior could have been accepted as a campaign stance. However, now we are days away from the inauguration, and he continues with the insults and the inane tweeting.

One prays that President Trump wakes up on Monday morning; by the way, have you heard that the Trump Presidency does not begin until Monday, due to celebrations? Again, wakes up Monday aware of the enormity of his position - aware that this is no slap-stick comedy, but real life - aware of someone other than himself.

Toot Your Own Horn! (Tales of the Shameless Self-Promoter and a Gracious Public Servant)

The past few days have been filled with nostalgia for Barack Obama. Not only have we acknowledged his steadfast dignity, oratorical skill and optimistic stance, we have also finally discussed his many accomplishments. Too little credit, too late, as it turned out. Why did we not praise him to the heavens when he prevented a second major depression? When he saved the auto industry and saw to it that millions of folks would work, somehow this news also was relegated to a footnote.

I'm reminded of the example of some bratty, privileged teenager, who when given a turquoise-laden bangle-bracelet responded with a half-hearted thank you, but soon opined that diamonds would have been nice. But it's not just that the public wishes all problems to be fixed completely and instantaneously, as if great prosperity could be ensured with a simple statement: "Your wish is my command." More precisely, the public fails to remember history in order to understand the genesis of an economy gone awry. Because past governments are out of our reach, many express their frustrations where they have access, in other words, toward a sitting president, one who inherited strife and sought to ameliorate it. Unfortunately, Donald Trump capitalized on this specious "blame-game."

Trump fanned the fire of disappointment while eschewing any sort of specific plan or intellectual exercise. He simply said: "Your wish is my command!" - or words to that effect, but heavy on self-aggrandizement: "Only I can fix it!" Prior to his candidacy, Trump attempted to undermine "the thinker" with his egregious "birther" lie. So, we cannot discount completely the intelligence of Donald Trump. However, we must understand fully that self-enhancement is the only driving force behind Trump's intellectual forays. And we must understand, too, that Trump abhors rigorous, creative thought. After all, he embraces mindless entertainment while others deny such pastimes for something deeper, more provocative.

When Trump declared that he might cut spending for the National Endowment for the Arts /Humanities, I shuddered. Is this simply ignorance at its worst? Poking intellectuals in the eyes for the fun of it? Or does such a move attempt to deliberately shut down dissention or creative ideas – and/or intellectualism, generally speaking? Is this a way of erasing history? These questions demand attention, it seems to me.

In the way of human regret, for example, "I never truly appreciated so and so until I lost him," many more will finally appreciate President Obama. I wish Obama had tooted his own horn more often, though perhaps such behavior goes against the grain, being unseemly. But look where it got Trump? Obama saved millions and millions of jobs over the past eight years, among other accomplishments; Trump took credit for thousands of jobs at Carrier, and enjoyed a shameless victory lap in the process. I guess a marketing degree beats a law degree - at least in the minds of some folks. However, soon we will witness the beginning of the end of Trump's presidency. I do believe that when all is said and done, the law degree will be revered once more. Perhaps, we can also take solace with the notion: Sometimes anticipation feels worse than the actual event; though such a notion

DOES NOT preclude continued vigilance - and protest, when necessary!

Inauguration Day

A gloomy, gray day here in the East, but I shall take a long walk nevertheless. The peaceful transition of power is essential.

I wish to embody a magnanimous spirit, to wish all well. And I do. Yet, ironically, given the title of my entire collection of thoughts, I cannot bring myself to "bear witness" today.

Another After Word

Bill, my mainstay, asked me the other day: "Have you ever before been so politically motivated?" My immediate answer was "No." Though quickly I amended my response with recalled memories of a protest against Johnson with regard to the Vietnam War - and my then visceral dislike of Nixon. I concede now that Johnson's legacy, while tainted, included a domestic agenda of social reform, most notably, civil rights legislation. Even Nixon can be credited with continued support of desegregation, the creation of the EPA, detente with the USSR and the beginnings of a relationship with China.

Of course, in the end, ignominy ended Richard Nixon's tenure. Perhaps some parallels can be drawn between Nixon and Trump, not the least of which may turn out to be impeachment. Yet, it must be remembered: Nixon evinced intellect that, on occasion, benefited this nation. We have seen no such indication of thoughtful reflection in Trump's demeanor or behavior. Though I have grown exceedingly tired of the word, unprecedented, Trump's accession engenders disbelief. Such disbelief rises from the demonstrable fact: Trump's deficits are truly shocking.

Incredulity became my motivation: to bear witness, to write (in real time, episodically) about essentially surreal turns-of-events. Even now, January 21, 2017, Trump's presidency seems impossible. I feel as though I'm living some sort of hallucination; surely the electorate did not choose an inexperienced, vindictive, intellectually inferior and self-absorbed wannabe?!

Reality sets in: Today Donald J. Trump is the 45th President of the United States of America.

Today is also the day of the Women's March. Over 200,000 women will raise their voices today. I'm fortunate to be able to state that I know three of them personally. Their ages are 67, 67 and 73. My generation... I think of their service as a reunion of sorts - a revisiting of past protests that resulted in remarkable, glorious change. I am so proud of their commitment.

And, today I take a page from President Obama's optimistic "book." The world hasn't ended. I, too, believe in the basic goodness of our citizenry. Yes, we will!

Part Three: The Early Days of Trump's Presidency

(Introduction: Meant to provide copious detail as to the first days of the Trump presidency, the reader might conclude that I have displayed a relentless hyper-vigilance, and the reader would be correct. Whole days were spent consuming print as well as broadcast material.

Though such an experiment proved to be finite in nature, it underscored the massive amount of information constituents could consider. I salute the fourth estate in its relentless pursuit of detail, in its dogged protection of democracy.)

Day #1 (actually, technically, day 1 and a half)

I tuned into the prayer service held at the National Cathedral this morning (1/21). Naturally, Trump et alia were in attendance. The opening prayer for the country was pointed, to say the least. The church leader prayed for an end to arrogance and walls that separate peoples; he prayed for peace, unity and respect for all. I hoped that President Trump was taking it all in, though I wondered, too, if he would respond in some way.

I watched the Women's March exceed 200,000. At last count, close to a half million individuals are protesting in Washington. Other gatherings throughout the country, too, are exceeding expectations of participation. From New York City to Minneapolis to Los Angeles - and too many other locations to list easily - women and men are making their views known in peaceful, respectful cadences. I believe this is just the beginning of full-scale resistance.

I viewed President Trump's remarks at his first meeting with the CIA. He deplored the media, per usual, accusing them of underestimating attendance at the inauguration, among other complaints. He pledged his great love for the CIA. Then he went on to praise himself: his inaugural address, his intelligence - also reminding us of his fifteen appearances on the cover of *Time* magazine. Frankly, it was embarrassing. I found myself muttering: "He's truly off the rails!" - or words to that effect. And all the while, his audience hooted and hollered with glee. (Who were those people?)

Surely, this cannot go on indefinitely...

An aside: Madonna's F-Bomb (dropped at Women's March)

If I were to have at the world's microphone (hardly likely to happen) I would hope that I'd be able to contain emotion to the extent that I would eschew the F-Bomb. In the first place, such a rhetorical device dilutes the important message one is trying to impart through thoughtful concern and action, namely, the demand for respect. By resorting to crass, emotional language, one is visiting "Trump world" where inelegance of speech and basic ignorance reign. It is most Trumpian to believe one can say or do anything - wherever and to whomever - one pleases.

Don't get me wrong. I'm not a prude, nor am I promoting the language police. Though I used the F-word liberally during the past election season, I relegated it to where it belonged, my space, not the world stage. Remember "indoor voice" versus "outdoor voice" when we were kids? Well, this is the opposite. When "outdoors," I would advise circumspect rhetoric. Let's not give loud mouths the satisfaction of stooping to their level or, even more to the point, any ammunition with which to dilute the message of protest.

Day #2

I call it the audacity of the dope. Unfortunately, it is a calculated audacity, a deflection away from Trump's plans for self-enhancement at every turn. And yet, in a strange way, it is both a deflection from real issues, depriving folks of their health care and, in general, undermining the rights of "the other," even while stating openly and brazenly: "It's all about me."

This morning we are not talking about the specifics of health-care; we're talking about numbers in attendance at the inauguration. Our eyes are off the ball; therefore, we are supporting Trump's overall plan. Even his surrogates openly admit that Trump "is all strategy" - as if governance is one big game of grab the ball and score. Trump wants us to forget the "shining city on the hill," to forget "I have been to the mountaintop." He is playing the child's game of "King of the Mountain" masterfully.

Citizen Trump is smart enough to know that he has the media between a rock and a hard place. They feel they must report on his inane speeches of self-aggrandizement, but air-time given to this endeavor is air-time spent away from eliciting Trump's agenda - pushing for cogent answers, asking questions such as: What.do you hope to accomplish as you sign the first papers of repeal of Obamacare? My advice? Do not accept the inevitable response - "I will save all with my plan." One should ask how today's signing will impact specifically tomorrow and the next day. Reporter and citizen alike should attempt to unpack Trump's strategy. Even if he cannot or will not respond, the process will reveal something akin to substance.

Trump has demanded and received attention, on his terms, from day one of his campaign. It is time we come to the "business table" with our own terms. The press no longer needs to report on Trump's idiocy. He has won the election. That game is over. Trump's relentless pleas for attention as to the "unfairness" of news outlets must be ignored now and countered with relentless questions about each and every move he makes - the old "who, what, where, how and why" questions. I ask that we please end the reality show/shell-game at this very moment in time, lest we lose all sight of real issues: transparency, fairness and freedom.

An aside: portion of email to friend

I agree with you about Pence. Watching him yesterday as he backed Trump's idiocy at the CIA meeting (in Pencian, oily fashion) prompted me to surmise that the vice-president may be paving the way for his eventual day in the sun. And, Pence is terrible, for sure. His take on education, in addition to all that you mentioned, is offensively egregious. Yet, an "off-the-rails" Trump poses a real threat that cannot be discounted. At least with Pence, one might put away thoughts of a psychotic episode - though, presumably, such a breakdown is too fanciful a fear. Yet, I shudder to think how Trump will react if and when he discovers he is not, in fact, king of the world.

Day #3

A day that engenders dizziness. It seems to me that Trump is throwing multiple ideas. against a wall in the hope that some will stick: NAFTA will be overhauled, corporate taxes will be massively cut, companies who work outside of the United States will be harshly penalized, business regulations will be slashed by 75 per cent, the US embassy in Tel Aviv may well be relocated to Jerusalem. One has to wonder about the sheer boldness of such an agenda and note, as well, the inherent difficulty of simultaneously unpacking these wide-ranging possibilities.

Trump's style is problematic for two reasons. One: It negates requisite reaction-time - essential for those who deliberate as to policy; experts (and other thoughtful people) are facing a massive volume of topics - too many to consider in a measured way. A paranoid person would suggest that this scenario is no accident. Perhaps the paranoid person is correct. Two: Little credence is given to the complexity of issues,

106

and this reminds me, sadly, of the bombast of Trump's candidacy. The possibility of unforeseen outcomes of policy-decisions needs to be carefully considered even at the outset of discussion.

On the surface, promoting business growth with tax cuts sounds promising. However, we have a deficit to consider and the notion that perhaps, once again, average citizens will be called to fill the void - though Trump says not. I mean, revenue has to come from somewhere, does it not? Relocating the United States Embassy to Jerusalem is not a new idea; other presidents have considered doing so. But now? In midst of Arab unrest and the real threat of ISIS, would this not further enhance the recruitment arms of any number of terrorist organizations?

Admittedly, I am no expert in economics or foreign policy. However, I maintain that governing without measure and bragging about boldness is dangerous. Perhaps, pointing out President Trump's seemingly short-attention span is an unkind denigration. Yet, I wish to see President Trump recognize complexity. I wish to see President Trump concede that he may not have all of the answers. I hope that perspicacious individuals work hard to ensure a vigilance regarding all that is being presented, despite the manic pace.

Research tells me that President Obama's first four days were less frenetic. He accomplished the following: suspended military commissions for 120 days, signed an executive order on ethics, ordered the US intelligence community to adhere to the US "Army Field Manual," ordered the end of the "Mexico City Rule" and addressed the nation on its economic situation with the hope of presentation of an economic recovery plan within a month. Well, that was then. To be sure, the times were different. Yet, it is quite clear that the styles/personalities of Obama and Trump offer a stark contrast - a profound understatement if there ever was one...

Yes, President Trump deserves a respectful chance. However, it's difficult to embrace a "honeymoon period" in the midst of multiple plans and the less than measured "roll-out" of these plans.

An aside:

I do not envy Mr. Spicer's job. As press secretary, he is the true surrogate of President Trump. As spokesman, he must relay the president's stance on a host of issues; also, he must mirror Trump's style. Clearly, President Obama's press secretaries spoke much the way he did - slowly and in a particularly circumspect manner. In contrast, Mr. Spicer speaks at a brisk pace, is less circumspect, sometimes protective of his boss to the point of combativeness.

Spicer's first performance on Saturday was rocky. Today he presented a more genial presence. Yet, once again, the press secretary stood firm on the media's portrayal of President Trump's inauguration with respect to ratings, specifically, crowd numbers. He stated that the media's presentation of comparison photos of the respective Obama and Trump audiences was "demoralizing." And I immediately thought: For heaven's sake, we're not dealing with a pep-rally here. Though it sounds harsh, few are concerned about Trump's or his staff's emotional reactions.

The great irony is that President Trump, an attention-seeking individual, has prompted many to pay close attention to his each and every move. Such a response is perhaps not what Trump envisioned, for inevitably there will be criticism - comes with the territory. One hopes that Trump and surrogates learn to respond only to what is truly important. To do otherwise would endanger their own well-being as well as the well-being of the country.

Day #4

Last night President Trump once again railed against the outcome of the election - specifically the popular vote - by repeating that same old unsubstantiated claim of illegal immigrants voting. This time he upped the number to three or five million. But let me move quickly away from this nonsense, for it is simply a major distraction - not worth discussing, really. Pathetic but not profound in any way...

Today Trump will meet once more with titans of industry. This represents the second piece of bread in an economic sandwich - the union leaders' meeting of yesterday falling as it did between two sessions with top brass. Somehow the access of union folks, the small guys, feels like a token gesture - an optics-move of little import. Once again, the average Joe was relegated to window-dressing. This has been a major problem for both parties lately. When one notes how Trump's cabinet appointments are playing out, Trump's professed love for masses is suggestive of broken promises, a manipulative sham.

That Trump will give credence primarily to the honchos should offer no surprise. Yes, he will threaten them. Perhaps he truly believes that he can force corporations to hire American. However, I suspect that the president misunderstands the effects of globalization and automation. Moreover, as has been noted by many others, Trump's Cabinet, if it be comprised of billionaires, will offer a billionaire-outlook. Let's face it, Trump is most comfortable with his own crowd. At the very least, visually, this set-up is entirely too cozy. It is perhaps redundant to mention the general lack of diversity inherent in Trump's choices.

How to insure the little people have a hand in their own destinies? That question represents the conundrum of politics and governance. The simple answer is that there are many more of us. If the grassroots-contingent observes, assesses and then responds both by way of demonstration and outreach to those currently in power - tirelessly and with creative fervor - just maybe things will change. First, the great hump of small-minded nationalism, a notion that President Trump embraces (for selfish reasons) must be scaled. Folks must realize that they have more in common with other marginalized people, as opposed to the kings of Wall Street - that jingoistic patriotism, in the end, represents the death knell of the very premise of this country. Well, we'll see...

An aside:

I often wonder why I am doing this writing. To what purpose? I do not think I am merely writing for selfish gain. Writing clarifies my thoughts. And, fundamentally, I believe that creation denies destruction - that somehow making something, even if that something is of a critical nature, prevents a kind of nihilism. I must admit, also, that I like to play with words. Often, I share with my mainstay, Bill, who appreciates what I write. But, of course, without a larger platform, my writing amounts to simple entertainment. I have to acknowledge that...

This latest section of *Bearing Witness,* "The Early Days of Trump's Presidency," continues in the mode of a journalistic recounting of in-time reaction to what I perceive as a debacle. Small portions of the earlier writing, having to do with Trump's candidacy and the transition, "saw the light of day" as several entries were published in various Connecticut newspapers and one online. Whether or not anyone's thinking was affected, I will never know.

I do this because I believe that even the average citizen needs to be acknowledged. Is there not a place for the musings of one who has led a relatively pedestrian life? Do we not deserve to be heard? I guess the hard part is figuring out how to call attention to the views of a mere

Jane. Perhaps I should consider a blog. Though that notion strikes me as essentially self-serving. I mean, who would read it? Maybe I will inundate my state representatives and other people of political persuasions with daily "briefings." It could become annoying, I am sure, and perhaps I would be simply ignored. However, one never knows. It is slightly possible that one, little, incessant voice would prevail in the long run. It never hurts to try.

Day #5

"Fast and Furious" has a whole new meaning today. Trump is vigorously attempting to project a BOLD persona. He is still furious about various perceived slights. He is on a mission to prove that he keeps his promises and is no fool. Hold onto your spinning head, for he is certainly not holding on to his. The order has been signed for the pipeline. "Jobs, jobs, jobs!" Only problem is, while thousands of construction jobs will be created for the building of this unnecessary expense, more on that later, only 35 permanent jobs will be needed for the running and maintenance of the pipe-infrastructure. Ranchers and farmers in Nebraska are outraged by the prospect of eminent domain. Native Americans worry about danger to the water supply. Someone ought to haul out that old advertisement for fire prevention that showed a dignified and tearful Indian as he surveyed a land choked by smoke and carnage. Remember that ad? The thing is, while this pipeline will support the oil industry, it is an "export" pipeline. In other words, not to be used for US consumption of oil. (Therefore, not necessary.) As the US moves toward isolationism under Trump, one wonders exactly how the exportation of this oil will work. OK, perhaps that last line was a bit too glib.

But speaking of walls, or alluding to them at least, Trump will sign his wall order today. Another case of unnecessary expense - and what an expense! Supposedly funds will be moved from other government agencies in order to start the process. Care to hazard a guess as to who will lose funding? The president may tackle additional immigration issues - but just more on the notion of border-enhancements. Ditto the previous question. Back to the "great wall of Trump" - a two-thousand-mile wall that will eat up a sizeable chunk of American revenue. For what? I am not witnessing hordes of Visigoth-style terrorists breaching the ramparts of the US. And I believe that drug smugglers have many options; their activities will not be substantively curtailed by a single barrier. This wall-idea is an outrage; we are witnessing a grown man playing with Legos.

By now, you've noted that fast and furious has rubbed off on me. I am angry and the previous words of today's entry have taken me just 20 minutes to write. Taking a page from Trump's penchant for hyperbole, let me suggest that those of you who are holding series EE bonds convert them to cash ASAP. Trump has stated that perhaps the value of those bonds could be renegotiated. I'm not kidding, though I seriously doubt that the faith and full credit of the country is up for grabs. And as to additional funds that will be needed for the wall, Congress will have to approve such an appropriation. Highly unlikely, wouldn't you say? So, the sky is not falling today... However, if my optimism and/or belief in the intelligence of a Republican-dominated Congress is misplaced, then fear takes hold...

In the wee hours Trump tweeted about the very troubling murder rate in Chicago: "I will send in the feds!" Another example of BOLD. Guess he'll get that parade of tanks, after all... But seriously, Trump's fast and furious persona is worrying. The man needs some sleep. He needs to get off his PR shtick for a moment. This is not all about him and his image. Thousands of anti-Trump organizations are coalescing as I write. In February citizens will descend on the offices of many and various legislators to demand the reigning-in of Trump. Actually, the early phase of this campaign took place yesterday. Many people are furious, and they are moving fast. Power to the people!

An aside:

A bit about the current White House web site in comparison with Obama's web site... To be fair, Obama had eight years to perfect his pages and links. Trump hasn't been in office eight days yet. However, it is interesting to note that while Obama's staff provided 114 links just prior to the transition of power, hours later the Trump administration offered a mere 38. In other words, a whole lot of deleting took place. All mention of climate change has been purged. The page on Americans with disabilities is gone as is the page that promoted LGBT work-opportunities. And there is no longer a Spanish language option. A paranoid person might note that Trump appears to be settling some scores...

Yet, it is the tone of Trump's link titles that is most telling: America First Energy Plan, Trade Deals Working for All Americans, Making the Military Strong, Standing Up for Our Law, America First Foreign Policy, etc. In contrast, President Obama's links featured: civil rights, health care, climate change, economy, education, gay rights, ethics, disabilities, etc. Trump's titles read as campaign slogans while Obama's web site provided spare topics of concerns. By the way, one can no longer access Obama's White House web site - even as a retrieval. It has been thoroughly scrubbed. Enough said, perhaps...
Oops, not quite enough as it turns out. Just learned that President Trump has ordered an investigation into voter-fraud as to the election he won. Guess he's not going to quit gnawing on that bone. He has also called for a temporary ban on refugees.

Day #6

A banner hanging from a crane and visible from the White House said it all: "Resist!"

The privileged, petulant president is about to hear "NO!" at every turn. He is not going to enjoy the experience; we know this, for he has been spared revolts throughout his life. Money enabled him to escape retribution on many an occasion. However, in this new position, money alone cannot save him.

Trump's latest schemes and pronouncements have engendered vociferous "blowback." Some examples follow: Mere hours after Trump called a halt to "sanctuary cities" with the threat of withholding federal assistance, many more than several mayors ignored Trump's mandate and vowed to shelter vulnerable citizens. Their reactions can only be described as fierce. Little time had elapsed when the president of Mexico rebuked Trump's reiteration of Mexican wall-payment. When Trump stated that "torture works" and spoke of reopening CIA prisons, John McCain responded with alacrity and passion. A former prisoner of war, he is not about to countenance barbaric stupidity. When Trump foolishly spoke once more about taking Iraq's oil, Iraqi social media compiled a montage of Trump's campaign statements in that regard; the product of this compilation revealed a blowhard who knows nothing about sovereign nations.

In other words, "NO, NO, NO and NO!" One more than a trifecta! The resistance has begun in earnest. Meanwhile physical demonstrations continue. Thousands of anti-Trump folks turned out in New York City once again last night, for example.

When Garrison Keillor stated: "Help us GOP, you're our only hope!" he was advising people like Paul Ryan to "man-up." So far Ryan has refused to do so. However, he and others will find it increasingly difficult to parry the concerns of the many. Witness this idiotic response of last evening when pressed on Mexico's reimbursement for the wall: "There are different ways of defining how exactly they (Mexico) pay for it." Pure gobbledygook - and a mirroring of Trump's non-reflective, bombastic stance - though quieter. But, how long will Republicans agree to inhabit the roles of court-jesters or fools? For that matter, will the inner-circle hold? The dance that Spicer has performed is fast devolving into a spectacle devoid of rhythm and grace. KFC (Conway) - I like to call her "the way of the con" - seemed somewhat muted yesterday. Of course, Steve Bannon lurks in the background; though, even he was called out for being registered to vote in two states - a bit embarrassing for Trump as he has deemed such an oversight a crime. In short, and quoting Riley (from "The Life of Riley") Trump finds himself immersed in a "revolting development." Get it? Revolt developing? I believe we are witnessing the beginnings of massive resistance...

An aside:

I am a bit worried, however. I fear that Trump is heading for an epic "meltdown." When alternative reality is replaced by the real thing - the realization that he is not omniscient - Trump is going to feel real pain. I am not looking forward to witnessing this, despite my relentless criticism of his rhetoric and behavior. First of all, he will not go gently. Many others will share his great discomfort. Second, I take no joy in watching the downfall of another. I do not cheer in the movie theater when the villain is dispatched. I think taking joy in others' pain and suffering takes us back to barbaric practices: public hangings, Christians fed to the lions, etc. Such stances are more than unseemly; they diminish souls. In many ways, I see Trump as a King Lear character. We should not forget the tragedy of Trump even though his ways have hurt many. When we fail to see another human

115

being as a human being, we become less "human" ourselves. I take a page from those magnanimous parishioners in Charleston who forgave Roof mere hours after his capture. As for Trump's eventual comeuppance? I hope that the last sentence of my Trump-writing reads something like: "He walked away. It was all he could do."

Day #7

We are heading for a full realization of the scenario: The (big) cheese stands alone while we stand together. Trump's isolation is a combination of his preference and the result of days of mad (both misguided and angry) decisions. When the president held fast to his promise that Mexico would pay for the wall, predictably his counterpart baulked. Rumors soon flew as to the cancellation of Trump's early meeting with yet another head of state. Not wanting to appear weak, Trump opined that it would be better not to meet should Mexico adhere to a "we're not paying" stance. Naturally, Mexico called off the meeting. We knew they were going to do this. Trump fooled no one in trying to save face. We also noted that he had failed miserably as "Negotiator-in-Chief." Considering a 20 per cent tariff on Mexican goods that would punish American consumers further indicated that Trump is essentially impulsive and averse to carefully-wrought strategy.

Two instances of the walling-off of Trump's team highlight a penchant for divine rule. First, he called for the resignations of bipartisan, career professionals at the State Department. Evidently, Trump wishes to put his own people in place. Knowing his comfort with his crowd of billionaires, one assumes that he will offer some the chance of an interesting hobby. But seriously, to let go of people who understand the workings and the history of diplomacy in order to ensure one's own comfort level (and control) is profoundly dangerous. It also creates both Trump's and national isolation.

116

Trump continued along this path when he slashed the workforce and the budget of the EPA. Incidentally, he also proclaimed that all studies and other information of the EPA must be vetted by Trump's political staff before release to the public thereby curtailing free communication of scientific thought. Again, dangerous. The public has the right to know the thinking of experts; the White House should not practice propaganda primarily. To save face? To undermine democracy? This preference for absolute control is evident elsewhere.

Steve Bannon regards the press as the "opposition." Far from concluding that a free press promotes dialogue and discussion, Bannon takes a page from Trump's playbook with such a stance. (Or, more likely, the other way around.) Bannon appears to want to crush all who disagree with him with the argument: "The press got the election wrong. The press now is merely attempting to assuage its embarrassment" - or words to that effect. Both Bannon and Trump will soon learn that strong-arm tactics involving "gag orders," in fact, orders of any kind, will not stand in the long run.

The rest of us are beginning to stand together in ways that cannot be ignored. The demonstrations continue. The press is working overtime to provide thoughtful commentary - despite the frenetic pace (probably deliberate) of the Trump administration. Online petitions in opposition to Trump are growing by the day. What follows are some specific examples of resistance.

Former Secretary of State Albright has declared that she will register as a Muslim should a registry for Muslim-Americans materialize. Thousands of women have called for a reversal of Trump's reinstatement of "the global gag rule," a measure that would deny medical aid to poor women in venues that dare even to mention the word, abortion, thereby causing many deaths due to HIV, lack of prenatal care, etc. The voices of women will definitely be heard on

117

this one. Meanwhile the ACLU and other civil liberties groups promise to litigate. "See you in court!" They will stand together to see to it that laws are obeyed.

In short, many citizens of the United States are coalescing in ways and numbers previously unseen. I believe that this represents a true challenge to the cheese who, by and large, is standing alone. (Though he probably does not realize the full import of his isolation just yet.)

All of the above is unnecessary. Much of what has energized Trump has to do with his quest to be "alpha-dog." For example, in his mind, any vestiges of Obama's tenure must be expunged. This goes beyond policy arguments entertained during Trump's campaign that included the repeal of Obamacare. Trump is systematically opposing Obama's humanitarian efforts, such as scrapping CIA torture prisons and assuring women's health care in foreign lands. To put it crudely, Trump is marking his territory in an attempt to create the full allegiance of US citizenry. Allegiance does not work that way, as Trump and his surrogates are reluctantly discovering. In fact, vociferous voices are multiplying. We are not cowed or engaged in a retreat. Just the opposite. We are learning to stand together.

An aside:

The silver lining of Trump's destructive candidacy and ensuing presidency has to do with renewed public engagement with governance. The unprecedented and dangerous turn of events has prompted many to become involved: in learning more, in keeping track of day-to-day developments - as never before.

It is essential that news outlets feed the public's hunger for veracity in an age of "alternative reality." During much of Trump's campaign,

I was dismayed with the overwhelming coverage of his antics. I wanted to hear more from other candidates. Unfortunately, reality-show mentality and/or entertainment won out on too many occasions. Jessica Yellin of the New York Times has written eloquently on this subject in "How to Save CNN From Itself." To be fair, CNN could not conceive of a time when bombast and lies would triumph in a presidential election. Many did not want to believe in this possibility. But it happened. No need to rehash the reasons for the outcome here. The point is, now more than ever, the public clamors for reality-based news that can only emerge from rigorous, investigative reporting. Now is not the time to fall for the distraction of Trump's inner turmoil. Now is the time to focus on that which he and his team would like us to ignore.

With a strong press and an engaged public, this unprecedented nightmare will eventually be over, for many have already awakened. I even wonder what the results would be if we were offered the opportunity of a "do-over" election - this after just one week of Trump's presidency.

Day #8

Two glimmers of hope to report. President Trump will defer to his secretary of defense on torture; that is, Mattis will be able to follow the "Army Field Manual." Water-boarding will not happen. As Trump has stated that he believes "torture works," this capitulation is important. Kudos to him for that. Also, when engaged in a joint statement with Prime Minister May, Trump remained quiet as she stated that our president had "given strong backing to NATO," and Trump even contained himself with her admonishment as to keeping Russian sanctions in place. (Later Conway would report that sanctions will remain under consideration.)

119

Yet, Trump's statements in the company of May were less than dignified or gracious. One was embarrassed when our president remarked: "I don't know this woman. We might get along or we might not." It must be said: Trump's speech was less than elegant; in fact, it was unseemly, which leads me to Nikki Haley, our new ambassador to the U.N. She seems to have jumped on the bandwagon of graceless rhetoric. When she declared that we would want to know that the U.N. "had our back," once again, I was embarrassed. Yes, the normally elegant, President Obama used that phrase as well, and I found this to be jarring at the time, but he uttered the slang in the context of a domestic audience in less formal situations. Haley's speech essentially reflected her inexperience on the world stage. One does not assume that the world-community is conversant with American jargon - or would want to be. Haley's inelegant threat: "I'll be taking names," projected a belligerent stance, a bit of Trumpian bullying-behavior. Threats as to withholding funds indicated an ignorance of the workings of the U.N. In fact, as the bulk of these funds fall under the umbrella of "assessed contributions" agreed to by the U.N. General Assembly, they are not voluntary. In a nutshell, amateur hour was on full display. Voluntary contributions do exist in the form of funds for such endeavors as UNICEF. Would Trump/Haley deny children to make a point? Unfortunately, other situations overshadow the notion of inappropriate diplomatic behavior - presented here in an order of ever-increasing concern.

First, Trump stated that the annual March for Life would possibly exceed the Women's March in participation. Another falsehood and a savvy distraction. Pence used the march to further his agenda to defund Planned Parenthood, an organization that does so much more than provide counseling for the procedure and safe abortions: pre-natal care, contraception, cancer screenings, etc. At this moment in time, abortion rates have fallen to a record low. Should Planned

Parenthood be eviscerated, one can easily conclude that the lowering-abortion trend will not hold. Moreover, many women will suffer needlessly as to broad health issues. We would have a classic example of unintended consequences.

Second, it was especially striking to learn of Gorbechev's concerns as expressed in the following statements: "It looks like the world is preparing for war. No problem is more urgent than the militarization of politics and the new arms race. Stopping and reversing this ruinous race must be our top priority." These remarks underscore the urgency of our predicament. Coming as they do from a former prime minister of the USSR who no longer wields power, they should be considered as much more than merely note-worthy. They are courageous. One even entertains the notion that Gorbechev may have put himself at personal risk in speaking in such a forthright way, for he speaks not only to Trump but to Putin as well.

Finally, President Trump's refugee ban is profoundly egregious. Not only are our ideals denied with such a pronouncement, in so doing we sow the seeds of discord around the world. By ignoring our responsibility toward the disenfranchised of dictatorships, we place an unfair burden on our allies. We also pull away from our alliances in Europe and elsewhere. Additionally, we are perceived as waging a war - not on violent extremism solely - but on Islam as a whole. In other words, we are perceived as engaging in a religious war, and, as a result, we give credence to the very terrorists we wish to defeat. As to "extreme vetting," the American public appears to live in a hysterical mind-set. The chances of being killed by a refugee is approximately 1 in 3.6 billion. Furthermore, it has been noted that many refugees have, in fact, enriched this country economically and in other ways, as they have always done, I might add. Once again, I am reminded of unintended consequences... President Lincoln, a preeminent sage, once stated that America would not be destroyed

121

from without but needed to guard against destruction from within. Our government must behave in measured, circumspect ways. To bow to hysteria and less than rigorous thought is to sow the seeds of destruction.

An aside:

Though Trump's deference to Mattis was heartening, the lack of experience evident in other Cabinet nominees is, in a word, horrifying. Clearing the decks of "Washington insiders," in order to appease the disgruntled, exemplifies short-sighted thinking. Draining the swamp of the experienced is fool-hardy, to say the least, for expertise is thrown out with the swamp water. As it stands now, for examples, we have a former denier of civil rights nominated for attorney general, a climate-denier suggested to be in charge of the - soon to be eviscerated? – EPA and a defamer of public schools on tap as secretary of education. Need I go on?

It almost does not bear thinking about, but think we must. Let us question the motives for such dystopian choices. Let us stand together to ensure that amateur-hour does not devolve into utter chaos.

Day #9

Amid all of Trump's talk of "buy American," the hypocrisy of his foreign-made hotel-furnishings, while emotionally satisfying to unearth, is relatively unimportant in the scheme of things. Rather, the focus should remain - with laser-beam clarity - on the stark reality: Trump is "in way over his head" with regard to topics of globalization, trade and security. One hoped that the president would see fit to rely on those who are knowledgeable in such arenas. However, he is guided by sycophants or by puppet-masters. Neither scenario is acceptable. When the president tweeted about a "failing" *New York Times*, he sounded very much like Bannon: "They got the election wrong. Fake!"

KFC's sycophancy was on full display with her comment: "Get used to it. He's just getting started." I wish Conway would remove the smirk from her face. It is annoying in its willful arrogance and, now, in its brazen stupidity. Another Bannon puppet?

It is human nature to assume that an emerging idea is necessarily a good idea, especially if one is self-enamored, and we all must concede that many ideas do not befit navigation in a complex world. Governance requires honest reflection as well as the input of perspicacious individuals who often reside outside of one's immediate sphere. I knew I was a grown-up when I realized that I knew enough to know when I knew nothing. Unfortunately, Trump does not evince adult proclivities. This is especially unnerving as a full-blown crisis is in the making.

The blowback with regard to Trump's ban on refugees, as well as Trump's trade policy, has been swift and sure. Pragmatist Rouhani, who helped to broker a curbed nuclear program in Iran, stated the following: "To annul world trade accords does not help their economy and does not serve the development and blooming of world economy. This is the day for the world to get closer through trade." Instead, this is the day when the US denies ties of friendship with those who need us most.

It is absurd to note that a green-card-carrying Iraqi, who had worked for years in the employ of the United States, was detained at JFK airport and denied entry. Fortunately, those who revere our constitution of civil rights responded appropriately and in good time with massive demonstrations and a court order. Of course, the greatest

123

absurdity has to do with the seven countries affected by Trump's ban. None of these countries has produced successful terror-operatives in the US. 9/11 was carried out by Saudi nationals primarily, for example, and Saudi Arabia is not one of the countries banned, nor are any of the other middle-eastern countries where Trump conducts business. Trump is not making us safer; rather, he is inflaming tensions with his inept and (perceived as) anti-Muslim stance.

Additionally, the response of those implementing Trump's order indicated the profound ineptitude of Trump and his inner circle. In fact, it was reported that agents were unsure of just how to proceed; the Department of Homeland Security and the State Department appeared to be in disarray. (Remember the resignations at the State Department?) Such ineptitude signals a distinct vulnerability to our enemies. To say such an inept operation is a dangerous business is an understatement of the broadest order. Meanwhile, our good neighbor to the north exhibited laudable statesmanship with Trudeau's tweet: "To those fleeing persecution, terror and war, Canadians will welcome you, regardless of your faith. Diversity is our strength. #Welcome to Canada." I imagine that Canadians are feeling both proud and safe today.

I have little faith in Trump's presidency. However, Congress remains. It is beyond time for Republican leaders, who dominate both the House and the Senate, to "man-up" - to save our standing in the world - and perhaps, in the long run, our democracy itself.

While the court order staying Trump's ban on specific nationals indicates that our checks and balances-government still works, in fact, the detained remain in limbo. What will become of them? Not sending individuals back to their countries of origin does not mean acceptance here, and other previously-vetted asylum seekers face grave risk as well.

Because our government finds itself in crisis, the whole world is in crisis. Ineptitude as exhibited in the first nine days of Trump's presidency amounts to much more than simple humiliation; it conjures up dire scenarios, the complexities of which we have only begun to ascertain. America's people must stand up for the righteousness of our Constitution. America's people must demand that members of Congress finally put aside selfish, partisan behavior in favor of statesmanship. It is self-evident that the emperor wears no clothes. Will others don the apparel of altruism and intelligence? The world is watching.

An aside:

Any document, be it of a religious nature (Bible, Koran) or a political one (Constitution), is subject to interpretation. Occasionally, faulty interpretation results in pure evil. We decry the interpretations of radical jihadists, for example, as we most certainly must. It is essential that we also realize the fallibility of our own interpretations - of Christian and other dogma and of our understanding of our Constitution. We are not "radical" or "un-American" when we question - when we seek ethical stances and/or truth.

We are, in fact, truly American when we work toward global understanding and justice for all - this in a quest for peace.

Day #10

Trump's need for constant attention may have resulted in unintended and unpleasant consequences for the new president. Today marked a day of standing up against his administration's travel ban, noted with vociferous demonstrations throughout the country and, indeed, not far from the back yard of the White House. Ordinary citizens in the tens

125

of thousands focused attention on the ham-fisted practitioner of orders and edicts. Leaders of many persuasions chimed in as well. Christian spokesmen decried the notion of welcoming Christians over Muslims in the seven, named countries sited for the ban - pointing out that such a plan, profoundly un-Christian in its tenor, would have the unintended outcome of putting remaining Christians in predominately Muslim countries at greater risk.

Lawmakers, too, came to the fore with arguments blazing. McCain was especially chagrined and disgusted with the Iraq ban noting that it was egregiously counterproductive. Indeed, why would the US insult a partner engaged with us in the on-going fight against ISIS? Priebus was met with salient questions such as: Why were Pakistan and Afghanistan, countries that have harbored pockets of extremism that have occasionally launched attacks in the US, exempt? Priebus could only counter with: "Perhaps they will be added." Meanwhile, numbers of lawyers made their ways to airports in order to assist detainees. This action was not coordinated, by the way, but rather occurred spontaneously. NYC taxi-drivers, too, displayed solidarity with detainees by way of a work stoppage. In short, the country "was up in arms."

We would learn of Steve Bannon's presence on the National Security Council's "principals committee" and the thereby rather diminished roles of the Chairman of the Joint Chiefs as well as the Director of National Security. Staunch Republicans, John McCain and Robert Gates, both felt the need to comment negatively on such a strategy. Interesting to remember that President Bush had concluded that his counterpart to Bannon needed to be excluded from the "principals committee" stating: "The decisions I'm making that involve life and death for people in uniform will not be tainted by any political decisions."

So much for a quiet Sunday...

An aside:

One should take special note of the machinations of Trump and his staff. As Trump's primary need is loyalty, he is averse to broad participation and/or rival thought. Unfortunately, this penchant connotes a preference for isolation; the resultant curtailed mind-set is counter-productive for players in a large and complex world, perhaps indicative of presently-practiced isolationism in the age of globalization, more suited to the 19th century than our time.

Steve Bannon relishes such a state of affairs, for this player, who is not Senate-confirmed, gains inordinate power in such an atmosphere. Protesters' placards reading: "Stop President Bannon!" are not hyperbolic on some level, for this unelected individual appears to be steering the ship of state. That he jokingly refers to himself as "Darth Vader," should elicit a shudder or two. Certainly, his history as an alt-right promoter and conspiracy-theory impresario via Breitbart News should give pause. Moreover, it is fair to say that both Bannon and Trump use manipulation and falsehood to feed their needs and further their agendas. An editorial in the *New York Times* provided an apt quotation emanating from the late investigative-journalist, Wayne Barrett: "There is no check to power except reality." Obviously, manipulation, conspiracy theories and outright lies prohibit an understanding of what actually is reality. It should be noted: an isolated and apart group is requisite for the promotion of an "alternative reality."

Striking was Trump's own comment: "You know what's more important (than the veracity of claims of election-fraud)? Millions of people agree with me when I say 3-5 million voted illegally." This

127

more than cynical quotation prompts me to relate a human-interest story that underscores a basic truth: Those who are not to be trusted often admit to their untrustworthiness. It seems that they feel somehow exonerated when they own culpability. I recall a woman whose husband forthrightly told her that he would engage in an extramarital affair; she was meant to accept his decision and applaud his honesty. Of course, she did not. To be fair, the situation was more complicated than I have described here. However, it is fair to say that betrayal, more often than not, destroys relationships (and governments). In other words, this story is meant to work as a cautionary-tale for these times of self-absorption and resultant betrayal.

I wish to "come back at" Kellyanne Conway's smug rejoinder: "Get used to it." My response? "Get used to a public that is watching your administration's every move. Oh, and, incidentally, I believe your inevitable failure will serve ultimately as the singular cautionary-tale of our time, a lesson for generations to come."

Day #11

The blowback continues. The Koch brothers' "Americans for Prosperity" is working to kill the Republican "border-tax plan." Brothers Koch are also against Trump's travel ban. Career diplomats plan to release a memo decrying the ban as well. And Starbucks has vowed to hire 10,000 refugees.

Meanwhile, the press continues to educate the public both as to the feasibility of the Trump agenda as well as the unintended outcomes of his edicts. For example, the mere stroke of a pen will not, in itself, result in slashing environmental regulations such as the Clean Water Act or greenhouse gas regulations. (Evidently Trump's team does not understand the workings of government.) When floating the idea of tariffs, Trump's team failed to realize that most probably these import-taxes would be mirrored throughout the world to dire effect. (Evidently, no one in authority understands basic economics.) President Carter's federal hiring freeze (appealing to Trump) resulted in the unintended consequence of the increase in part-time hiring which proved to be even more expensive for the US. (Evidently, the president's team is ignorant of history, too.) Oh, and jihadist groups have already hailed Trump's travel ban as a "victory," while the Iraqi parliament considered "retaliation."

Most worrisome is the fact that America's credibility is now on the line. Many such as: Iraqi interpreters, small countries bordering Russia, Mexican entrepreneurs, etc. are wondering whether or not America is to be trusted; in other words, will promises now and in the future, be taken seriously and honored? This is a serious business. Loss of faith in the integrity of the United States will mean the collapse of our standing in the world. Terrible for America, indeed, terrible for the world.

The salient question then comes to the fore: How will Trump and his team respond to blowback? Well, for one thing, they will try to maintain their frenetic pace. More and more "stories" will hit the airways in the hope of saturating and thereby exhausting both the public and the press. They will also continue to lie. Examples follow: A. "Trump scored a mandate." (when 51% disapprove of his policies) B. "The problems at the airports, with regard to the ban, were the fault of a Delta computer outage." (Give me a break.) C. "Only 109 people were affected by the ban." (And the moon is made of cheese.) These would be deemed laughable attempts at double-speak if the stakes weren't so high.

Additionally, they will resort to Trumpian insult so as to entertain their base. For example, when Senator Schumer spoke against the travel

129

ban in the company of those actually affected, Trump couldn't resist the snarky - really nasty - rejoinder: "I know him. He cries 'crocodile tears.' " It should be noted: Many responded to this latest comment by the "enfant terrible" in the following way: "Ho, Hum. Trump's being nasty again. Doubt very much that Schumer's feelings are hurt or that he will be deterred."

Finally, repetitive obfuscation will be evident at every turn, especially evident with Spicer's meetings with the press. Examples follow: A. False equivalency: comparing Axelrod's presence on the National Security Council with the position Bannon will hold. (Axelrod did not experience permanent status and was not invited as a member of the "principals committee.") B. Exaggeration: The travel ban, in Spicer's words, speaks to a dire "safety issue." (Not the case. These are not the days following 9/11, and the chance of an American citizen being killed by a refugee are 1 in 3.6 billion.) C. Stone- walling/obfuscation: When Spicer was asked whether Homeland Security had been consulted prior to the roll-out of the travel ban, he answered "yes." When confronted with the reported denial of people in question, he merely asked whether his questioner had contacted all 500+ employees. Needless to say, Spicer did not provide the names of those supposedly consulted.

It is clear that this country is in for continued confrontations. The press will not back down despite what Bannon says or does. And if government officials won't respond to the egregious nature of the Trump regime, US citizens will. In trying to save the power of WASP men so blatantly, Trump / Bannon have miscalculated. That ship sailed on a 51% disapproval rating. Our strength as citizens exists in our diversity, and many WASPS are joining the fight to maintain American values - simply because it is the right thing to do. Trump's frenetic plans will inevitably (and ironically) hit walls.

An aside:

It is no secret that social media has played an important role in Trump's rise. He masterfully garnered inordinate attention with his asinine tweets, unfortunately. Before this, Bannon used the megaphone of Breitbart News to create an "alternative reality" by way of stoking fear, anger and resultant prejudice. However, social media promises to be a two-edged sword. Citizens are able to readily ascertain heartening facts such as the ACLU received $24 million in donations on the weekend of the enforcement of the travel ban, and one million British citizens signed a petition to ban Trump from Britain. The glories of the computer... Google celebrated the birthday of a Japanese-American who successfully saw to it that the internment of Japanese-Americans, near the end and after WWII, was overruled by the Supreme Court. That heartened us as well.

That news outlets are updated during the span of a 24-hour day means citizens have easy access to each event as it unfolds and therefore are able to respond accordingly. Witness the speed of blowback to the enactment of Trump's ban; the whole world is keeping pace with the frenetic pace of Trump roll-outs. As more and more become alarmed by the perceived changes in our democracy, the tide will turn. My advice to law-makers who support Trump/Bannon and those who remain on the fence for political reasons? Take note. The populace is engaged more, and in more ways than ever before. We are watching, and, as much as it pains me to reuse Nikki Haley's words, we are taking names.

Day #12

I am setting aside my usual synthesis of important, news-worthy developments today. I do so in order to consider two "puppet-masters" who stand behind the president but, nevertheless, guide Trump's every move.

We know that Trump displays childish qualities such as self-absorption and unchecked impulsivity. Unfortunately, he is lacking in another quality often noted in children, a positive one: curiosity and/or interest in a world outside of himself. He does not read, is not conversant with history or even current facts and events. He responds only to news items that refer directly to him. He is not intelligent - sly, but not intelligent. Therefore, we must conclude that others are feeding him his "lines" as to behavior and even rhetoric.

Steve Bannon and Jeff Sessions have happily taken hold of the marionette-strings. What follows (quotations) may shed an important light on these ambitious players. Much more investigation as to the backgrounds and penchants of these individuals needs to follow - preferably as quickly as possible.

Read these widely-disseminated quotations (and weep?) Better yet, read them and find ways to resist blatant misanthropy.

Steve Bannon:

In the reported words of a conservative talk show host: "He (Bannon) is a vindictive, nasty figure, famous for verbally abusing supposed friends and threatening enemies. He will attempt to ruin anyone who impedes his unending ambition, and he will use anyone bigger than he is - for example, Donald Trump - to get where he wants to go."

From Bannon and/or Breitbart: "Are there racist people involved in the 'alt right'? Absolutely... But that's just like there are certain elements of the progressive left and hard left that attract certain elements."

"They're either a victim of race. They're a victim of their sexual preference. They're a victim of gender. All about victimhood..."

"There's no hiring bias against women in tech; they just suck at interviews."

 Jeff Sessions:

On civil rights: The NAACP and ACLU – "un-American" and "Communist-inspired."

On immigration: "Fundamentally, almost no one coming from the Dominican Republic to the US is coming because they (sic) have a skill that would benefit us."

On protesters against the Iraq War: "I frankly don't know what they represent other than to blame America first."

We must consider whether or not Bannon and Sessions have or will renounce these misanthropic and un-American statements - this as we witness the unfolding agenda of the Trump administration.

Who am I kidding? Not myself, at any rate. I believe that these men pose a real and present threat to domestic and world equanimity.

Day #13

I had made the decision not to write for some days, though vowing to remain vigilant as to unfolding events. However, soon thereafter I reversed my plan deciding that I needed to make note here of several Trump "near confirmations" (cleared committees) and one actual confirmation by the Senate: Tillerson as secretary of state (confirmed), Sessions as attorney general, Price as secretary of health and human services and Mnuchin as secretary of the treasury. Having witnessed at least a portion of the confirmation hearings, I remain skeptical as to the character, background and experience of too many of these men. Examples: I don't need to reiterate my concerns as to Sessions, and it seemed to me that Mnuchin presented a flawed presentation of financial transparency, to say the least.

The only candidate for a Cabinet position who looks to be on track for possible failure is Betsy DeVos. This should come as no surprise, as she is supremely unsuited for the position having no experience of public schools, a history of dealings with for-profit schools (a conflict of interest if there ever was one) and a performance of extreme ineptitude during the process of questioning, to include concerns of plagiarism. However, with nearly all of Trump's Cabinet picks expected to be confirmed, it appears as though Senate Republicans have ensured that the Trump juggernaut has found its footing.

I also happened upon an interview on CNN'S Jake Tapper hour that absolutely dictated that I write today - disturbing as it was. Though I do not recall the name of the man in question, I'm quite sure I have not seen the last of him. He was the consummate spokesperson for the Trump-team. One easily remembers the early days of Kellyanne Conway, her coolness under pressure. Well, the gentleman in question surpassed Conway by leaps and bounds when it came to presenting talking-points. He is a pro.

His measured tone was perfect, an art form, really. He made ridiculous statements appear cogent. He mirrored Trump's stance to a tee and then some. For example, the "fact that only 109 people were impacted by the travel ban proved that, in fact, the roll-out was a huge success" - or words to that effect. "Only 109 out of the thousands and thousands of travelers..." In addition, this spokesman claimed that Iraqis are pleased with the travel ban - as "they, too, are most concerned about keeping the bad guys out." He stoked up the fear factor, making it seem as though we are experiencing an imminent threat to rival anything seen in France or Germany. For good measure, he told us of his immigrant status; he wore this mantle proudly.

However, when he claimed that the media had all of the facts wrong, I knew that he had over-played his hand. I am supposed to believe him over all of the news sources I access daily - newspapers, news broadcasts, etc. I don't think so... It is quite clear that Bannon et alia would like to discredit the fourth estate in the quest for public acceptance of an "alternative reality." I and many others will continue to value investigative journalists, for we support the necessity of a free press. We know that a free press stands between us and would-be "in control" manipulators of truth.

It was interesting though, this interview, for it indicated that the Trump administration, well aware of a 51% disapproval rating, realized that it must cross the next line. It is no longer enough to rally the base. They are going to have to play "hard ball" indefinitely.

An aside:

Many of us have experienced an "I wish I'd said that" moment following an argument or a debate. Thinking on one's feet is difficult. Much easier, by far, to engage in writing, for one has the luxury of time to present a cogent argument complete with researched facts in support of said argument. Tapper was at a distinct disadvantage in his interview with the Trump spokesman. It was obvious that the interviewee had prepared his talking points in advance while Tapper had no prior knowledge of what his guest would present. At times, Tapper appeared to be caught off-guard. Moreover, he had no time or way to fact-check. Also, Tapper was charged with presenting an unbiased response while the interviewee had no such constraint. In a word, Tapper was relegated to defense. "Pro" played offense, and some might say he was offensive in his presentation. I imagine that

135

Tapper knew very well how he was being positioned, but he knew as well that he could not respond as an ordinary citizen might have done. Newsmen are expected (really called upon) to be circumspect when it comes to blatant accusations of obfuscation and subtle manipulation, as Jake Tapper's performance most certainly indicated.

Day #14

"Do as I say, not as I do" - an apt adage for the Trump-team and perhaps the Republican Party as a whole.

Last night the campus of the University of California-Berkeley erupted in protest against the scheduled talk of one Milo Yiannopoulos, a right-wing Breitbart news editor. There was some violent behavior, though it should be noted that the protest began peacefully as 1,500 students, professors and others expressed their outrage with the views of Breitbart and Donald Trump. Eventually the campus was put on "lockdown" and the talk called off. The would-be speaker's response? "They are absolutely terrified of free speech and will do literally anything to shut it down." Now that is really rich - coming from an outfit that routinely characterizes the broad media as perpetrators of "fake news" in a not so subtle attempt to undermine, if not destroy, the free press.

Meanwhile, Republican leaders have the temerity to accuse Democrats of abjuring their responsibility in attempting to block the nomination of Gorsuch for the Supreme Court. This after their refusal to vote - even on the opportunity of a hearing for President Obama's nominee - some ten or eleven months prior to the president's departure from office. Aside from the blatant hypocrisy on display for all to see, Republicans appear to have no sense of history; in fact, they have no sense of yesterday - or of that which is barely history. Yet, in a larger sense, this is the way of double-speak.

Additionally, and along this line of thought, we learned that Trump participated in, actually precipitated, contentious conversations with both the prime minister of Australia and the president of Mexico. Remember Trump's statements on the order of: "If they're not nice to me, I will come back swinging, and if they're nice I'll be nice"? Once again, "Do as I say" and once again, hypocrisy and denial of history.

While Trump behaves in a childish fashion, he treats American citizens as though we were children - unlucky children called upon to merely follow didactic instruction. With such a stance, infantile Trump gives the concept of irony a whole new meaning. Yet, we are not children. We are able to discern the hypocrisy, the idiocy and the evil intent behind all of it. Americans will not be corralled into a box where thought and belief is verboten. Rather, we will say and do what is right.

An aside;

Early on in my high school teaching career, I realized that the school-place functions in many ways as a microcosm of larger society - both in its structure and with the examples it provides as to changing mores. To spend time with adolescents is to spend time with those who exude the pulse of change. I must admit: Sometimes our roles were reversed, for the teacher would learn much from her students with regard to human relationships and also as to variant ways of viewing the world. Let me enlighten you with one bit of truth: Teaching is often a humbling experience.

I look back now with the realization that the authority that comes with being a teacher is largely misunderstood. On more than one occasion, the authority I enjoyed was enhanced with a "life lesson" learned from a student. Ironic that. When I listened to a student's concern or suggestion and then followed through with changes in my behavior, I often gained traction in my attempts to become both a role-model and a benevolent leader. Though my students were not my equal in the sense of the equality of peers or friends, their roles as arbiters, of at least some of what went on in the classroom, could not be denied. This is as it should have been.

I am reminded of one particular student who stated, "You teachers have just got to realize that you're not really in control." I knew what she meant. This was a wise statement, for, indeed, a teacher cannot and should not attempt to control, in a solely didactic manner, the developing minds of her charges. Nor is it possible for a teacher to control all of the events that may occur within the walls of the classroom. Teaching involves reaction to a great extent. One is called upon to listen, assess need and then respond as best as one can.

The aforementioned is meant to raise the notion of the necessary component of respect that exists in a thriving democracy; respect is a requisite for any sort of social system that enables freedom of thought. Indeed, respect is the hallmark of benevolent, adult behavior. So, when I note disrespect in the rhetoric of supposed leaders. I am alarmed. When I note "strong-arm" tactics used in order to gain a kind of control, I become incensed. When discourse is cheapened, when games are played in an attempt to obfuscate reality, when a leader is enamored with the notion of absolute control and the exclusion of those who do not fall in line, we are witnessing the demise of democracy.

Those who would attempt to gain this sort of mesmerizing, but ultimately unrealistic, really impossible, control, would do well to listen to the admonishment of my former student: "You're not really in control." Unfortunately, for the rest of us, the fruitless quest for control of a would-be autocrat causes hurt and damage, possibly irreparable damage in some instances. However, history, that which he/they appear to deny, will judge them with a truth that cannot be denied. In the meantime, many are watching and resisting the nihilism inherent in the process and example of unenlightened disrespect - and an obsession with control.

Day #15

Let me indulge in yet another little conspiracy theory of my own - just for fun. Though I normally eschew background nonsense, that which I readily regard as mere noise, I will consider a rumor that is swirling around: Melania Trump may not join her husband as a resident of the White House, even in the long run.

One immediately wonders about the state of the Trump marriage or one wonders whether the situation portends something entirely different. Perhaps the Donald has no intention of serving out even his first term as president. Perhaps he remains true to his first love, amassing wealth. If this be the case, perhaps he sees his unexpected win as a literal windfall. He could somehow set an agenda, put his people in place and then reap an enormous benefit money-wise.

With this scenario, Trump becomes the absolute "reincarnation" of the mythic Midas-character (symbolized with Trump's bizarre penchant for gold that cannot, in good taste, be used to encase the White House). Money is Trump's life, his god, after all is said and done.

How's that for a nifty conspiracy theory? Not nearly as outlandish as the stuff Breitbart is spewing, I say in my defense while noting that it would explain Trump's extreme reluctance as to letting go of his former life.

Absurd times call for absurd writing-detours on occasion; this is my actual defense for the above.

******** *** ** *** ** ** *** ***

Is it too much to ask that Trump and his team think for more than several minutes before reacting to the words or behaviors of others?

For example, Trump has intimated that he could cut federal funding to the University of California-Berkeley in the wake of a protest held there last night (resulting in the cancellation of a speech by a Breitbart editor). First of all, Berkeley had allowed the man on campus with every intention of enabling his speech. The talk was canceled only for public-safety reasons. Thus, officials were not curtailing free speech per se. I doubt very much that a court would find U.C. Berkeley in violation of the First Amendment.

Flynn's response to Iranian missile launches was bellicose in a vague way. Given the blundering nature of the execution of Trump's travel ban, perhaps one cannot be faulted for assuming the worst - thereby questioning Flynn's competence. One was prompted to wonder: Did he review the nuclear agreement arranged during the Obama tenure? Did he engage in discussions with diplomats or Iranian officials before spouting off? International affairs, from the US perspective, should not amount to a replay of an old advertisement - complete with an "alternative" slogan: "We speak. You listen."

After the short span of two weeks, our government must appear to the world as one disorganized, anti-intellectual mess. While I am, at least obliquely, on the topic of diplomacy, let me express concerns about this administration's lack of decorum most recently displayed with Trump's behavior at a prayer meeting. He used the meeting as an occasion to avail himself of yet another self-absorbed rant, choosing his replacement for the "Celebrity Apprentice" television show as his target. In the parlance of today: "You can't make this stuff up!" "Celebrity Apprentice" and prayer meeting in the same breath?

As for KFC's predictable input: "Democrats are a bunch of cry-babies," KFC, your routine is becoming stale. No one is listening. Our slogan is: "You talk. We flip to another channel." Better yet, we take time to research law, history, diplomacy, etc. If you all refuse to think, we citizens will gladly pick up the slack - and then follow through by way of well-thought-out activity. Furthermore, we will ask questions such as: Who elected or confirmed Bannon? Why is an individual of limited military experience and a promulgator of conspiracy-theories allowed within one mile of National Security Council meetings? Meanwhile, please note that the demonstrations continue with variant groups coalescing nicely. Also, the courts have lifted the travel ban. An auspicious beginning, I'd say.

There is an irony at work here. Trump claimed that he would give government back to the people. As a result of his inept and bullying ways, many citizens have become more aware, and, significantly, much more engaged in the political process. Perhaps government will, indeed, belong to the people, but in a scenario not envisioned by Trump and his cronies.

I remain hopeful.

Day #16

Trump's impulsive language continues to wreak havoc or at least is the cause of much concern. Two recent examples come to mind. In an interview with Bill O'Reilly, the president once again spoke of his admiration/respect for Russia's Putin, a suspected proponent of violence with regard to his political adversaries. When pressed on

Putin's reputation as a "killer," Trump responded: "We're so innocent?" Clearly this public denigration of the United States is troubling in its glib quality. You will recall that the extreme right excoriated President Obama's mention of instances of past US behavior which he deemed as less than perfect. They shouted: "Obama is un-American!" - or words to that effect. I wonder how these folks feel about Trump's Putin remark.

When Trump referred to a sitting federal judge as "so-called," he essentially denigrated one branch of our system of government. Did that precipitate blowback from his own party? The answer to that question is mixed. McConnell's usual tepid rebuke made an appearance: "I think it's not best to single out judges for criticism." Pence supported Trump with the following statement: "The President has every right to criticize other branches of government." Republican legislator, Ben Sasse, on the other hand, was not so sanguine. He stated: "We don't want 'so-called' judges or a 'so-called' president."

The existence of stubborn party loyalty is obvious in the McConnell and Pence statements. Therefore, I raise the question: When is loyalty detrimental to an ethical stance? Throughout Trump's campaign, transition and now presidency, many have turned a blind eye toward his questionable - in some cases, clearly egregious - remarks. Is this not wrong? I am reminded of the recollection of a family-abuser. Said abuser was able to continue his reprehensible behavior because there existed a code of family loyalty that precluded a speaking-out and the resultant cessation of hostilities. The aforementioned example is not meant to equate the abuser and Trump per se, but to point out the ethical implications inherent in the practice of stubborn loyalty.

Free speech continues to be a topic of concern and confusion. Trump accused U.C. Berkeley of a First Amendment violation while attempting to undermine the free press with his next breath. Meanwhile, a Michigan state legislator opined that "a bullet would stop student demonstrations" (referencing the shootings of students at Kent State some 48 years ago). Will said legislator be charged with inciting violence? More likely, an apology or explanation of "poor wording" will suffice. Where does "yelling 'fire' in a crowded theater" fit in? Is hate-speech lawful? These questions have yet to be considered adequately.

Yesterday a small pro-Trump demonstration occurred outside Trump Tower in NYC. Though I am quite sure that Trump supporters still exist, perhaps in large numbers, I couldn't help but wonder whether this particular protest had been staged. Though I freely admit that I could be engaging in a dreaded conspiracy-theory here, I noted the following sound-bite: "I like everything he is doing!" Everything?! I thought... I also recalled the story of the neighbor of a friend in Massachusetts who gleefully reported that she'd been paid handsomely to erect an enormous Trump campaign-poster in her yard.

Again, my conjecture may be unfair, indeed, factually wrong. Perhaps other pro-Trump demonstrations will pop up in other parts of the country Considering the massive rallies that Trump was able to precipitate or orchestrate during his campaign, I'd say that his base has been notably quiet (in comparison) thus far. Resting on their laurels? - or having second thoughts?

An aside:

Quiz for Trump Supporters

Part One (Yes or No Questions)

Do you admire/accept the following?

1. joking about sexual assault

2. name-calling

3. bragging about real or imagined accomplishments

4. refusing to pay back debt to others

5. singling out groups for disparaging remarks

6. "getting even" behavior

7. joking about shooting someone and getting away with it

8. bold, but not well-thought-out, action

9. public venting of frustration

Part Two: (Essay)

Assuming that your answers to the above fell mostly (even solely) in the "no" category, why did/do you support Trump?

Day #17

Today illustrates a rather schizophrenic political reality. On one hand, all appears to be business as usual. Yet, with every exponentially more ludicrous remark uttered by the president, we are witnessing, as well, a particularly unusual use of power - one that may simply indicate the evident self-absorption of Trump or, conversely, a sinister deflection for eyes that otherwise would note with alarm the full scale of a Trump's agenda. Certainly, the public is flummoxed by this dual sense of reality. I sense that pundits, too, are grappling - working hard to understand the significance of the president's style and/or method of operation.

On the business as usual side, we learn that Trump is reverting to a Republican stance. For example, he will bring change to Obama's lobbying rules. As one person described such change, Trump will "keep the swamp alive." In other words, he will bring back "fat times" to corporate America.

That such a decision flies in the face of Trump's promise to "drain the swamp," appears not to matter to Trump; ergo, business as usual. By the way, the change involves removing the ban on lobbyists going to work for the agencies that they lobbied for the minimum of a two-year period. Trump would change the time frame to one year. As one analyst explained the result of Trump's tweaking: "It's as if their employers have embedded influence in the government." Business as usual?

On the ludicrous side, in a speech before military leaders at the US Central Command, the Pentagon agency charged with overseeing security interests throughout the Middle East and Central Asia, Trump put forth his latest conspiracy theory: "The press is not reporting instances of terrorism... They have their reasons, you know that." I'm

145

quite sure his audience had no idea what Trump was talking about, for just what does such a statement suggest? Is the press in cahoots with ISIS? If one were to believe such an "off-the-wall" statement, what other nefarious doings are implied? At first glance, Trump's accusation appears to be just another instance of attempting to maintain a self-importance, a desperate one at that. In so doing, Trump is teetering on the edge of farce. Or is he?

It is possible that this latest distraction will serve to dominate the news cycle and distract us from more important issues, many having to do with Trump's Cabinet appointees. For examples: EPA eviscerated? Public school system destroyed? Cronyism in treasury? etc. If you will recall, Trump's modus operandi has much to do with accusing his political foes of his very own attributes and actions. ("Lyin Ted," "Little Marco," "Crooked Hillary"). Is it a stretch to conclude that Trump is accusing the press of covering up while, in fact, he himself is attempting to cover up his own nefarious agenda?

On the other hand, I may be attributing a savvy to Trump that, in fact, is non-existent. He enjoys the show, after all, and he also enjoys an atmosphere of strife and confusion. Consummate con-man or churlish clown? We'll see...

In the meantime, it would behoove pundit and average citizen alike to take careful, detailed note of Trump's agenda as it unfolds while assessing the would-be success of his unconventional style.

Final Afterword

Arbitrariness occasionally plays a role in the decision to end a project. Indeed, this portion, this daily diary of sorts, could go on indefinitely. Yet, now is the time that I choose to stop. In part, my decision has to do with the recession of my incredulity with regard to the Trump presidency. It has happened. And while I sense that we are embarking on change the likes of which I have not seen in my lifetime, I note as well and as Obama stated, the world does not end until it ends. Though we may see more confusion and some frightening times, I sense that the frenetic opening-salvos of Trump's administration, the early days, are beginning to wane. And that is a good thing.

Trump promised to shake things up, and he has. He demonstrated an intuitive purpose as to disruption. What I do not think he envisioned was the awakening of a large segment of the population who became more engaged, those who saw fit to bear witness to his every move. The dangerous time of the transition of power has lapsed. Now we will take careful note of unfolding events. We have learned thus far that democracy is not fragile, but it is not a given either. I believe that the American experiment will proceed in a way that will result in a positive outcome ultimately. Our democracy is sometimes battered; it has not been irredeemably broken. It is up to us to ensure that some lessons have been learned; chief among them is the notion that nothing is promised. We all must remain engaged.

It is essential that we continue to revere history (the memories of others); it is also essential that we vigilantly review "near history," those details of our individual memory. This was the premise of my project: The notion that emotional as well as intellectual processes need to be expressed, shared and saved.

I do not believe that we are witnessing the "end of days" (despite the mention of the doomsday clock); rather, we are witnessing a momentous shift having to do with the revolution of information-technology expansion, among other developments such as the impact of a "smaller world" and/or globalization. Perhaps there is hope for a new world- order of a particularly constructive nature. It is my hope we will come to a better understanding of the diversity and resultant promise of this world. Easy and on-going access to information will enable this promise.

This is not the time for the man who would be king, who essentially embodies a regression of thought; this is the time for a cooperation, a hearing of many voices. This is the time for a coalition that will give birth to talent couched in optimism. I believe that we are just beginning to understand the potential greatness of our time. I remain hopeful, as I must.

Additional Asides:

Psychiatric Nomenclature

Psychiatrists/psychologists cannot agree as to the ethics of publicly assessing Trump's mental status. Some feel the need to warn the public; others have concluded that they should not diagnose from afar. The way I see it, psychiatric labeling is useful only in two instances: by the courts, when ascertaining criminal insanity, and in the psychiatrist's office when treatment is contemplated. Generally speaking, labeling is otherwise fruitless.

However, that does not preclude professionals from speaking broadly as to behavior that falls within the spectrum of emotional disturbance. In fact, considering such behavior is warranted, I believe. One could easily note and probably should speak to instances of mendacity, grandiosity, linguistic cruelty, misogyny and on and on...

From my laywoman's point of view, I prefer to focus on what I see as a severely emotionally-arrested individual. One who is self-absorbed, intellectually limited, morally bankrupt and so on... In other words, not a fully-formed adult. I also allow myself a bit of nomenclature to describe Donald J. Trump. With a nod to his Germanic heritage, I like to call him Bratwurst or the other way around.

I need not state, though I do: An emotionally-arrested individual is not up to the stresses of the presidency.

Seven Deadly Sins

A reminder: The seven deadly sins include pride, greed, lust, envy, gluttony, wrath and sloth. I figure Donald Trump is guilty of at least five of the seven. Most worrisome is his penchant for pride and wrath. More telling are corresponding virtues - that to which we all should aspire: humility (bravery, modesty, reverence, altruism), charity (benevolence, generosity), chastity (purity, knowledge, honesty, wisdom), kindness (loyalty, compassion, integrity), temperance (humanity, justice, honor, abstinence), patience (forgiveness, mercy), diligence (persistence, fortitude, ethics, rectitude). Unfortunately, Trump cannot be counted as a practitioner of these aforementioned virtues, at least in his public life. In fact, he is the poster-boy for behavior that demeans both himself and those he would lead. I need not recount specific examples of his egregious actions; we remember too well.

And yet... Trump is in many ways a reflection of the shifting values of our society. That is not to say that the seven deadly sins are new in any way. However, popular culture seems to eschew what was once deemed appropriate and inspiring. Those who garner attention often exhibit immense wealth but paltry morality and/or emotional intelligence. Witness the antics of the Kardashians, for example. Why are the teachings of Martin Luther King, Jr. regulated to lip-service only? Why did Donald Trump (a hedonist) resonate more widely than Bernie Sanders (a man of integrity)? We must ask these questions. We must consider our own culpability - as to choices made and values espoused.

149

We must begin to change the narrative and ultimately the slogan. I opt for replacing "Make America Great Again" with "Make America Good Again."

Soul-Searching

"Tree-hugging, animal-loving, union-supporting,

'other'-respecting elitist!"

- they sneered

- and then yelled: "America First!"

- and "Save our guns!"

Will they prevail?

Will our vast world

 - bounteous nature,

glorious, variously-hued people –

 survive the denial of history?

Sneering ruled before - and then came war.

Or will thought - couched in the integrity of benevolent impulse

- stand firm?

We know not what we do,

I tell myself

- when disgust with the very image of our president assails me.

I tell myself: I cannot hate

and thereby relinquish all that keeps me whole

- when fear takes hold.

When I know that intellect and humility have succumbed to base fear

- then and now.

I tell myself: I cannot thrive by way of ignominious fear.

Part Four: Fiction (*Animal Farm* Revisited)

 **Note to Reader:**

Being a former English teacher and a life-long student of literature has engendered my understanding and appreciation of the pleasure and promise inherent in the act of reading fiction. One is entertained, of course; however, there exists a far more important impetus for partaking of literature (and the arts in general), for these works offer truth and hope for a better human-experience. Born of the very real experiences of individuals, these stories not only point out how not to live, but indicate, through their examples, the possibility of transcendence.

From the so-called "low-brow" detective stories of Agatha Christie to the esteemed genius of Shakespeare, such art-forms offer an important understanding, as they provide us with intellectual/emotional history as well as artistry, the pleasure of witnessing another's vision.

For years I have pondered one such work, *Animal Farm*. This easily accessible bit of literature lives on - perhaps because George Orwell captured the human condition so well in his tale of "animal" behaviors. How often have I noted similar behaviors - both in my personal life and in my assessments of world figures to whom I have no personal access. And though I am far more optimistic than Orwell appears to have been as to the future of mankind, I am forever grateful for his clear-eyed observation and for his courage in telling his truth.

My homage to George Orwell and specifically *Animal Farm* follows. Orwell spoke to his generation, but it seems to me that he was prescient - that he speaks as well, perhaps even especially, to us. Perhaps like Shakespeare, indeed, like many other talented artists born of integrity, Orwell is destined to be remembered indefinitely.

Napoleon's PR Headquarters

Napoleon (also known as 1%) gathered his pig friends together in the former house of Mr. Jones for a very important meeting. It had become clear to him that PR was important. So important that a headquarters needed to be established and various jobs created to cope with a persistent - though so far manageable - questioning (and rumblings) by the others - those animals needed to work the fields and, in general, provide for a comfortable pig existence.

"Squealer," Napoleon began, "You have done well with double-speak. 'Four legs good. Two legs, better!' was a stroke of genius. Slogans always get the attention of our minions - especially when they are reduced to very simple but lively ideological statements." Squealer allowed himself a puffed-out chest and a deceptively modest smile. "However, we must follow up with television news programs that will further our cause," Napoleon continued. "Remember, the medium is the massage."

Napoleon spoke to a particularly adept pig - one who understood electronics and could run a DVD player with perfect ease. This pig also was capable of erecting a giant screen that would serve to mesmerize even the largest of the animals with its magnification of the pigs' stature and power. "Balderdash, I want you to keep in mind that the other animals will succumb to flash and gadgetry. It is essential that you impress them with your magic. They'll wonder how they ever survived without the constant reminder of pig elegance and stature."

"I haven't forgotten you lady pigs," Napoleon proclaimed in an oily fashion. "You must know that we love ensuring the progeny of our pig way of life with you. You are the best! However, the time is now for you to practice your wiles in another vein. Specifically, I want you to 'turn on' our less fortunate comrades. You must doll yourself up. If possible, tease your hair so that it resembles my 'cheeze-it' do. You will deliver the news with flair, painlessly inflicting our agenda on an unsuspecting audience. The males will desire you (and believe you). The females will aspire to your fashion sense (and believe you)."

"Back to you Squealer," said Napoleon. "Double-speak must be stepped up. When the other animals express concern as to the disparity of the distribution of food-stuffs, you must point out that they are inciting 'class warfare.' None of them want to go to war again, so they will reconsider their complaints - especially if they know what's good for them," added Napoleon in a low, menacing voice. "Remind them again that they were once enslaved by Mr. Jones. That old saw never fails. Tell them that they are exceptional. Also, pump up the notion of the wonderful world of entertainment inherent in the news. Show them movies that depict the miserable suffering of animals in other lands - so as to remind them of their good fortune and their inherent status as members of Pig Farm."

"Finally, we must crush all educational endeavors that purport to teach those who are not pigs," Napoleon warned. Only education that furthers our cause will be provided for them. Yes, it's important that they know enough to carry out simple tasks - though soon we might be able to send those tasks 'off campus,' so to speak, for our benefit - but that trade topic is for another time." (Napoleon didn't want to play all of his cards - even with his cadre of pigs. It was best to horde a few surprises *when* one practiced autocracy.)

"You see, pig education implies that our little piglets will be taught to think for themselves, so as to procure their rightful places into posterity. But mere animal education is quite different, indeed. Think

157

about it; there is only room for a few generals in an army, a captain and his mate on a ship, a president for a country, etc. The 'regular' animals will be assured that their contributions are vastly important, sacred. They must be called heroes at every turn. That is very necessary for continued peace and acquiescence."

Napoleon went on: "But the 'regulars' are getting wilier, despite an increased work week and the food that we provide them - essentially devoid of brain nutrition. It's very vexing, really. And their concerns might morph and become our concerns. Heaven forfend that we get into a discussion about the true meaning of socialism. To that end, we must indicate our awareness of their children's futures by way of a new plan for improvement of 'regular' animal education. I here and now choose Da Boss to be our education secretary," stated Napoleon with great authority. "She will follow Drunken's agenda." (Remember Drunken? Though his name was misleading, for he rarely drank, he might as well have for all of the get-up-and-go he expressed in the intellectual department.)

"Da Boss," Napoleon said in a stentorian tone, "Simply create some more tests for the regular-animal schools. Ensure that animal students fail these tests. This will allow us to confirm that regular-animal schools are broken. We'll step into the breach at such a pronouncement with our own ideas for improvement. Once and for all we'll get rid of those pesky teachers who want the animals to think on their own. They actually have the audacity to think that education can be life-affirming, creative, an enhancement for every individual. The nerve! Anyway, once they are gone, we'll set up computer schools that will ensure intellectual isolation - especially considering the computer-programs that we will develop. Easy-peasy. Can you handle that, Da Boss?" Da Boss thought she could.

Napoleon returned to his secret room where he did all of his ruminating. "So far, so good," he thought. Of course, there was so much more to be done. Even his cadre of pigs did not know that Napoleon had much larger plans for the future. He'd lately become bored with his smallish pig-fiefdom. He knew that out there in the broader world were others who had amassed great wealth and power. He longed to form a league of power-holders who would rule the planet. He realized that probably such an occurrence would not take place during his lifetime. However, he had produced piglets ripe for greatness. He would have to consider the development of an elite (and true) education for Napoleon II, Stalín and even little Maggie.

No Heart News

Napoleon had gone against his better judgement by aligning himself with Cannon, the particularly volatile pig who ran NoHeart News. "Yet, holding onto power sometimes means sharing the spotlight," he thought to himself. Normally, Napoleon liked nothing better than to wield his power - demanding and getting attention. He especially enjoyed saying, "You're fired!" As a matter of fact, he often strolled about the farm looking to dispatch workers (who were essentially dispensable, after all). This activity made him feel like a big cheese. The element of surprise? A bonus; all were kept on edge, playing defense, as it were.

But lately, Benjamin, the donkey, was raising questions and causing problems for Napoleon. As the oldest living animal on the farm, Benjamin recalled the time before Napoleon, not with nostalgia exactly, but with the notion that life now was much worse, truly terrible, under Napoleon. In the past, Benjamin had evinced little interest in governance - being somewhat cynical: "Things will go on as before. That is, badly."

However, lately he found himself singing a different tune, for finally he was fed-up enough to need some sort of release from his ever-growing annoyance. Benjamin's ways were sneaky as far as Napoleon was concerned. They amounted to funny, little comments made at Napoleon's expense or the telling of fables that used humor to skewer Napoleon's style. Benjamin was extremely subtle; at first, Napoleon did not even realize that he was the object of ridicule. And though many of the other animals were also immune to Benjamin's wit, Napoleon eventually concluded that he'd be wise to counter in some way.

Enter Peeved Cannon. P.C., like Napoleon, enjoyed attention, and he also secretly coveted Napoleon's position. Cannon was an angry sort of pig, and his venom was used to fuel NoHeart News. He especially enjoyed the art of the insult coupled with outrageous examples of alternative reality. He also knew that many animals nurtured a simmering resentment as to their lots in life. He would use their emotionalism to create havoc. "Divide and conquer" emerged as the underlying strategy of his campaign for power; P.C. was nothing, if not ambitious. Thus, he and his acolytes disparaged female animals, believers of various religious-sects and, most telling, any animal that did not look like P.C.

Soon the animals on the farm were looking at one another askance and with suspicion. It was easy then to stoke up the fear factor: "The other is out to get you!" As time went on, many animals fell under the spell of NoHeart News. They loved slogans such as: "Feminism: Worse than Cancer!" They especially enjoyed NoHeart's cartoonist, who illustrated "enemies" in a particularly ugly fashion. Eventually, some animals exhibited symptoms of blind rage; and then P.C. knew he was "golden."

Meanwhile, Benjamin continued with his own campaign of "truth through good humor" via several news outlets of his own. Benjamin would disseminate cold facts couched in jokes and small riddles with which other animals eventually became enamored. Even Napoleon found he looked forward to the attention he was engendering (not realizing that Benjamin's message was essentially subversive). That was the genius of the "new" Benjamin. In the past, he had been a dour cynic. But now? Not so much. Benjamin had learned that a negative outlook was counter-productive. He had also learned that maintaining a compassion - even towards one's enemies - enabled clear thinking and good results. Napoleon could not help but admire and like Benjamin; therefore, Benjamin could continue with his mission of relating truth and conjuring, as well, plans for a better future. These plans included demonstrations and even work-strikes.

At the same time, Benjamin noticed that Napoleon was ceding his power to Peeve Cannon. It became evident that Napoleon was merely serving as a mouthpiece for NoHeart News, as his very speech echoed P.C.'s words and philosophy. Noting that Napoleon still viewed himself as the big cheese, Benjamin hatched a plan. He would kindly point out to Napoleon that he was being usurped. Benjamin knew that Cannon's influence would only result in a further disintegration of society, and he wanted to prevent increasing hardship for his fellow animals. He also suspected that with Napoleon's understanding of the betrayal of his "so-called," supportive friend, confusion would ensue, and Napoleon's power would be diminished. Spoiler alert: That is indeed what happened.

Soon Napoleon's eye was not on his subjects but on one Peeved Cannon. An all-out battle for control followed, and Napoleon was victorious as it turned out. Yet, he was left with the conclusion: "I can trust no one!" Much to Benjamin's relief, it had happened. The cheese stood alone. You see, Benjamin had understood that one pig could not oversee and control the minds of all of the animals on the farm. Moreover, these same animals slowly had become educated as to the real reality of their governance. They were united, and they were strong.

In time, alone and overwhelmed, Napoleon lost the last vestiges of his control, and his reign collapsed like a house of cards. Benjamin, remembering his vow of compassion, allowed Napoleon to walk away with impunity. Napoleon had lost everything that mattered to him. Further punishment would only be gratuitous and unseemly - or so thought Benjamin.

Muriel's Take on Things

Muriel, the wise goat of Animal Farm, was worried. As far as she could tell, Napoleon was, in a word, nutty. How could the other animals be sure he wouldn't do something really crazy - like start a war with the denizens of a neighboring farm for no good reason? One thing for sure, he wouldn't fight himself. Young, starry-eyed animals would make the ultimate sacrifice. Such a thought made Muriel very sad.

Napoleon's behavior during his brief tenure so far had been nothing short of flamboyantly erratic. "I mean," Muriel opined, "what sort of animal breaks out in hives over every little obstacle that presents itself? What sort of animal rarely sleeps, preferring to blast out messages to real and imagined enemies all night?"

If one were to judge the character of an animal by the company he kept, Napoleon would have come up very short. His cronies were a bunch of lying sycophants who were just along for the ride and the perks of power. Certainly, not one of them gave a hoot about Napoleon. This worried Muriel, as well. Napoleon always referred to his many friends, but he was deluded in this thinking. Napoleon had no friends. Somehow, he had managed to scuttle nearly every relationship that came his way. "And how does one operate without the support of others?" Muriel wondered.

Muriel wasn't the only animal who was worried. The hens, after noting that Napoleon never kept his promises and, in fact, took advantage of them, had already decided to dig a great bunker underneath the hen-house "just in case of a horrific emergency." Even the dogs, who had previously been a part of Napoleon's inner circle, had taken to meeting secretly - drawing up plans in the event of a "Napoleonic meltdown." Needless to say, the other pigs, specifically Napoleon's second and third in command, were already jockeying for advantageous positions. "This is a truly ugly situation," Muriel thought. "I must think about what I could do to change the course of things."

The only idea Muriel could think of was to befriend Napoleon. This would not be easy. First of all, Muriel really disliked Napoleon, and she was concerned that he might hurt her in some way. "I'll have to take the chance," Muriel said. "Someone has to step up to the plate. There's so much at stake." For days and days thereafter, Muriel made her way to the Farm-House in the hope that she would see Napoleon. And for days and days he refused a meeting. "I'll have to think of something to get his attention," Muriel decided.

Knowing that Napoleon took great pride in his appearance, especially his hair, and knowing, too, that Napoleon took some sort of drug that supposedly enhanced hair growth, a medicine not without worrisome side effects, Muriel decided to work on her own remedy. Her medicine would not involve synthetic drugs but would come from the natural world. Luckily, Muriel's father had been a farm-renowned herbalist. Muriel was pretty sure she'd find something in the notes he had left her - something that would enable her to enhance hair growth and/or restoration. And she did find good notes, and Muriel was able to concoct a remedy.

Muriel created an elixir that tasted very good and, more important, really worked. She tried it on herself first and found that it worked on her rather too well. Muriel's hair grew in thicker and thicker. "If I'm not careful, I'll soon look like Roseanna Danna," Muriel concluded. So, she stopped taking the herbal treatment, but not before making it known that she had discovered this wonderful product. Muriel even sent away for a patent. Soon all of the balding pigs made a bee-line for her door. In each case, the elixir was successful. Soon Napoleon's cronies were sporting luxuriant 'dos that rivaled anything ever before seen. Think Elvis, or the Beatles when they were young, for examples.

Not one to be left out, Napoleon soon approached Muriel. Actually, he summoned her to the Farm-House. Muriel stood in wonder as she perused the "family quarters." Never had she seen such a plethora of gold ornamentation! But that is beside the point; Muriel quickly got down to business. She carefully explained the dosage-regimen to Napoleon, wished him "good luck" and was on her way. (Muriel's mother had taught her early on to "always leave while they still want you to stay.") Napoleon enjoyed a wonderful resurgence of hair growth almost immediately. He also found himself intrigued by the personality of Muriel. He regarded her as someone who was not looking for something from him, a novelty. And so, he asked her to visit him in the Rose Garden on occasion.

As it turned out, Muriel was able to convince Napoleon, in time, to seek the counsel of a new doctor who would not simply tell Napoleon what he wanted to hear. This physician ascertained that Napoleon was clinically exhausted, sleep-deprived as he had been for a number of years. He also suggested that Napoleon consider therapies that would enable him to control his temper and ease his manic behavior. At first,

Napoleon balked - seeing such a decision as less than "manly." However, the doctor was firm: "If you do not change your ways, and soon, I will not be held responsible for what befalls you."

In the end, Napoleon took the advice of the doctor. The result of his treatment? A whole new outlook on life. As a matter of fact, Napoleon came to the conclusion that he had been "living all wrong." "There is more to life than gold acquisition and power. I want to have some fun, some joy in my life. I want not only to love what I do, but also those that I'm with." Within a few months, Napoleon came to the conclusion that he really did not enjoy the pressures of running Animal Farm. He resigned. It would take some time before Napoleon slept really well and repaired broken relationships, but it was a beginning...

(A simple fairy tale? Perhaps. But, one can still hope.)

The Story of the Sheep

The sheep of Animal Farm had endured many hardships over a long period of time. In fact, they had been ignored or ill-used by most who had governed them in the past. Denied education beyond the rudimentary, they were born and raised to provide for privileged others. Their wool had kept other animals warm under the very old regime, for example. Moreover, at times their offspring had been sacrificed for the nourishment of their "betters." It was an unfair existence, to say the very, very least. Unfortunately, they had no memory of life beyond abuse or neglect. They had, more often than not, given up hope for a fair chance. Once in a while a member of their flock was singled out for special treatment - when these individuals exhibited "good looks" or an inherent talent or a proclivity for leadership. These animals were whisked away to foreign climes, and they usually were never seen or heard from again.

The bottom line was this: Some animals had made inroads as to their relationships with the governors, for examples: dogs, cats - even horses - but the sheep had been relegated to the back pasture - taken for granted as steady providers. Some have concluded that the sheep were too clannish for their own good, but that was not the case. They had no choice but to huddle together when nights were cold and they had only inadequate shelter. Make no mistake, they did note that the cats and the dogs slept well, in cozy beds, no less.

Some have characterized the sheep as stupid animals. Nothing could be further from the truth. The sheep understood their plight, but marginalized as they were - stereotyped - not allowed to venture outside of their pack while denied educational and work opportunities, they remained "boxed in." It is true that sheep were, for the most part, docile animals; perhaps this characteristic was the result of years and years of being herded by others.

Some think that the sheep suffered from low self-esteem. Again, this is not true. They evinced and believed in values of "clean living." They knew they were worthy. They also knew that had those who ruled not been so selfish and keen on hoarding, all of the animals would have been better off. What the sheep hadn't figured out was how to break through the fences that held them back. The other animals, seduced by their privilege, failed to grasp the idea that there was plenty for all. So, you see, the sheep, in fact, were both smarter and better adjusted than most.

Occasionally, the sheep's hopes for a better existence were raised. Occasionally, very occasionally, a leader emerged who took notice of their plight. There were practitioners of vegetarianism, for example, and the believers of animal rights who supported PETA. However,

166

more often than not, would-be leaders simply used the sheep as stepping-stones in their quests for power. To garner votes, they promised the sheep interesting jobs, access to education and improved housing. Usually, these ideas failed to materialize. It's true that some of these leaders cared about the sheep and tried to make good on their words, but change was complicated, and the selfishness of those many who lived a charmed existence could not be discounted.

Just when the sheep, sick and tired of the gridlock of government, had enough and were in the mood to do something to change the status quo, a different sort of would-be leader came on the scene. He spoke their language - no "high-falutin' " words. He knew exactly how to win the hearts and minds of the sheep. He tapped into their long-simmering discontent, and he somehow convinced them that he "alone would make things right." He also expressed what the sheep felt: "Things are terrible!" He repeated this slogan over and over again. Soon the sheep were repeating it as well, along with: "The cheaters must go!"

On top of all of the hardship long experienced on Animal Farm, at this particular point in time, there existed a threat from outside. The sheep understood that as bad as things were, they would become even worse if outside zealots took over. Napoleon tapped into that idea as well - repeating ad nauseam: "It'll get worse!!" He also said: "I alone can protect you! I am smart!" And the sheep thought that, just maybe, Napoleon was smart and strong - that he would protect them and enhance their lots in life. They had watched him get rid of "losers" in the past with the words: "You're fired!" What really impressed the sheep was Napoleon's repeated use of the word, "unfair," for the sheep, perhaps more than most, had lived the reality of that word. The upshot? The sheep voted for Napoleon in large numbers, and he came to power.

For a while the sheep celebrated. However, the honeymoon period was short lived, for quickly the sheep realized that Napoleon was not all-powerful. The promises he made were shot down for lack of good planning, among other deficiencies. Moreover, he filled his Cabinet with pigs, privileged folks who spoke in a "snooty" way (unlike Napoleon), but like Napoleon as to looks and experience. Needless to say, there were no sheep in the Cabinet. There was one stupid hen; otherwise the Cabinet was comprised of pigs only. It was then that the sheep began to experience doubt as to their choice of president.

As time went on, Napoleon fought with everyone who disagreed with him, and in so doing, he blatantly ignored the sheep, his supporters. Napoleon was evidently in this gig only for self-enhancement, or so the sheep then thought. He wasn't their champion at all; in fact, he was a "wolf in sheep's clothing." The sheep's disappointment was profound and "so sad." Napoleon was what he had labeled others to be - a "disaster!"

In time, the sheep began chanting their own slogan: "Liar! Liar! Liar!" And then; "Loser! Loser! Loser!" They knew that the latter chant would hurt Napoleon the most. The sheep eventually understood that for all of his bluster and bravado, Napoleon was neither self-assured nor strong. Rather, he suffered from low self-esteem and, more to the point, he was weak - ironically far weaker than the sheep, as it turned out.

Snowball's Failed Coup

Perhaps you recall that Snowball was an important player in the original plan to take over what would then be known as Animal Farm. A disciple of the movement's esteemed leader, Old Major, Snowball had great visions for a magnanimous, animal society - a society that would promote freedom, prosperity and peace. This vision was born of old Major's wonderful teachings. But Snowball's vision and his very place on the farm were quickly expunged. His rival, Napoleon, sensing Snowball's idealism and charisma, quickly moved to have Snowball removed from the premises. You see, Napoleon wanted all of the glory; first and foremost, he wanted to become a big cheese. To that end, Napoleon took action - literally chasing Snowball off the farm; actually, his henchmen, the dogs, did the actual chasing. (Big cheeses delegate - especially when it comes to dirty work.)

While in exile, Snowball endeavored to enhance the lives of those on his adopted farm, and they were grateful. But soon word of Napoleon's tyranny reached Snowball's ears. Snowball became incensed, and he wept for all of his old friends who had remained on Animal Farm. Snowball understood well that all of Old Major's dreams (and teachings) were evaporating. Napoleon had taken them back to the "old ways" and worse; the animals were suffering. Then Snowball became embittered. He had suffered himself, after all. And he remembered, as well, the strategy Napoleon had used to destroy him: character assassination through name-calling and disgusting lies, and then false promises made to counter all of the negativity. Napoleon was absolutely unprincipled - and ruthless to the nth degree.

So angry was Snowball, that he decided to use Napoleon's very strategy against him. He would become ruthless, too. First, Snowball created television shows for the citizens of his adopted farm, knowing

169

that, in time, these programs would become known to Animal Farm. One game show involved contestants who tried to outdo one another in the recollection of Napoleon's crazy behavior and statements. It was called, "Loony Tunes." A bio-pic on Napoleon featured clips from his most unsavory and/or unflattering days: These included an example of his violent behavior caught at the venue of the WWF as well as footage of his many court appearances and/or news coverage pertaining to accusations of fraud, groping and other instances of misconduct.

Not satisfied with his initial ventures on television, Snowball also commandeered news programs. There he willfully lied about the situation at Animal Farm. He reported that Napoleon engaged in cannibalism - eating the hens' eggs for breakfast. He also implied that Napoleon was on crack, and that he was, in actuality, Darth Vader come down from outer space. Well, the news and other television programs were soon leaked to Animal Farm and elsewhere, and what followed was absolute turmoil.

Not only did life come to a virtual standstill on Animal Farm, but the neighboring farms, some of which were especially bellicose, saw an opportunity to undermine the standing of Animal Farm; they even considered invasion. During his reign, Napoleon had sought to isolate his farm; in fact, the farm existed almost entirely on its own. Snowball quickly realized that his quest to unseat Napoleon, coupled with the weakness inherent in an isolated state, would have dire effects on his friends who remained. This was not the result Snowball had in mind!

Just in time, Snowball awakened from his vindictive mind-set and ill-conceived plans. He thought back to the credo of Old Major: "One must always remain righteous as well as humble." Snowball knew very well that good leadership had nothing to do with notions of becoming a hero. Snowball rued his temptation, and he mended his ways. He stated: "When fighting for the cause of justice and goodness, one must never stoop to misrepresentation, lies or evil strategy. Doing so would be a form of self-defeat." Snowball had realized, just in the nick of time, that the coup that he had planned, as a follow-up to his preliminary strategy, should not occur. The coup would not be bloodless. Moreover, it would not have been precipitated by righteous thought but by the way of untruths and despicable behavior that, ironically, was identical to that of Napoleon. Snowball had learned a great lesson.

Still, Snowball remained convinced that he must do something to help his friends on Animal Farm. To that end, he decided to revive the memory of the teachings of Old Major. He would write the definitive biography complete with Old Major's benevolent wisdom. He would publish this tome at his own expense and see to it that it was disseminated far and wide. Though a resultant, happy outcome would take much more time to achieve than a spectacular (but otherwise ill-advised) coup, Snowball understood he was not engaging in the fight for accolades or self-enhancement; the benevolent result would be, and needed to be, bigger than he could ever dream of himself becoming. Much more important, Snowball steadfastly believed that ultimately Old Major's vision would prevail.

Though many animals, especially the sheep, had no memory of Old Major's message of goodness, one that promised unity, prosperity and peace, it had come to Snowball's attention that Clover, the kindly cow who was in possession of the few remaining copies of writings attributed to Old Major, all along had been sharing Major's thoughts with her off-spring who listened with wonder. Truth could not be buried completely, and Snowball knew that somehow Truth would emerge again as has happened so many times before.

The Rise of Snowflake

Snowflake, Snowball's bright and engaging niece, admired her uncle immensely, for she had spent much of her young adulthood learning of old Major's teachings via Snowball's tutelage. Ultimately, Snowflake would articulate a few ideas of her own, for Snowflake was not just a synthesizer but a creative thinker.

Of course, much of the following occurred after the end of Napoleon's reign - an ending that initially involved a complicated process, but then a speedy conclusion. As it turned out, the premises of old Major's views held firm. Napoleon was unable to dismantle the three branches of government, and the fourth estate, the press, was largely responsible, through its investigative journalism, for the resurrection of belief in the system of checks and balances as well as the resurgence of hope and the justifiable pride experienced by the citizenry at large.

But it hadn't been easy. By the end of Napoleon's tenure, many folks were emotionally exhausted and physically spent. Yet, the young, Snowflake's generation, were somehow energized. Perhaps youth, often the practitioners of idealism and optimism, saw great opportunity in repairing the psyche and general well-being of the electorate.

Snowflake's mission was particularly all-encompassing. She wanted to speak for the previously ignored; she wanted to save the planet, and she wanted to reestablish alliances with other benevolent countries of the world - countries that had been insulted and then eschewed by Napoleon. And while some older, tired constituents smiled benignly at Snowflake's "dreamy" nature, there were others who supported her positive outlook and tireless activism. Fortunately, she enjoyed many mentors along the way.

Snowflake's work began in a small community. As a young adult, she had the time to spare for the learning of disparate experience. She attended town hall meetings and came to know of issues of concern. She taught youngsters for a while in the public schools, thereby reaching an understanding of the two-tier power structure (administrators versus teachers) that made little sense to her. She eventually sat on the school board and was able to convince others to see beyond a bureaucracy that had stymied many a creative thought.

Later on, Snowflake attended law school. She was particularly interested in international law as well as the particular national issues addressed by the courts. She was less interested in probate and business law. When she completed her studies – admirably in the eyes of many - Snowflake became a law clerk for a female Supreme Court Justice of noble bearing and prodigious intellect. And this is where we leave her for the moment.

However, it is safe to say that after deeming herself educated in the ways of law and having continued to engage with the concerns of community, Snowflake will once again return to her dream of improving the governance of the underrepresented. She will run for office: first at the local level, followed by a governorship or a stint in Congress. Eventually, she will consider her ultimate goal: to be the first female President of the United States, though she will quickly relinquish the idea of that distinction in her quest for a national fulfillment rather than a personal one.

Part Five: Parting Shots (of Unfortunate Duration...)

Message to Congress

I say to all of the male members of Congress, especially: Now is the time to act forcefully with integrity. This attempt to replace our democracy with a plutocracy, perhaps in cahoots with the most notorious plutocrat of them all, Putin, has persisted for far too long; its existence is dangerous and imperils our very future. Have courage!

Should you not act decisively, and with wisdom born of magnanimous, benevolent thought, the "Clovers" of this world - the mothers, the nurturers - stand ready to come to the fore. Now is the time for the often gentle, yet intellectually strong. Beyond time, in fact.

(Note: Some nascent seeds have been planted. For example, two Republican Congresswomen, Susan Collins and Lisa Murkowski, stood up and voted against the confirmation of Betsy DeVos.) Too little, to be sure, but surely it is not too late...

Congress, do your job (a letter to the editor)

Remember when a two-bit burglary brought down a president?

I remind you that Nixon's downfall had nothing to do with foreign entities. It is beyond incomprehensible that the Republican-dominated Congress has the temerity to go along with "There's no there."

The emperor with no clothes resides in the White House. He may have egregious ties to Russia's Putin.

Meanwhile, Congress members join Trump by forming their own nudist colony.

A true investigation is in order.

Start by demanding to see Trump's tax returns. This isn't rocket science. Do your job.

The visual of you unclothed - having no adult common-sense - people in Congress is too much to bear.

Apt Quotations and Thoughts

"Political language is designed to make lies sound truthful and murder respectable, and to give an appearance of solidity to pure wind." - George Orwell

(We must eschew mere politicians. It is beyond time to demand an end to dirty and fruitless game-playing. Identifying and supporting statesmen/women of character and good will has never been more necessary.)

"Power concedes nothing without demand." - Frederick Douglass

And it bears repeating: "Ask not what your country can do for you; ask what you can do for your country." - John F. Kennedy

(As citizens, we must bear responsibility for the fate of our country: continue to LEARN - noting on-going developments, to THINK - employing intellect rather than mere emotion. We must DEMAND truth, integrity, thereby procuring justice for all.)

"It is said an Eastern monarch once charged his wise men to invent him a sentiment to be ever in view, and which should be true and appropriate in all times and situations. They presented him the words, 'And this, too, shall pass away.' How much it expresses! How chastening in the hour of pride; how consoling in the depths of

affliction! "And this, too, shall pass away.' And yet, let us hope, it is not quite true. Let us hope, rather, that by the best cultivation of the physical world, beneath and around us, and the intellectual and moral worlds within us, we shall secure an individual, social, and political prosperity and happiness, whose course shall be onward and upward, and which, while the earth endures, shall not pass away."

- Abraham Lincoln

Final Aside

I. Integrity Has Two Meanings

I have been labeled as an idealist by some - idealist in the sense of being a Pollyannaish figure rather than a pragmatist. However, if being a pragmatist means going along with those of little character in the hope of "mixing things up" while ignoring flaws of hubris and selfishness, then I wear the appellation of Pollyanna proudly. I firmly believe that those who would lead or govern must exhibit integrity, first and foremost.

Also, "progressive" is not a naive state of being, for presumably progress - as to the human condition - engenders, above all, a broad gain to mankind; one cannot govern in an intellectually honest (truly pragmatic) manner if one is bereft of the dream for the betterment of "others' " experiences as well as for those described as "our people."

When those governed are content to overlook short-sightedness, immorality and mendacity in their leaders, they consign themselves to living in a wolf pack - destined to guard forever a small existence, often by way of expressions of vitriol and naked hatred - this leading to ultimate and pervasive destruction.

179

Simply put, the house cannot hold - has no integrity (structural stability) - without a moral practice born of integrity (honor, rectitude).

II. In Praise of Progressive Thought

I'm about to state the obvious - at least that which should be obvious - but, unfortunately, that which is not seen by many. All too often, folks focus on the social conventions of others while ignoring their own biases and proclivities. Take, for example, the notion of gay rights. Why do some heterosexuals decry the state of homosexuality? Why do they care about what others do in the privacy of their own homes? No one is asking straight people to become gay, after all. Has it ever occurred to judgmental people that homosexuals feel as they do - that practicing an unnatural (to them) sexual life feels wrong?

Sometimes denigrating attitudes, as to perceived as abhorrent practices, are born of fear of losing accepted norms of society. Remember when interracial marriage was deemed to be miscegenation? Why did some people care about others' choices of loving across racial divides? Such decisions did not affect their own personal lives in any way. One suspects that such blowback was conceived in racial prejudice - seeing the other as somehow unworthy. Or, in some cases, seeing one race as the "pure" race not to be challenged. It doesn't hold up. Is skin color so different from eye color? Are we to shun those hybrids of hazel eyes?

Fortunately, life has a way of moving beyond preconceived terrors to a place of acceptance of that which benefits culture. As an example, not so long ago, adoption was seen as an unnatural decision. My own adoptive parents told no one outside of trusted friends of their plans to welcome me. They knew all too well that their own parents would rail against such an endeavor. Better to present a healthy baby as a fait accompli. (It worked, for who can easily eschew a defenseless baby?)

180

Yet, how many children languished in orphanages prior to an enlightened view of adoption?

In all three of the aforementioned examples of prejudice, those who judged failed to note that decisions made were based on the capacity and practice of human-love.

Why are we often fixated negatively on differences? And why are we wedded to preserving the notion of apartness? Such a belief would appear to be fundamentally counterintuitive. Certainly, we do not expect to develop into clones of our ancestors; much as we may love our parents, most of us view ourselves as unique beings capable of individual enlightenment. And yet, more often than not, family lore or tradition is viewed as worth defending, sometimes even when such tradition bars a positive reaching beyond established conclusions. "Our people" may have a negative connotation when it comes to ideation and the practice of false assessment. Why assess at all - if assessment means denigration of cultural implications such as the practice of particular religions? Why the need to establish a "one and only" way to salvation on any number of fronts?

I maintain that such thinking is born of a pack-animal mentality as well as a false reverence for the notion of superiority. Moreover, acceptance of provincial thinking has no place in the establishment of a world peace, for it engenders jingoistic talk over broad-minded listening. Jingoistic thinking revels in fear rather than possibility. Meanwhile, all of the energy expended on protecting the norm precludes an expansion of individual development, both intellectual and emotional. Let's finally admit that it is easier to sit in judgement of others rather than to enlighten ourselves. Would that self-reflection trumped the fervor of practiced superficial-patriotism - mere flag-waving.

I sometimes imagine a world where individuals seek a personal betterment, are concerned with cleaning their own houses rather than attempting to destroy the houses of others. I imagine a world where clans are replaced by true communities, where countries celebrate diversity of culture - are eager to learn of different perspectives. Ironically, I believe that such practice would enable us to discover that which exists in all cultures and potentially within us as individuals: a reverence for beauty, truth and love.

No Respite: He's At-It Again

Trump has tweeted, suggesting protesters on "Tax Day" who demanded the release of his tax returns had been paid to protest. Once again, Trump has accused others of deeds he is either committing or has committed. (See "Antithetical Reality.") Allegedly, during the campaign season, the Trump-camp paid property-owners who agreed to display enormous, Trump lawn-signs, specifically in areas of the country likely to support Clinton.

Now Trump maintains that others are using a similar pay scheme. Of course, it begs the question: Where and how did Trump obtain such information? My source for the lawn-sign caper is a friend whose neighbor allegedly (and reportedly gleefully) related and celebrated her loyalty-reward from the Trump organization. With an abundance of caution, having heard this story secondhand, I included the word, allegedly, in the telling of it. Trump has no such compunction; he never uses that word. More to the point, I have concluded that Trump simply makes up stories or excuses out of whole cloth whenever he feels threatened. We've come to expect this. Nothing new. Remember Obama/Clinton, the "founders of ISIS?" and Cruz's hapless father, connected with the JFK assassination? Trump's middle name should be Balderdash or the more sinister-sounding appellation, Machiavelli.

182

One might speculate that Trump, so immersed in his own wishful reality, may indeed believe the palaver he spews. However, the salient point has much more to do with Trump's own behavior. I suggest that whenever Trump accuses an entity of a nefarious deed, one quickly considers Trump's own past or recent behavior; with all that has been said and done, we are left with the following notion: Apparently, Trump understands "dirty tricks" and less than honorable action all too well.

Update: Trump and "P" Words (Exclusive of That One)

Donald Trump, a pampered, powerful would-be potentate, promised to put the proletariat first. His plebeian and sometimes puerile language endeavored to put pomposity in the dustbin of discourse. He also knew that parading a pulchritudinous daughter could only pump up his image.

In his mind, power resided in the pedestrian past-times of an already pugnacious public. He would put forth puny plans by way of a people's entertainment - an updated version of pitting unfortunates against lions - a perfidious past-time, indeed, reminiscent of a pernicious play, known for paucity of politic points presented, hardly a promotion of peace.

Post-election, his prepubescent party in primary-land persisted: publicizing petty poison, pondering pulverizing punches. And when our eyes were feasting on that pointless pseudo-punditry, in the days of paltry sunlight, plutocracy plunked itself down. Puffed-up princes of Wall Street purloined positions of power.

With the preview of pined-for-summer, the promulgator of "P" words posits pathetic, pointless pronouncements that preclude a powerful US position per the world. Presently, President Trump presides over problematic and portentous pot-holes passes on the Pope, panders to, then later provokes, Pyongyang and tries to powder the press, though they passionately and patriotically persist.

Not promptly - positively plodding, in fact - though pretty soon (I pray) - perspicacious, peaceful people of "land of the Pilgrims' pride" will prevail. Yet, should progression be poky, "from every mountain side let Freedom (of the press) ring" - lest we phony up our precious power.

Jettison Theater of the Absurd for Reality

"Kim Jong Un (potential nuclear-war enemy) is a smart cookie." President Duterte (self-admitted murderer) is invited to the White House. The man who claimed President Obama was born in Africa and was a "founding member of ISIS" calls for changes to free-speech laws having to do with slander. And all of this has occurred in the past few days...

For levity, Trump produced another campaign-rally. When the going gets tough, throw a party; I guess that's the point. My point? We are witnessing a theater of the absurd. It would be amusing if the stakes weren't so high.

The press is between a rock and a hard place. The Office of the President must be respected. Every tweet, every statement, every action - no matter how offensive - has to be reported with a modicum of deference. In a different venue, a boardroom or a classroom, for examples, the disrupter would be sanctioned immediately or sent to the guidance office.

Does no one in government dare even speak of impeachment - predicated on incompetence, mendacity, conflicts of interest to include possible collusion with Russia, nepotism, denigration of the courts and possibly the Constitution itself with an attempt to rewrite the First Amendment?

Though the waters be uncharted, they must be navigated - and soon.

Comey and the Cat (Letter to Editor)

Re: the firing of FBI Director Comey

I am reminded of a cat I once had, Fred, who closed his eyes while inching toward a verboten platter of turkey. He figured if he couldn't see us, it stood to reason we couldn't countenance his nefarious act. Cute in a cat... Dangerous in Trump with a "Russian ties" investigation ongoing. The timing of Comey's firing is more than curious, occurring hours after Director Comey requested additional support for said investigation. Additionally, the changing story as to how and why his termination was decided is ludicrous in its inconsistency.

To: Republican Congress

Open your eyes and find your moral center, please! Subpoena Trump's tax returns and all other pertinent documents. Get the questions answered. The watchdogs are watching.

Because He Can

Others, better educated in the climate change arena than I, will explain eruditely the debacle of President Trump's latest proclamation, and these opinions should be heeded. The way I see it, Trump pulled out of the Paris Accord simply because he could do so. Another example of marking his territory or covering over anything President Obama accomplished. He'll also insert some palaver about saving energy jobs: "America First!"

Trump felt a psychic need to flex his muscle, to proclaim alpha-dog supremacy; this behavior makes him feel better. I base this opinion on the myriad examples of his past reactions to his own frustration, in this case, a frustration having to do with an on-going investigation of Russia-ties and a failure to legislate anything. Remember all of those rallies held post-election and meant to boost his ego? These "show-boating" episodes inevitably occurred on the heels of bad news for Donald. Quick example: rally held the same day news broke as to out-of-court settlement of the Trump University fraud-case.

Now, he'll chortle: "See, I keep my promises," for all of the other promises have fallen short (health-care reform, travel ban). It is incumbent on us to remember that when President Trump is feeling passed-over, he will strike out for Donald. The rest of the world can go to hell in a hand-basket in these scenarios. He doesn't care.

Once again, we witness the spoiled-child syndrome, also on full display during his trip abroad. Perhaps shoving someone out of the way so as to procure a prime spot during a photo-op is not the most important faux pas in history, but it reprises the story: "It's all about me." It was particularly embarrassing to hear Trump exclaim publicly: "I'm President, can you believe it?"

As to "America First," how short-sighted. More to the point, how ignorant, for this stance is not based on thoughtful reflection. An isolated nation is a sick nation; witness North Korea, the most extreme example of thoughtless nationalism.

President Trump, we don't believe that job prospects will be improved with head-in-the-sand notions of renewed coal production. You can lower standards for emissions, isolate us from the rest of the world, beat your chest 'til the cows some home, but even "Big Oil" knows that this latest display of impotent machismo is pig-headed, wrong and will not improve job prospects - not one iota.

On days like this I will President Trump back to his gated-community existence. I also shall seek the names of those Republicans who back him on this latest and future stupidity. Someday, when this nightmare is over, I shall want to remember the enablers, lest they somehow manage to hold onto congressional seats. It is stand up and be counted time.

Those who continue to play the game of unconscionable deals must wear forever the uniforms of self-absorbed shills, the moronic emblems of the anti-patriots, for patriotism is not about flag-waving in the end.

Patriotism requires intellect, a willingness to listen when those in the know speak, scientists and others of experience, for examples. And patriotism often requires sacrifice - the antithesis of the self-preservation President Donald Trump constantly seeks by way of his quest for applause and adulation.

The Fall-out of Comey's Testimony

The chess-game continues. Listening to commentary in the wake of Comey's testimony (made available through various networks and newspapers) leads me to the obvious conclusion: We are living in a realm of incredibly all-too pure partisanship. Moreover, the current, evident war of words primarily serves as deflection, this with regard to the larger concern of presidential requirements.

One may latch onto the word "hope" (as in "I hope you will let Flynn go") and conclude that President Trump was engaging in mere wishful thinking with regard to the cessation of the FBI's investigation of Flynn, rather than overtly applying coercion. However, such an argument is specious. At the very least, Trump's behavior and words were improper; this is a non-contestable fact. So, while a largely futile discussion of semantics bubbles on - so, too, does an exhaustive, overall investigation, one prays.

Will the public demand behavior that is fitting of a president? Propriety nourishes diplomacy, egalitarianism and rule of law, that which defines our country. Propriety is not a question of style; it is a need requisite for decent and productive governance. Sadly, President Trump has seen fit to relinquish both the understanding and practice of this essential requirement - in his divisive speeches, his less than forthright and/or inappropriate actions and behavior. He is, to be sure, an improper president. The chess-game will eventually end. Will probity and propriety win?

Beloved Leader

A recent cabinet meeting, televised for all to witness, was and remains especially chilling. An entire coterie of Trump sycophants pledged allegiance to the "beloved leader" without reservation - save Mattis who pledged devotion to US citizens. One could not help but see a parallel between this spectacle and the over-the-top adulation of Kim Jong Un of North Korea. As Kim sees himself as divine, so must Trump.

The salient point has to do with Cabinet members' willingness to "drink the Kool-Aid," however. What were they thinking? Are they still capable of thought? Such a display of fealty is meant to shore up the ego of one man; it accomplishes nothing else. Frankly, I cannot imagine relinquishing self to that degree for any mere mortal, for to worship in that way is to deny autonomy of thought and emotion. It ultimately means denying one's own destiny.

Perhaps it is not hyperbolic to recall at this juncture the instance of a mass suicide precipitated by a mad, religious leader (Jim Jones). At the very least, I am most appalled by the lemming-like or zombie quality of the participants in Trump's latest self-love-fest. In his quest for ultimate power, President Trump has seemingly mesmerized a remarkable number of (presumably) heretofore intact personalities.

The worst of the flatterers, Pence, may have his own eventual beatification in mind. Perhaps he is simply waiting in the wings - subversively undermining Trump with a faux loyalty that sends Trump into further raptures of self-regard - a less than rational stance that may ultimately squash not only Trump but the Republican agenda as well; at some point hyperbole and manic behavior will be seen for what it is, crazy.

But what is in it for the others? Dreams of increasing power? As Orwell suggested (and Lord Acton stated): "Power tends to corrupt, and absolute power corrupts absolutely." How can they not realize this truth? Oh, I momentarily forgot. They drank the Kool-Aid.

Incredulity and the Republicans: Time to Read *On Tyranny*

We learned today that 60% of Americans disapprove of President Trump's behavior at this point in time. We also learned that Attorney General Sessions refused to answer direct questions as to conversations with Trump - not citing executive privilege, not because the substance of these conversations is in any way classified; he merely cited Department of Justice protocol. Needless to say, Sessions was unable to produce documentation of said protocol.

We watched another day of spectacle. Certainly, Democratic senators hammered hard, seemingly incredulous that for the second time in as many days witnesses refused to discuss interactions with Trump, though Coats, at least, offered to do so in a closed-session setting.

189

Meanwhile, Republicans sought to downplay any possibility that their leader, Trump, could be culpable in any way as to anything. Team sports.

My concern has to do with this notion of spectacle - that which amounts to quasi-entertainment signifying nothing. And though my feelings as to Trump's oily ways are obvious to those who have read prior essays, I am especially dismayed when so many Republican senators are adamant in their defense of him - when control of an agenda negates the notion of getting to the bottom of Russia's influence in our elections, by the way, something President Trump seems not to care about - not one whit.

Does the notion of "running the clock" - a plan of providing day after day of strategy usually applied to a basketball game - invoked for a reason? Is it meant to exhaust the public, so that folks throw up their hands in frustration? It seems to me that democracies can be undermined and toppled by way of any number of subterfuges - not the least of which occurs when congressmen place party above principle.

Of course, foreign intervention in our elections is particularly worrisome. An on-going tit-for-tat display or competitive sport demoralizes citizenry. Accusations of "fake news" further confuse and exacerbate rifts in a society predicated on the necessity of unity. Into such an environment fear (masquerading as hatred) and paranoia creep.

Yes, in large measure, I hold responsible those Republicans who blindly support Trump. Frankly, I am surprised that the previously mentioned 60% disapproval rating has not triggered a response. Would an 80% number do the job?

One final note: Now is the time to read Timothy Snyder's *On Tyranny* if you have not done so yet. In confusing, frightening, incredulous times one must review history, as Snyder does amid practical suggestions for citizens, for it is true: "There is nothing new under the sun." There is much to be learned and understood if one leaves the basketball-tourneys behind, if one commits to participatory democracy through education (recalling history) and thought - if one is willing to see the significance of the larger picture.

I Ask You, Republican Members of Congress

Would you reward a three-year old for having tantrums or calling others nasty names? (insulting tweets, "Lyin' Ted")

Would you countenance a middle-school boy who flattered the school-yard bully in order to procure a sense of safety and power? (praising Putin)

Would you accept the behavior of a teenager who celebrated poor school-performance by throwing parties or cruising about town? (post-election rallies)

Do you revere mendacity, obfuscation, ignorance, threatening behavior?

Members of Congress:

Haul out the "time-out" chair.

Monitor "friendships."

Take away the car keys and venues for parties.

More to the point, work against Trump's contempt for balance of power and freedom of the press.

You must take on parental roles now lest you relinquish your positions as "the adults in the room." The current state of affairs (post-Comey) is beyond belief, beyond understanding, indeed, beyond any semblance of integrity in a democracy.

I should not have to ask you to reflect the will of concerned or appalled citizens, now nearing two thirds of the electorate. What are you waiting for? Trump's implosion? A full-blown citizens' revolt. An incursion by an adversary who views our government as rudderless and therefore weak?

Obviously, none of these potential outcomes is acceptable, nor is the non-action of those who should know better.

To Donald J. Trump, Would-Be King: You Did Us a Favor, Mate

Without your conscious knowledge, you may have unleashed a true revolution - a call to one and all to "Make America Intelligent Again." Your rhetoric and behavior - so outrageous - so lacking in subterfuge as to your true strategy - to save everything for Donald - that finally all is revealed to an electorate who has too long turned a blind eye to the shenanigans of a governing class, a class that rewards the wealthy and ignores or takes advantage of those less fortunate.

It should be obvious: This nation is predicated on the notion of equality for all - abjuring a take-over by the powerful elite - an aristocracy. (Check your history books and thoughts of John Adams, in particular.) Yet, in the past decades we have been witnessing (or not witnessing as the case may be) surreptitious attacks on the premise of the "American dream." Clearly, we have relinquished any notion of a level playing field. Upward mobility is no longer a given for those who dream big and work hard.

An experiment built on the premise of a vital middle-class, the ethos of this country, has steadily crept toward plutocracy. Those of fortuitous beginnings often view themselves as presumptive leaders, a group apart in education and wisdom. Such people carefully guard their advantage - and have done so for some time. Let's face it, the tax laws have not been just for decades. The wealthy often protect their treasure through "legitimate" loopholes, off-shore stashes and the like. Nothing new. Even those who would run for office (and not merely needing the largesse of the wealthy) have seen no problem with investing in the Cayman Islands rather than their own nation. This behavior, in a potential public servant, is particularly arrogant.

And now you come along. You take arrogance to the next level; you refuse to share your tax history with the American voters. Why this audacity was accepted is a mystery to me. And yet, there may indeed come a time when such records necessarily become common knowledge. Perhaps your business dealings with Russia will demand the unsealing of your tax returns. If not, the public will still come to realize that the notion of plutocracy is real. They will come to understand that "Citizens United" does exist, your Cabinet is filled with billionaires and so on... That so much of your wealth has accrued through dealings with Russia - a nation of plutocrats and deniers of democratic values - ought to - and is - raising eyebrows.

Though your behavior - rhetoric and behavior that indicated a supreme arrogance born of a spoiled child: "I can say whatever I want to whomever I want!" initially titillated and amused, soon it will be evident that impulsivity and authenticity are not one and the same. As your bombastic promises fall by the wayside due to your incompetence, all will become clear. Citizens will determine that they are no longer enamored with a celebrity and a, so-called, business-success-story. And when they feel duped? Watch out!

My hope is couched in the belief that your bragging ways, often more revealing of your modus operandi than you know, will eventually enlighten those who previously ignored and/or accepted a plutocratic infringement on our governance. Sometimes the "Classic Comic" - a watered-down and easily accessible version of a truthful story - fills the bill. Though some may overlook the story of *King Lear,* all will recall the outcome of King Trump. Unfortunately for you, in the end, your ratings will not be favorable. But you will have done us a favor, mate. In one sense you have been more honest than some of our previous plutocrats. You were unable to hide your true agenda - the crowning of Donald Trump - and this has proved to be your fatal flaw - but a boon for us in its obvious unveiling.

Revisiting "The Mentality of the Game": The Use of Superlatives

Recently, psychologists and the like have commented on Trump's use of language - specifically his penchant for declarative sentences and his use of superlative vocabulary: "the best," "the greatest," etc. In fact, those who study speech have noted that Trump's speech may indicate a cognitive decline - that his current use of language differs markedly from his elucidations of the '80s, '90s. Does this indicate age-related decline? Is it indicative of stress-related dysfunction? Regardless of causes, Trump's inability to see beyond superlative thinking presents a worrisome liability.

But, as "The Mentality of the Game" sought to point out, superlative thinking has infected many in American culture. I maintain that competition - revering "the best" - serves to limit intellectual capacity. We don blinders when we speak of the US as "the best" or when we throw around words that promote "the exceptional," when we rest on the laurels of having attended a superlative university, for example. Such thinking leads to a moral deficiency as well, for in assuming the

194

mantle of "the best" we eschew the ideas of those who have something to contribute. Our intellects become narrow and selfish. Additionally, we celebrate a class system that is inherently biased and ultimately short-sighted, for grace and insight often reside in the (presumed) unlikeliest of places or with those that provide wide experience best contemplated for egalitarian understanding.

We all play roles in the undermining of a democracy, often unaware that we are doing so. We must listen, as best we can, to the voices of those too often overlooked. Authenticity resides not in puffed-up proclamations that serve to feed the ego, but in the careful weighing of the ideas of the many by way of noting the important contributions of a diverse and variously-experienced populace.

The worst of superlatives indicate "run-away" ego - the delusion of assuming omniscience - an omniscience that none among us can honestly claim.

The Donald

The New York news media of past decades got it right when they labeled Trump "The Donald." The president's entire life has been predicated on preserving his inner id - the childhood place where the predominance of a given name resides, and I can imagine his supporters screaming: "Psycho-babble!" as I write this. Yet, my opinion is not one of a licensed-psychotherapist; it is based on the assessment we all employ as to others' behaviors. We do this in order to understand our places with regard to those we encounter. Sometimes in the process we learn something about ourselves. Sometimes the exercise is vitally necessary.

It is vitally necessary today as we attempt to sort out the actions of one self-absorbed man - a man who never questions his own motives, never retracts even innocuous misstatements - a man who lives for self-preservation's sake solely, for like it or not, he is our leader.

Of course, we all are interested in preserving our being at the basic level. However, those who would be leaders must commit primarily to the well-being of those represented - those beyond self. Presidential leadership means relinquishing privacy as well as many personal comforts. It also demands a tamping-down of the id.

I inevitably come back to Abraham Lincoln, the example of super-ego: the questioner, the practitioner of intellect over raw emotion, the adult wary of his own weaknesses and frailties.

And why is it that so many leaders of integrity: Lincoln, Gandhi, Mandela, for examples, suffered degradation - even death - in their quests to be heard? I think we must look long and hard at ourselves in times of fear and strife, lest we, too, regress to living solely by the id - this in response to that which we would rather not contemplate (our own proclivities for selfishness, for example).

Ultimately, thinking and questioning are moral acts predicated on reality beyond self.

Get out of the Sandbox

It's very simple, folks. Go back in time for a moment. You're playing in a sandbox and Johnny throws sand at you. Incensed, you retaliate in kind, and at this moment your mother glances your way seeing only your action. Naturally, she is upset with your behavior, and makes her feelings known. Your response? "Johnny threw sand at me!" Her rejoinder? "That is no excuse! Get out of the sandbox," she demands - leaving no room for argument. And she is right. Only an emotionally regressive individual would deny the fact - to quote an oft repeated adage of the nursery - "Two wrongs don't make a right."

196

And, even this analogy, in the wake of President Trump's vicious and personal attack on Mika Brzezinski, is inaccurate and more than generous to Donald Trump, for Brzezinski, though critical of Trump's behavior and policy, never engaged in vicious gender-bashing. Clearly, Trump cannot abide criticism of any sort. His world view begins and ends with his need for adulation. This is the way of an emotionally-stunted individual.

So, when Jeffrey Lord or Sarah Huckabee Sanders, try the four-year-old's ploy (recalling bad behavior in others) in an attempt to support Donald Trump's vile tweets, we must react with adult circumspection. There is simply no excuse nor room for behavior befitting a toddler in one who represents our country, both to US citizenry and, indeed, to all citizens of the world.

Juvenile behavior in a president is unseemly, unintelligent, and ultimately immoral. Those who would say otherwise are practicing expediency to an absurd degree. For what? One envisions the time when all of the excuses are recalled - a future that will determine that not only Trump, but his surrogates as well, are relegated to a shameful footnote in history.

Can't come soon enough for me.

Jane Marple

Sometimes I identify with Jane Marple of Agatha Christie fame. You remember; she was the elderly detective who lived a circumscribed life in a small English village. Yet, this village, a microcosm of the world in the eyes of one who had lived long and thoughtfully, provided a harvest of human nature - examples of behavior that Christie's Jane called upon when solving conundrums.

I've always enjoyed detective stories, starting with Nancy Drew during childhood. Nancy appealed to me because she led an adventurous life. At the same time, she seemed on par with the boys of her acquaintance - if not one step ahead. I liked that. Later, I concluded that detective fiction spoke to my need for seeing justice served. Still later, I noted that "mysteries" reflect the mores and concerns of the particular societies depicted. (Just for fun, read an old Perry Mason book from the fifties; you'll discover what I mean.)

So now, I have retired and have left frenetic work-life behind. Like Jane Marple, I have the luxury of time and the perquisite of decades of life-experience, including the reading of fiction and non-fiction, upon which to draw. And I note that those in positions authority, for example, Trump - though initially viewed as startling - are in reality retreads of many characters that have lived before. In Trump's case, King Lear comes to mind along with the memory of a former boss who managed to create a toxic environment and, in the end, an isolation that could not be sustained. I remember well the damage that can be wrought by one, lone individual. Though toxic individuals inevitably self-destruct, the pain caused by their wakes is real and sometimes long-standing.

Trump's story suggests two outcomes: 1. He will eventually leave the world-stage, I imagine under circumstances that will be extremely detrimental to him. 2. He will have left us to pick up the pieces, to bind the wounds and to carry on. The latter may prove difficult. However, I do believe that when all is said and done - when the crucible has been acknowledged and met - we shall have learned to consider (potential presidential) character differently. We shall have attained a wisdom.

In the meantime, this former English teacher urges one and all to consider the many stories of various people, those made available in literature that exists in vast dimensions. To do so is to discover a universe of experience, examples one might draw upon when considering the behaviors of those who seek power.

Elegy for a Madman (Response to Shooting of Republicans)

Hate the act not the man

For he was no longer a sane man - forfeiting rationality in the throes of pain

Do not hate his once intact soul - lest you mirror his illness
- lest you, too, become mad.

****

Deny creeping fear - the stoker of fiery violence

Envision a once-man (and former child) as you realize your enemy

To dehumanize him is to create a faux monster

- a personified evil - an illicit license for violent retribution

Fall not victim to violence by creating it anew

Be wary of the sickened soul - the contaminant of humanity

But do not hate - lest you forfeit humanity itself.

****

199

Be mindful of ideation, language

Irrational thought and word - precursor-weapons

 - the tracer-bullets of ruin

enable humanity's devolution and the demise of the soul.

Trump's Version of the Three Rs: Relentless, Reckless and Reprehensible

Donald Trump's education was sadly lacking. He did not study history, philosophy, literature - or anything else remotely tied to the humanities. Yet, he purports to be a leader of humanity. Trump's lack of awareness, his practiced dearth of curiosity as to the workings of governance and leadership, his unwillingness to engage in self-reflection present a woeful and dangerous situation. His three Rs, hubris-inspired, require careful monitoring by the public at large, for these attributes are insidious precursors to our democracy's demise.

The drum-beat of relentless lies, antithetical reality, delivered with wrath and bombast, serves to entrance the consumers of such rhetoric. A key ingredient of such verbiage lies in its relentless practice. Trump's mantra appears to be: "Never back down. Repeat, repeat until misinformation is so firmly remembered that it takes on a life of its own." Like the steady drip of a leaking faucet, what was once deemed innocuous, even ludicrous in its practice, becomes a mechanism for erosion - even of the strongest surface.

Reckless spectacle is meant to additionally mesmerize an audience. Trump understands the power of spectacle; he seeks to obfuscate truth by way of an entertainment that recognizes frustration and discontent. Trump's own fearful and angry response to feeling less mirrors our own, though his is couched in a charade of omniscience. Spectacularly

200

inexperienced as to governance, Trump must produce a show of grandiosity. And this show must exponentially evolve. The genius of ever-evolving, reckless spectacle has to do with the (to be expected) incredulous response of those who are reasonable. Forever responding, forever surprised, the audience remains engaged rather than questioning and then denying recklessness. The spectacle becomes the story. And some otherwise perspicacious individuals are even drawn into a "tit-for-tat" scenario, that which further gives credence to essential absurdity, approaching full-blown delusion.

Reprehensible behavior provides the fuel for the aforementioned, two Rs. Born of limitless self-regard (extreme selfishness), this behavior includes obsessive denigration of all who question the viability of Trump. It is pernicious in its cruelty of words. It plays with notions of violence. Given free rein, it will lead to destruction in real terms - as well as the destruction of our worth. Citizenry must choose a path forward. Shall we accept Trump's faux and ultimately immoral "education?" Or shall we make known our desire for humanitarian goals - ideals that reflect altruism and integrity. Shall we stand together with belief in and reverence for our democracy? Or shall we fall apart?

A Cry for Help

Trump tops himself with a violent tweet depicting his beating of a stand-in for CNN. Not literally, of course, but as a symbolic gesture. If this isn't a cry for help, I don't know what constitutes the message: "Please, someone rein me in!"

And the pundits on Sunday morning news programs attempted to reasonably discuss this matter. However, such a display in a sitting president fits not within the realm of normalcy. Either Donald Trump

201

truly believes that he can literally do anything he pleases, presumably (in his mind) appealing to his base, or he is subconsciously willing the adults to step in and end his charade of a presidency.

I do not for one minute, think that Trump's base is truly base. At some point, enough will be enough. Yet, it doesn't serve to report on this situation in the vein of "just another Trump outburst," for to do so is to lend credibility to the essential unraveling of a man.

Meanwhile, Newt Gingrich has a new book on the *New York Times* best-seller list that purports to explain Trump's agenda and ethos. What ethos? What agenda? We've observed Trump waffle on any number of issues. Moreover, the president spends his time tweeting rather than working through policy matters. Our leader is literally out-of-control. This latest depiction of metaphorical violence illustrates the reality of his emotional state.

Will no one help this man?

Get Out of the Sandbox: Part Two

Donald Trump Jr. met with a Russian lawyer. Amid the conflicting stories as to the purpose of this meeting comes a new twist on an old tune: "Clinton had untoward connections with government officials of Ukraine." Aside from the obvious use of deflection, we have one more example of "This is beside the point."

Remember the ten-year-old argument put to your mother: "Everybody's doing it," whatever "it" was? Presumably she retorted: "And if everybody is jumping off a ten-story building that makes it sensible?" With the current government in place, we are prompted to revisit childhood arguments, a truly juvenile turn of events. Or is it? We appear to have been engrossed with juvenilia since the beginning of Trump's entry onto the world stage. How many times did Trump utter the word "unfair" during his campaign? How many times did he state: "She started it" - or words to that effect? I am aware of day-care situations that evince more in the way of cooperation and intelligence than Trump and his surrogates exhibit.

Yet, the aforementioned is my soft take on Trump's possible collusion with Russia, with its assumption of the president's juvenile, self-absorbed stance coupled with spectacular ignorance as to the workings of government, history and so on. Should investigations reveal actionable evidence of collusion/conspiracy with the foreign entity, then it becomes clear that this childish behavior may well serve as a cover for a truly sinister campaign of willful disinformation.

The practice of ammunition-gathering as to the supposed culpability of Trump's foe, Hillary Clinton, and other Democrats as well, may have dual purpose: deflection (muddying the waters) and enhancement of public division (leading to the undermining of citizens' confidence in our system of government). The constant puerile rejoinder: "They did it first" becomes an off-the-current-topic refrain, a convenient "alternate" reality - a relinquishment of focus - a focus obscured by the practice of sleight of hand. At such a juncture, intellectual rigor may well be forfeited; therein lies the potential for our democracy's demise.

PostScript:

Ted Cruz, when pressed on current issues having to do with Russia, responded as one might have expected. He accused Obama, Clinton and Kerry of appeasement with regard to Russia's annexation of Ukraine. According to Cruz, the Obama administration offered an "off-ramp" for Putin - a diplomatic approach that Putin ultimately declined. Aside from the reasonable practice of diplomacy first, my question for Cruz is simply: "What specifically should our government have done?"

The salient point? We are no longer living under the Obama administration. But then, said Republican would rather engage in partisan argument than speak of issues of current, particular pertinence. Additionally, in praising Trump's prepared Poland speech while invoking words of Pope John Paul in the process, Cruz provided yet another example of manipulative deflection and relentless obfuscation.

Will we begin to demand more than partisan politics from those in positions of power? Will we demand straight-forward intellect?

PostScript #2:

When all else fails, Trump acolytes address raise concerns as to Trump's behavior by hauling out the old "Get over the election" gambit - as if all could be explained away with accusations of "sore loser" or poor sportsmanship - once again, falling victim to (or enhancing) obfuscation.

Unlike the president, most are no longer focused on the defeat of Hillary Clinton; rather, legitimate issues as to the future of this country have emerged. For example, will Russia succeed in influencing future elections? Will their cyber-activity morph into breaches of our infrastructure?

Unfortunately, the current situation is not a replay of the post-election activity following Bush v. Gore where, by the way, there were no accusations of "sore losers" with regard to Democrats amid sporadic demonstrations. Normally, this country quickly offers support for new presidents. Sadly, this time around, any number of missteps, if not something much worse, coupled with Trump's own incendiary language have fueled a proclivity for unprecedented concern among large swaths of the electorate; this concern provides a bright light in an otherwise dark place.

Trump's on-going behavior either reflects that of a chucklehead or a modern-day version of Caligula. One hopes, the former. Bad enough.

Trump Has Finally Found His Ideal Squealer

George Orwell's *Animal Farm* continues to resonate with an uncanny accuracy. In Anthony Scaramucci, Trump has found his ideal Squealer, a mouthpiece bent on procuring unprecedented power for the president by way of brazen propaganda the likes of which we have not witnessed since Squealer proclaimed: "Four legs good; two legs better."

Move aside, KFC; super-sycophant is in the house, the White House, unfortunately. With KFC's trademark smirk, the Mooch begins his war on reality. His arsenal of gimmicks? Very much like Trump's: outrageous, deflective accusations of the supposed malfeasance of opponents, off-the-wall proclamations in the nature of "black is really white" - all delivered with colorful and entertaining verbiage. His nuclear weapon? His disdain for the give-and-take of conversation. One cannot converse with the Mooch; one simply listens, for he denies all counterpoints - cutting off conversation by way of interruption. He is very rude. He is very aggressive. He alone knows everything. Sound familiar?

I am reminded of a nagging child who understands well that simply digging in and repeating demands, if carried out long and loud enough, will cause utter frustration in a rational adult, for there is no reasoning with such a willful entity. What Scaramucci must realize is that adults will respond to "bratty behavior" in one of two possible and divergent ways: The weak or overwhelmed folks will give up and give in to demands. The resilient will react punitively, knowing that the "time out" chair has its place. Scaramucci is betting on the former.

In a sense, it all comes down to power. The toddlers, Trump, KFC and the Mooch love the game of accruing power, and each sparring session affords them a taste of dominance. Their behavior goes beyond the unseemly; it engenders an anti-intellectual, emotional world of "I want." Such a world has no space for others. Such a world is antithetical to democracy. Unless the adults take control, and very soon, we will see the diabolical results of this reincarnation of the despotic pigs of *Animal Farm*.

Another Outlandish Conspiracy Theory: The Cheese Stands Alone

"Off with their heads," said the orange king. "No fealty, no job!" One by one those who serve the president are being fired. Soon the big cheese will have produced a long list of has-beens. What to do? If the presidency becomes truly irrelevant, due in large part to infighting and no comprehensive plan for governance, unable to do anything except pronounce edicts, some of which will be shot down, then the country is in peril; for one thing, Congress and the courts cannot function adequately "on a dime" should an emergency occur. In a nutshell, the presidency must be saved. Should Trump be unable to replace working parts of his administration appropriately after multiple firings, then the door opens for his removal, for the third prong of the government will be salvaged one way or another.

So, here's the conspiracy theory: A virtual "mole" will pledge loyalty to the mad king, but this fake sycophant will behave as a turncoat undermining Trump's power in covert and overt ways. The result? Another resignation or firing. This process will be repeated for as long as it takes, for the patriots lining up to become moles will exponentially increase as Trump's tweets become ever more bizarre. Eventually, the cheese will stand alone as all failed or would-be despots must. No longer president, and to his dismay, no longer relevant or even mildly interesting to others.

An Eerie Comparison

Nearly thirty years ago, as part of a curriculum project, I wrote the following, part of an essay on Charles Foster Kane, as played by Orson Welles in the film classic, *Citizen Kane*: Perhaps *Citizen Kane* depicts the corruption of the American dream. More likely, it asks us to question the very premise of the American dream, for in *Citizen Kane* the dream of prosperity and influence, the American version of success, is inexorably linked with the demise of interpersonal relationships and personal values. When the public persona of Charles Kane emerges, the private persona is diminished proportionately, and thus it appears that public success and private success are mutually exclusive.

It is ironic that a newspaper reporter interviews those closest to Kane in hopes of finding the man behind the public image, for "the man" had ceased to exist - or perhaps never truly existed. Kane's dying word, "rosebud," signifies not only a longing for values of a lost childhood, but the realization that true adulthood was never experienced. The child never developed into a man capable of love, friendship, or, ironically, in a newspaper czar, successful communication. The public, power-wielding individual simply manipulated people as a child manipulates toy soldiers. In fact, Kane saw no difference between people and objects; both were mere extensions of his egocentric personality.

207

Though one might hold Kane's mother responsible for Kane's arrested development, noting her misguided decision to separate Kane from the family at an impressionable age was devastating, one must also note the emerging public man was deemed successful by society, and/or his egocentric behavior was not only condoned by society at large, but often applauded.

Kane's pursuit of happiness resulted in his deadening isolation, and though this is tragic in itself, the essential tragedy of *Citizen Kane* concerns the destruction of those myriad others caught in the devastating web of false values and lost idealism. In short, Kane's loss of idealism symbolizes America's loss of idealism and/or the essential flaw of the American dream."

Having occasion recently to reread this, my curriculum unit, a project that considered short story elements (such as point of view and symbolism) and film elements (such as uses of lighting and camera angles) within the context of the late 1930s/early 1940s, I was struck by the many similarities between Charles Kane and Donald Trump. One could easily substitute our current president's name in the essay and not be far off the mark.

Considering the themes that emerged in the study of short stories created in the time period leading up to World War II, along with the film, *Citizen Kane*, prompted additional comparisons to our time: the emergence of fascism, a great disparity of wealth, isolationism, both nationally and among segments within American society and, once again, generally-speaking, the loss of idealism.

If history is seen as cyclical in some regard, one might entertain the notion of revisiting *Citizen Kane* in order to better understand both the psyche of Donald Trump and the tenor of our times.

He is a Human Being

I find myself observing Donald Trump, during what I believe are his numbered days in office with trepidation for him, with compassion. This is the way of seeing an end to fear. One does not easily practice compassionate viewing when lives are at stake - when a perpetrator causes anguish to the powerless: immigrants, the poor and other marginalized people, and when sheer incompetence threatens our nation's future. However, when the danger appears to be passing, my thoughts turn to the individual, another human being, flawed, but not evil incarnate.

I do not relish Trump's self-destructive tendencies, as he continues to dig himself deeper into controversy. His emotional and intellectual limitations prohibit a true Machiavellian stance. He is at sea, still relying on the bullying ways of his business experience, still longing for the regard of others, still hoping to become a human being worthy of accolades and love. This unfolding and/or unraveling is difficult to witness. It is a personal tragedy.

Who among us has not dabbled in hubris? Who among us is truly self-less? Who among us can with perfect right judge another beyond the deeds he commits? When Donald Trump fails, is humiliated - though he may well couch his departure in another light, he will know failure - I suggest one not celebrate the comeuppance of a man but rather, celebrate the strength of democracy.

PostScript: Remembering We're Not There Yet

In the meantime, we must not fall victim to exhaustion due to the emotionally-driven, intellectually-bereft, hubris-enhancing rhetoric that surrounds us. We must continue to resist all that threatens our nation while remembering to replenish ourselves - noting and appreciating: the promise of our days, the premise of our country and those who support the vision of a "more perfect union."

Metaphorical Sports

I have never been a fan of football: too violent, illustrating (largely) brawn over brains - all about grabbing, holding and blocking. Visually, football offers the picture of war. Baseball, on the other hand, metaphorically-speaking, is all about returning "home." It seems to me baseball is more civilized fundamentally and offers more opportunities for individual successes (notwithstanding the role of the less-violent quarterback in football). With baseball, the opportunity exists for spectacular, individual talent as to pitching or hitting the ball. Violent contact is reserved for an inanimate object.

If you recall, baseball has been dubbed "America's pastime," though lately I wonder if it has been usurped by football. Extending the metaphor to current governance, I also see a cruder, more war-like mode of operation there - akin to football. Once again, baseball offers the ideal of "home" (a unified place) and space for individual enlightenment (talent). I see very little in the way of baseball in our government at this point in time. I long for a Hank Aaron, or a Jackie Robinson, or a Ted Williams, a break-out star who would exhibit talent by way of sportsmanlike behavior.

A concern that arises with the sport of football has to do with brain injury, now generally considered to be widely prevalent. Well, what would one expect? All this violent contact of war-like maneuvers is bound to result in some sort of loss, just as current displays of players in our government result in the loss of cogent thought. We witness absurd strategies based on denigration rather than creative talent. We witness language that befits a bar-room brawl rather than the rhetoric of true statesmen. Brawn over brains. "Home" is forgotten with the chaotic tackles of opponents and with the resultant injuries that ensue.

When will the public demand an end to brain-injuring sport? We need to find home again. We need to return to America's pastime of fair play within the scope of civility and peace.

Trump's Cronyism: The Worst of Swamp Politics

Did anyone notice that Jeff Sessions' response to humiliation and denigration at the hands of the president was blatantly weird? The attorney general is still supporting the man who rewarded his misplaced, early support and on-going loyalty with absolute disdain. No hard feelings... Well, now there's talk that Sessions will not be fired as attorney general; rather, he will simply move to another Cabinet position, Homeland Security.

It is clear that Trump will do anything at all to ensure that his business dealings with Russia or otherwise will not come to light. What's next? A new attorney general who will get rid of that pesky Mueller? If Sessions is indeed going along with this disgusting game of political "musical chairs," we will know once and for all that he has little character, despite what his colleagues in the Senate have proclaimed lately.

Speaking of senators, when will Republican senators find their moral compass? The idea that Cabinet positions are viewed as mere perks or rewards for faithful service to the party, and are therefore interchangeable, is anathema to those of us who believe in the notion of requisite experience for important positions. But then, look at Trump's Cabinet; a secretary of education who does not believe in public education, a secretary of the interior willing to debase our public lands, for examples. And the Senate confirmed these folks with nary a hiccup. Cronyism, pure and simple...

The swamp has a new alligator in Trump who, let's not forget, promised to "drain the swamp." Now the swamp is murkier than ever with possible Russian collusion. If senators do not stand up for principle should Trump figure out a way to halt the independent investigation, we will know once and for all that corruption and cronyism define our government.

Are you watching, America? Well, are you?

Remember: "by the people, for the people" and remember, also, that democracy is dependent upon its citizens ultimately. My fellow Americans: Please resist when it is necessary to do so - at the ballot box, with letters to editors, petitions to congressmen and in any other lawful way open to you. It is up to us, as it has always been. Now more than ever before, unfortunately.

Steve Miller: The Deflector's Not-So-Secret Weapon

Have you ever had occasion to debate an opponent who offered a seemingly erudite rejoinder? His argument appeared to be cogent - especially when delivered in a particularly patronizing manner. Two minutes later, you realized how you could have adequately responded. Such was the experience of Jim Acosta at a recent press briefing when faced with Miller's momentarily adroit deflection with regard to a legal-immigration plan and the issuance of green cards. Miller had called for new rules: Those seeking green cards would be required to speak English and present with necessary skills for employment, middle-class employment, it would seem.

When Acosta, quite rightly, suggested that such a policy was antithetical to the spirit of the poem associated with the Statue of Liberty, Miller spoke of a numbers game: "Was the spirit of liberty invoked in past times with fewer allowed immigrants?" - or words to that effect. Miller's argument was beside the point, obviously. Had he simply called for a reduction of allowed immigrants his rejoinder conceivably could have been seen as apt. But Acosta was not speaking of numbers; he was speaking of spirit - or a credo that

enabled the United States to welcome "poor, huddled masses yearning to breathe free" irrespective of mother-tongue or skill level. On the other hand, Miller's "numbers" defense of a class-oriented immigration policy, offered mere obfuscation; moreover, it was, at its heart, disingenuous - even deceitful. This is the way of obfuscation, a necessary ploy from Miller's perspective. Would that Acosta had labeled Miller's argument as mere deflection; though, given Miller's constant interruptions, even brief counter-argument from Acosta proved to be next to impossible.

More to the point, the roll-out of this legal-immigration policy, a supposed boon to American workers, occurred at a time when Trump and his cronies would rather we turn away from current concerns: health-care issues, Russia-probe and general administrative chaos - not to mention recent criticism of the president from law enforcement, the military, transgender folks and those associated with the Boy Scouts, no less.

Especially galling was Mr. Miller's pronouncement that the majority of Americans support his heartless plan. Mr. Miller does not speak for us; rather, with the forked-tongue of the obfuscator, he speaks for the "Deflector-in-Chief." By now, many of us are not buying the tired uses of deflection and obfuscation. If Trump sees fit to continue to pivot, perhaps he should roll out a plan for infrastructure policy next, a policy less associated with people directly or with Americans' dearly-held beliefs.

Update: Trump blew his chance of pivoting to infrastructure during a news conference designed for said pivot. Instead of staying on message, he chose to dig himself deeper into a hole of stupidity and immorality by equating Nazis, the KKK and other extremist groups with counter-demonstrators in Charlottesville.

Trump's Recipe for Disaster: A 12-Step Process

Step One: Bombastically pontificate. No special ingredients necessary.

Step Two: Backtrack when some folks raise issues having to do with faulty thinking.

Step Three: Repeat Step One.

Step Four: Repeat Step Two.

Step Five: Beat in (or on) an inconvenient egg-head.

Step Six: Repeat Step Two.

Step Seven: Throw out (fire) any ingredients that cause personal angst.

Step Eight: Re-engineer ingredients (widely accepted credo).

Step Nine: Repeat Step Two.

Step Ten: Repeat Step Seven.

Step Eleven: Repeat Step One (for old time's sake).

Step Twelve: Admit defeat as none of the ingredients ultimately met with your approval. Find another recipe - preferably in the business world - presuming business-ingredients remain intact.

(By the way, and to state the obvious, the disaster-recipe fed no one.)

The Hatfields and the McCoys

Remember the saga of the Hatfields and the McCoys, those feuding families of yesteryear who fought for so long that the genesis of their war was forgotten? Reminds me of modern-day Democrats and Republicans. Let's face it, the parties in their current manifestations do not resemble the entities of our parents' time. Yet, many cast votes as their parents once did, following a kind of family tradition. Like the Hatfields and McCoys, they "just know" the opposing party is bogus or worse.

Perhaps the two-party system exists today solely to provide a team to root for or a team to hate with a passion. Seems that way. Where is the party of FDR? Kennedy? Conversely, where is the party of Lincoln? Eisenhower? Gone with the wind of incivility, beholden to big-money donors, mere vestiges of what they once were.

What to do? Bernie Sanders was able to run for quite a while with the support of small donors. Though dismantling the current two-party system seems a tall order, we ought to be able to press for fiscal independence within the current system in the following ways: Revoke "Citizens United" for a start, rein in powerful lobbies, limit monetary contributions of lobbyists and wealthy entities. In other words, give the vote back to the people.

Additionally, the electorate must become educated as to the belief-systems of the parties. Talking points with buzzwords such as "big government" do not begin to explain the workings of a particular philosophy. At this juncture in time, we need articulate candidates who go beyond vitriolic sniping and sophomoric platitudes. President Trump is but a ludicrous version of the overall state of government; many others partake of the same strategies for winning by stressing team-mentality as though governance was a sport, in some sense, mere entertainment.

Many long for the statesmen of yore, those erudite people versed in history and philosophy, experienced folk of civil ways and creative thought, people who put others and our country first. The antithesis of the mentality of the Hatfields and the McCoys - the current manifestation of our political parties.

Amendment:

You can discount the tenor of the aforementioned to some degree. The truth is, I hold the Republican Party of McConnell and Ryan culpable for the current state of our union. Obstructionism to the tune of: "Our main goal is to deny Obama anything he plans to accomplish" is a governing concept steeped in cynicism - a concept that promotes self-preservation above all else. Such a concept prevents service to a broad constituency. It places power above probity, hypocrisy above honor. It is, in one word, despicable.

And yet, Democrats are not entirely blameless. By kowtowing, to a degree, to "big money," and with the practice of strategy over substance, they managed to confuse an electorate during the last election. Often appearing to overlook the working-class and the middle-class folks who had previously comprised their base, they, too, were perceived as cynical or shifty. I do believe that much was accomplished for working people during Obama's tenure despite the blatant disrespect he endured, and yet, no one was able to tap into his idealism - his ability to generate the optimism we noted in 2008. Perhaps the fruit of constant disparagement, denigration and disrespect is cynicism writ large, a cynicism that prodded voters to foolishly turn to an "outsider" bereft of both personal esteem and professional credentials.

Enough!

Now is the time. Much damage has been done. One cannot begin to discuss Trump's latest behavior in any other way than to say: He is out-of-control, beyond reason, beyond reigning-in by generals, Congress or the people of this fast-devolving nation.

How does one adequately respond to Trump's provocation of Kim Jong Un: "They will be met with fire, fury and frankly power the likes of which this world has never seen before"? How can one begin to react to Trump's thanking Putin for expelling 750+ diplomats from Russia? Taunting a mad man of nuclear capability... Cavalierly dismissing the notion of diplomacy with regard to both Korea and Russia...

Trump's behavior does not warrant discussion. It is beyond the pale, beyond reason. It is indicative of a president who is not well enough to serve.

It is time to consider the 25th amendment.

Spoken and Unspoken Words Matter

President Trump condemned hatred from "many sides" following the violent demonstration in Charlottesville. Clearly, he was equating counter-protesters with neo-Nazis, the KKK and white-supremacist groups. Of course, after consultation with staff amid understandable outcry, he spoke specifically of the aforementioned hate groups as having no place in this country. Too little, too late.

Some Americans will speak of Trump's acceptance of those in his base who support the denigration of a variety of minority populations in our society. Others will conclude that Trump is bigoted himself. Certainly, his mode of operation - aggressive, demeaning and bombastic - serves to heighten tensions among citizens of the US as well as tensions existent in the world at large.

I maintain that Donald Trump is sorely lacking in a basic moral-code inherent in the belief systems of the world to include: Judaism, Christianity, Islam and so on. Donald worships Donald. Such a stance denies self-reflection, intellect and emotional well-being. It is nihilistic at its core. Such a stance also precludes reasoned thought as well as articulate spoken and written words. Perhaps Trump's inability to put forth a healing message should be seen as the first symptom of personal and professional dysfunction.

The ability to unify a nation rests on leaders of lofty thought exhibited through oratorical skill, for such people shine a light on all that is good in our nation with compassionate, moral words emerging from a solid framework based on reverence for truth, humility and rectitude, ideals Donald Trump has not practiced nor, for that matter, has even accepted.

My Advice? It's for Your Own Good

Donald, are you not tired? You expend energy as a four-year old does - in more ways than one.

You must know by now that tweeting and impromptu speeches are, at best, only momentarily energizing.

Admit it.
In the dead of the night, you worry: "Who is out to get me now?" "Will I lose everything?"

"Is it worth it?"

I'll tell you what is worth it.

Your young son is worth it - by all accounts, a good boy. We have seen him interact with babies in your family. He is kind.

Your wife is worth it - a loyal, supportive entity - standing by you always - under trying conditions.

Recalibrate your priorities - while you still can.

Do not wait for an ignominious end but walk away with some semblance of dignity.

I bear you no malice, and this advice? It's for your own good.

Another Message to Cable News Outlets: Make Trump and Co. Irrelevant for an Hour

Ousted Steve Bannon is going to war with Republicans, Trump, etc. When isn't he at war? And the news pundits agonize over what this will mean. I understand that adequate news-coverage requires reporting on these folks - entities who are steeped in blind rage. However, the platform provided for them to work through their personal angst overshadows the many who are not engaged in personal power-plays and anger for the sake of anger, precursor behaviors that may result in a destruction that will affect us all.

I have a small suggestion: Provide one hour of coverage to those who are actually trying to construct rather than destroy, folks who are not caught up in personal self-aggrandizement stemming from who knows where. Perhaps, several senators who are diligently working to improve life for average Americans. Al Franken, for example. By the way, his latest book, *Giant of the Senate,* is worth reading, for one learns much about the workings of government as well as the trials of running for office, all in the context of honesty through good humor.

Franken is bright, astute and, most important, self-reflective. He even exhibits self-deprecation, a marvelous quality in a person of some power. At this time of governance, largely built on the influence of great wealth (let us not forget Citizens' United and the Koch brothers), Senator Franken comes across as one of us. He is a hip "Mr. Smith Goes to Washington" - sorely needed at this point in time, not just to remind us that idealistic public servants exist, but to change the overall narrative and thus enable healing as well as the potential for constructive legislation.

Give Al Franken an hour of your programming along with other emotionally-grounded people. I'm thinking, a few diplomats, scientists involved in the EPA, for examples. Let's hear what they have to say about how we might move out of the swamp of big-money and blind rage couched in power-worship.

In short, give us some material beyond reality-TV. Simply ignore the cynical ones for an hour, so as to encourage appropriately-engaged and, eventually, hopeful people once more.

Note to Anderson Cooper:

Dear Mr. Cooper,

Thank you for your professional demeanor. Where others exhibit smugness in the face of the outlandish words of our president, you react honestly, without rancor, though sometimes with incredulity. I remember an example of this: You couldn't help yourself when Trump complained: "She did it first," and equated Trump's response to that of a five-year-old. This was done with good humor, so that Trump actually reacted as a five-year-old would - that is, he was momentarily chastened. It was a great moment of clarity. And I think it worked because you saw Trump as a human being. You were not trying to trip him up; rather, you reacted to an individual who had lost his way - as any concerned person would under the circumstances.

Mr. Cooper, your strength is your ability to see people not positions. In that respect, you are much like Al Franken. How about arranging an hour-long, on-air conversation with Senator Franken? That would amount to TV worth watching.

Yours truly,
a US Citizen

Update: (11/16/17) Senator Al Franken will likely face ethics charges having to do with sexual misconduct. Disappointing, to say the very least, when one admired is unmasked as yet another abuser of male power.

★ **(To the Reader:** Please bear with me. I, too, am aware of the tedium involved in restating the obvious in seemingly endless multiple contexts.**)**

An Elitist to the Core

For all of his elitist-decrying rhetoric (a message to his base), Trump proves himself to be an elitist to the core, in the sense of wielding his wealth and position as one might wield a sledgehammer. Trump's latest behavior amounts to yet one more pathetic attempt to create an antithetical reality within the context of "unfair" treatment. Many remember that Trump has consistently attempted to project a "plain-man" or authentic image - supposedly fighting against the powers that be - one of us. In fact, he is not one of us; he is merely a privileged individual used to getting his own way, one who has managed to hurt others in the past while experiencing immunity for his actions due to inherited wealth.

The latest? Posting a meme that depicts the "Trump Train" running over a CNN reporter - this mere days after an innocent was killed in a terrorist-style attack by car. Trump is way beyond "tone-deaf." His focus on himself knows no bounds; he jettisons human decency, human intellect - all facets of human goodness -

222

in his quest for ultimate power and subsequent personal satisfaction of the particularly revolting kind, it must be said.

His response to an African-American CEO when said CEO pulled himself out of Trump's business council for reasons having to do with integrity- refusing to countenance Trump's obviously racist stance? Deride and attempt to destroy. Vintage Trump. White businessmen who subsequently followed suit met with derision as well, though they were not called out by name: "There are plenty of others to take your place."

Unfortunately, the craziness continues... But, not for long, I hope. Sooner or later, the penny will drop. For example, today Trump's approval rating sits at 38%. Eventually, many more will see Trump for who he is in reality, a particularly dangerous charlatan, and that is putting it mildly.

PostScript:

Trump has now reversed his Monday statement denouncing the KKK, Nazis and white supremacists by opining, just this afternoon, that "alt-left" factions were equally responsible for the Charlottesville violence. How can one begin to react to Trump's unhinged, erratic words? Perhaps, the end is near, the end of Trump's presidency, that is. Will his Cabinet and Congress react substantively? We'll see.

Plea to Congress, Courts

Now he has pardoned Joe Arpaio, the Arizona sheriff who openly admitted running "concentration camps." Can you not see tyranny knocking at the door? Stop Trump now!

For Trump, All is Small

I think the worst thing about Trump is his inability to get beyond small. Oh, he talks a big game, but that is only talk. Now he is considering halting DACA (Deferred Action for Childhood Arrivals). Trump doesn't understand the "dreamers." For one thing, his background ensured that he didn't have to dream about a comfortable or adequate existence. Unlike many immigrant-dreamers, Trump exhibits not one iota of "I want to contribute to this country that has provided an opportunity for me." Quite to the contrary, Trump has used this country and its people to enrich himself only.

Not to unnecessarily rehash previously stated concerns, I merely ask the reader to revisit Trump's behavior: fleecing of workers by way of bankruptcies, fraudulent Trump University, etc., and, once more, I suggest we ask why Trump refuses to release his tax returns.

To put it bluntly, I maintain that Trump is self-absorbed and small-minded in every sense of these descriptors.

Selfishness tends to limit both moral and intellectual development. Some disparagingly labeled Obama a dreamer (and an immigrant). Well, I, for one, miss the idealistic demeanor of President Obama. I miss his empathetic ways. He did not have to make second trips to disaster locales to get the empathy-message across. I miss Obama's dreams for a more inclusive nation, and, perhaps most of all, I miss his cogent ideas.

My cynical side has concluded that Trump's relentless disparagement of Obama, coupled with his obsessive need to erase his predecessor's accomplishments, stems from a real fear. Trump may be terrified that one day, sometime soon, the public will recall President Obama's legacy. We'll remember that, while not perfect in every way, President Obama was essentially large-hearted and broad-minded (intellectually-sound). I do believe that the pendulum will soon swing back to the less angry, more hopeful times inherent in a thinking-public; then Trump will run the risk of being hit by the pendulum's movement. That is Trump's real worry. Really, the only worry he appears seriously to countenance.

The Enamored State

Fake news, fake governance, fake love. Here we are.

Fake news is not merely an endorsement of Trump's stance. Fake news has to do with the reverence for reality-show hype and/or Trump's driving of headlines with his deflective tweets and infantile behavior. On the one hand, it is appropriate for outlets to report on these side-shows; with Trump, all we have is side shows. Yet, it seems to me that the glee, with which such wretchedly-entertaining drivel is offered, serves to bolster a populace all too willing to live in an alternative universe of people behaving badly. This is a problem. It is simply not appropriate to see governance as another "Housewives of Wherever" episode - or to sanctimoniously view Trump as a pathetic specimen of human behavior in the vein of a hapless guest on "The Jerry Springer Show." Which leads me to the question: from whence generally the shift from unifying, dare I say, uplifting programming to denigrating, divisive fare? (By the way, not a new phenomenon.)

Blame Trump all you want for the current debacle: legislature brought to a screaming halt, disconnection from key allies, a divided nation... But such a stance is too easy. This hollowing-out of the values inherent in the premise of this nation is not new but rather, has been

225

occurring over decades, and we all bear some responsibility for attitudes of denigration, divisiveness and incivility. Unfortunately, the words of Abraham Lincoln continue to resonate: "America will never be destroyed from the outside. If we falter, and lose our freedoms, it will be because we have destroyed ourselves."

We often hear people proclaim their love of country, but what do they mean by this? Too often folks are enamored by notions of our nation's great power - as if our standing in the world was created by force alone. The truth is: Real influence is born of altruistic behaviors and a government united in its quest for peace and prosperity for all. When governance and the will of the people engenders mean-spirited gamesmanship born of an "us versus them" mentality, we have lost our way. Love of country is not vain or "puffed-up." Love of country is not static; rather, it is evolutionary. Love of country is not selfishly-regressive, but expansive in its humility.

We Americans should not be enamored merely with a presumed image of this country. Appropriate and true love of country reflects the capacity of compassion in its citizenry: a love that considers others as well as ourselves, a love born of intellectual and emotional respect - respect that acknowledges the need for on-going development of the inherent virtues of our democracy.

March of the Sycophants

Those who align themselves with Trump stand to face ultimate abasement. Presumably, some of these people possessed altruistic intellect - that is, intellect beyond the practice of manipulation - prior to jumping on the Trump band-wagon. Some even evinced wholeness and/or moral centers. Some, but not all...

Of note: A number of individuals have left Trump's side for one reason or another. The list includes Flynn, Spicer, Scaramucci, Gorka, Priebus, Bannon, Walsh, Cohen-Watnick, Price - while many sycophants remain: Sessions, Mnuchin, Icahn, Pruitt, Perry, DeVos, Carson, Chao, and General Kelly, most unfortunately.

Kelly's defense of the president's clumsy condolence-call to a Gold Star family proved unseemly, especially when he invoked the Trumpian method of puerile name-calling, this with regard to a Florida congresswoman ("empty barrel"). Remember the old aphorism: "Lie down with dogs, get up with fleas"?

Respectfully, I maintain that the "best one-percent" of our nation (service men and women) as referenced by Kelly, is not the same one-percent President Trump reveres most of all, for Trump cares most deeply for himself and his ilk, mostly for himself. Therefore, loyalty to Trump will not result in reciprocity. To support Trump is to support the antithesis of unselfishness and honor.

Sycophancy is painful to watch. Sycophancy inevitably results in the negation of autonomy and all that this entails: loss of intellect, loss of precious values and, ultimately, loss of self-worth. Terrible for the sycophants, perhaps even more terrible for the rest of us.

Trump: The Brat Syndrome

He has always been a brat and he has gotten away with this. Why? We all know how relentless brats can be. The ferocity of a brat's anger and need, and the seemingly endless energy he uses to dominate his landscape becomes an exhausting proposition for his family, school, etc. At the outset, his outrageous behavior is not taken seriously, and eventually those in his orbit choose not to see it at all. This is dangerous. Whole families have been ruined by brats. Witness the English-nanny television-show, and you'll see what I mean.

Trump's entire shtick has been one long tantrum coupled with boasting. Early on, he stated he could shoot someone on 5th Avenue and folks would still vote for him. Why do we countenance such a person in the White House? His aforementioned statement is plainly that of a troubled person and insulting to the voting public, to boot. Since Trump's circus-days of the campaign, things have continued to deteriorate. His presidency has consisted of relentless (and dangerous) name-calling and lies too numerous to count.

A few of the adults in the room are running around trying to contain him. Others sit on the side-lines, wringing their hands in impotence. Some have their own selfish agendas and hope to profit from the chaos. All have become complicit, and that includes many of us. We're worn down. The public outcry of the early days has dwindled. The brat has won. Maybe.

I still hold out hope for the English-nanny in us who will confront the truth and call for the time-out room. By the way, any teacher worth her salt knows that an entire class of children should not be sacrificed for the need of one. Now is the time. Haul out your placard signs, write "The Brat Must Go" on them, show up!

Remembering (Accurately) the Good, Old Days

Many decry the current state of affairs. They long for the good, old days. For some, this nostalgia is code for a time when white men were in charge. In case you haven't noticed, they still are, with some notable exceptions. (So far, that is...) Yet, this issue of nostalgia has less to do with who is in charge, and more to do with how debased our culture has become, in large part due to the monetary-lust evident in America of late. Money is power. Money is worshiped. Please recall *The Apprentice* theme song: "Money, Money, Money, Money..."

Remember when lawyers gauche enough to advertise in local papers were derided as loutish, unprofessional hacks? Now, television airways are awash with "ambulance chasers." Remember when drugs were the domain of health professionals, specifically, doctors? Witness the many drug-pushing ads on TV currently. To add insult to injury, these ads are packed with warnings as to side-effects, primarily to avoid potential litigation. These advertisements inevitably lead to consumer confusion. (Why would anyone take Chantix knowing of the possible counter-indicators of suicidal thoughts or actions?) Physicians, not drug companies, should be advising patients. But I'm afraid the current state of affairs is all about "money, money, money, money..."

Remember when movies featured "everymen" of dignified deportment? Remember Jimmy Stewart in *It's a Wonderful Life*? And Gregory Peck in *To Kill a Mockingbird*? And Sidney Poitier in *In the Heat of the Night*? Though not all of today's films are given over to the crass, many are. Moreover, the likes of moneyed do-nothings are revered. Why is a Kim Kardashian given the time of day? Because she has "money, money, money, money..." Call me a dreamer if it makes

229

you feel better, but I shall still maintain that money doesn't create a "big" person.

I've lived long enough to remember a time of reverence for what are now viewed as quaint notions of honesty and decorum. I remembered the old-time heroes and heroines. They were not vulgar; they did not engage in power-mongering. Often, they were everyday folks, the preachers and the teachers. They provided hope and peace with their erudition. They did not peddle money-making schemes or seek monuments in their names. They were above all of that. They were gratefully respected, for they sought not world-wide fame, but merely the good-will of their communities.

We live in a youth-obsessed culture, so my words may not resonate with many in the here and now. Yet, I would remind all that our twin obsessions with eternal youth and money are bogus, for these specious goals are essentially bids for immortality or on-going fame, impossible achievements. We have lost our way. The last presidential election reflects the misunderstanding of a once proud and moral people, for what we have in Donald Trump is the antithesis of erudition, compassion, decorum and grace. We have a money-lauding, out-of-control and eternal man-child instead. He mirrors our regression and our precipitous decline. May we avoid autocracy as promulgated by the power-loving, money-grasping Putin, Kim Jong-Un, etc. now and in the future. May the "little people" (of Leona Helmsley's infamous statement: "Only the little people pay taxes") prevail.

To: Donald J. Trump, Person (and others of his ilk)

I do not hate you, though I find your words and actions abhorrent. I pity you. I will state my point in words that you might understand:

You are a loser at living, though you do not see this yet. Eventually, you will know.

You will understand that peace triumphs over a war of words and actions. You will understand that beauty is not bought with purloined gold. You will understand that you are not God.

In the meantime, you wield destruction in your bid for immortality. History tells us that this will not stand. What was once St. Petersburg, became Stalingrad only to become St. Petersburg once more.

You will dub me "snowflake." And I will accept the moniker. A snowflake is a particular individual in structure and therefore autonomous. A snowflake is also transitory. And this is the point. You cannot attain immortality. You are not God.

What do you know of love? In your human form, you seek love to assuage your need. When one is able give love in the moment of an overwhelming need to receive love, one glimpses the divine - as a brave soldier does with his sacrifice for a comrade in need - or a giving child at the bedside of a beloved, dying parent. We all struggle to understand and attain this notion of love, being imperfect. But once experienced, there comes a knowing: Those moments of attainment, transitory as they may be, amount to truth.

I wish you the experience of giving love at the expense of yourself. I hope that you will one day see beauty in the mutability of nature, or in the fleeting smile of another who appreciates your worth. I sense that one day you will accept your mortality, in the face of the immortality of the whole, as we all must.

Aphorisms for and about Trump

If ever there was a president who was in need of the wisdom of aphorisms, he is Trump. If ever there was a president who illustrated aphorisms, he is Trump. The thing of it is, Donald Trump is a caricature; put another way, our president lacks complexity wrought of thought. Therefore, the somewhat simplistic quality of aphorisms fit the bill. Additionally, it is conceivably possible he would take note of these brief forays into reading, brief being the salient advantage, for Trump is normally a television-hound. In other words, he likes to be spoon-fed, is intellectually lazy to an astonishing degree. (How have we come to this?)

Well-known aphorisms Trump should heed:

1. It's never too late to mend.

2. It's the empty can that makes the most noise.

3. Knowledge is power.

4. Handsome is as handsome does.

5. Honesty is the best policy.

6. Fools rush in where angels fear to tread.

7. Doubt is the beginning, not the end, of wisdom.

8. Easier said than done.

9. Don't make mountains out of molehills.

10. As you sow, so shall you reap.

11. A rising tide lifts all boats.

12. All that glitters is not gold.

13. Pride goeth before a fall.

14. You can't unring a bell.

15. You're never too old to learn.

Made-up aphorisms especially for Trump:

1. Your golden hair is not a crown.

2. Incessant repetition bespeaks an empty vessel.

3. Being a man means occasionally having to say you're sorry.

4. Gnat-like accomplishments: the fruit of "big" ideas from a small mind.

5. Bellowed words do not an erudite vocabulary make.

6. Better a boring intellectual than an entertaining sensationalist.

7. A roiling stone gathers ill-will.

8. Name-calling displays the arsenal of a weak man.

9. A mountain does not proclaim its majesty.

10. The ant is revered above the sloth.

11. Fame is fleeting; respect reverberates.

12. Illusion: the immortality of the ignominious.

A final wish and admonition for President Trump:

Speak wisely; govern justly.

Sarah Huckabee Sanders: The Human Shield

Rarely, do I advocate that reporters behave in raucous ways. But I'll make an exception for the press-corps folks who attend the daily White House briefing. Just once, I'd like to see decorum fly out the window. Just once, I would enjoy a retort such as: "Sarah, what you just said is a load of marbles."

Ms. Sanders is the master-deflector. One briefing is very much like all the others. At the outset of each of these events, Sanders inevitably proclaims some non-existent Trump achievement or another; then she proceeds to take questions. Often these questions point out Trump's inconsistencies, to put it softly or, more to the point, his lies. Ms. S handles these tough questions in three ways: 1. She claims that Trump has already spoken on the matter. 2. She refers to behaviors of others as a faux rebuttal. 3. She moves on to the next hapless reporter avoiding the substance of the original question altogether.

Sarah Huckabee Sanders represents a female version of Superman. Nothing penetrates her steely shield, and the White House press have yet to find their kryptonite, unfortunately. Somehow, I also am reminded of the tin man in the *Wizard of Oz*. However, that analogy does not really work. The tin man was looking for his heart while Sarah seems to have denied hers. Mostly, she reminds me of a terrible school-mistress from the olden days - one who refused to countenance questions, expected docile behavior from her audience - an autocrat, in other words. However, that analogy is not totally apt, either, for Ms.

Sanders is not the autocrat. She is merely the shield for the autocrat. And I am left wondering: What does she gain from this?

Though watching the daily briefings feels to me like a waste of time, for reasons articulated above, I shall continue to do so on the off-chance that the human shield is trying to wear down the resolve of those of us who are trying to make sense of the nonsense, all the while hoping we are not witnessing the demise of democracy.

Metaphor of the Mountain

Long ago, I watched my younger brother play "King of the Mountain" with his friends. The game amounted to dominance of a small hillock, and the achievement meant hurling off any would-be contenders for the position of "king." Needless to say, the victories were short-lived as the boys replaced one another with rapid regularity. "I'm King of the Mountain!" lasted only a moment or two. It was boring to watch, really. Pointless, too. Of course, this memory reminds me of Trump. His whole life has been one incessant game of "King of the Mountain."

I also remember the metaphor of the "shining city on the hill" - that which was employed by Ronald Reagan as a descriptor of the United States. We were meant to view our country as the consummate example of righteousness and probity amid a world of lesser countries.

Yet, the true metaphor of the mountain, an idea that provides hope and moral sustenance to Americans and non-Americans alike, resides in Martin Luther King's "I Have a Dream" message - when he proclaimed that he had "been to the mountaintop" - a place of universal peace. It resides, too, by way of the novel, *Cry the Beloved*

235

Country, specifically, in Stephen Kumalo's experience of contemplation and envisioned redemption atop a mountain.

Let us replace petty hills and selfish dreams with the known metaphor of the mountain where hope, redemption and universal dreams dwarf momentary victories. The truth is: Those hillocks, destined to be bull-dozed by those to follow, will be forgotten or, worst-case scenario, live on in ignominy - while the majesty of the mountain will ever endure.

(And on the practical side of things, let's identify, support and elect those who espouse larger, loftier visions.)

A Fall from Grace: A Matter of Degree?

I cannot condone the sexual-molestation behavior of Al Franken. In fact, I am of two minds as to whether or not he should resign from the Senate. Women have been victimized, for far too long, by their lesser status as to power-sharing in the presence of men. This must be acknowledged.

There exists the obvious disparity of physical strength, that which puts women at a distinct disadvantage. Certainly, women learn early that such disparity in dangerous situations can only be met with a carefully-wrought plan of intellectual parry. (I am remembering a near-mugging incident of my younger years that I managed to avoid with quick-thinking; realizing that my only recourse had to do with brain over brawn, I pretended to be developmentally-challenged. Somehow, my acting skills, far better than I had known them to be, actually worked. The muggers let me walk free.)

But what a way to live. Of course, power-sharing has always been an issue for women: in the workplace, in government, even in religious contexts. This is the point. The larger issue lies behind the egregious behavior of sexual misconduct: the second-class experience of women. Perhaps we are nearing another watershed moment, a time when women come to the fore in order to challenge the status quo. I applaud those of my gender who are speaking out now. May this continue with regard to all aspects of female-experience.

Returning to recent allegations of sexual abuse, it must be noted: A tipping-point appears to have occurred. The sheer number of allegations involving men of power, brought to the light finally, indicates a remarkable change of opinion as to the place of women. This is to the good. Women of courage who fight back against the abuse of power in sexual matters are also underscoring a general prejudice long practiced as to women's rights, or lack thereof. Respect should be afforded.

The history of the treatment of women ought to be revisited. What Al Franken (and others) thought was amusing a decade ago, is anathema now. Rightly so. Yet, I would point out that Mr. Franken himself has worked for the rights of women in this arena over the last decade, introducing legislation that serves to address the very conduct of sexual harassment. Perhaps Senator Franken is not the same Franken of 2006?

At the very least, he apologized and admitted the need for an ethics investigation. Contrast such behavior with the machinations of Roy Moore. Apples to oranges - as to the degree of sexual misconduct and, equally important, as to reaction to an allegation. One man seeks redemption in apology. The other plows ahead with denial and subsequent power-plays. One has introduced bills to empower women who have been sexually victimized; the other was concerned with rapists' rights in past judicial-decisions.

I do not condone sexual abuse in any degree. I do note that public opinion is fast-changing for the better. It is no longer merely "politically-correct" to eschew public humor that is particularly demeaning to women, for example. Certainly, violating a woman's space in any way is clearly egregious. To the point, cultural norms matter in the scheme of things.

I acknowledge Al Franken's misconduct - with disappointment and some sadness. In many ways, he has acquitted himself with admirable instinct and intellect as a US Senator. Perhaps he will be jettisoned or will resign. If so, I will miss his straight-forward thinking. I will remember, too, that he acknowledged his fall from grace.

To Be: Woman

Let us once and for all think about what it means to be a woman. Let us honestly assess our positions as to norms of behavior and thought. Let us aspire to enhanced self-respect.

Let me also state once again: We have reached a turning-point. Women are speaking up and exposing sexual abuse in droves. Yet, more often than not, degrees of wide-ranging sexual misconduct serve to misconstrue the message. To be sure, all examples of sexual power-plays are wrong. However, the discussion should center on the history of disrespect that has permeated the experience of womanhood.

Again, what once was accepted or regarded as innocuous, though potentially harmful joking, should be seen as something deeper, another way of curtailing the aspirations of women. Therefore,

Franken is not off the hook - even for some of his essentially adolescent-like exploits - though his fall from grace should not be equated with particularly egregious, criminal behaviors associated with child molesters and rapists. One suspects that the lately viewed, erroneous tit-for-tat messaging of right versus left, as to examples of sexual malfeasance, beyond the obvious false equivalency scenarios, works to deflect from the real issue: basic inequality experienced by women.

Though women managed to secure the vote, relatively recently in the scheme of things, women have yet to overcome a male-dominated reality that operates unchecked: in government, in the workplace, in a misunderstanding of patriarchal religious-construct and in the home at times. Such subjugation has worked to quell the dreams of women throughout history. Some women have assumed that their experience needs be subservient to the experience of men. Such acceptance has often resulted in syndromes such as the "Lady Macbeth" mode of operation - where a woman wields a hidden, spurious power - or the "supportive" syndrome, where the woman plays the nurturer behind all that is wrought by man. In some instances, this relinquishing of potential or self-actualization begets pathology.

Public examples of said pathology exist in the persons of Sarah Huckabee Sanders and Kellyanne Conway. Both women are twisting in the wind - defending the indefensible - while riding on the coattails of President Trump's current power. In doing so, they have relinquished their probity, their individuality and the truth of their important relationships as mothers, wives, co-workers and citizens. With their choices, women are once again demeaned and diminished on the public stage. Sanders and Conway are easily dubbed the handmaidens of Trump.

On a positive note, women have often reached their potentials in the world of arts and letters - by way of artistry and intellectualism - though occasionally under the guise of being male. (George Eliot comes to mind.) I need not list those creators of vision and enlightenment. They endure and live in parity with men. Long may this continue, for the wisdom of authors and artists results in redemption and hope. And those who pass on the words and the art of women and men should be lauded as well; teachers of all persuasions inspire and champion the best in us.

President Trump's wish to diminish or squash intellectuals and artists by threatening to deny funding for the National Endowment for the Arts and Humanities is telling. Doing so would provide cover for his deficits as to intellect and talent. Also, such an action might serve to prohibit progress and attitudinal changes that are unappealing to Trump and his ilk. More to the point, to deny intellectualism and expression is to deny the attainment of power of others beyond the president's kin and ken; power-sharing is anathema to his skewed reality.

Particularly at this juncture in time, women must look power square in the eye. We must recognize the potential of our procurement of power in a changing world. Now. The Women's March spoke to an awakening. Today the hard work begins. For the sake of the women who will follow, specifically, and for the sake of humanity as a whole, women must wake up, speak up and dream up.

Young women, especially, know that you are able to attain power: in government, industry - in all places of your lives. And when you do attain power, realize a paradigm- shift in the very notion of power that is yours to effect. That is, seek not power for its own sake, participating in power mongering as an end. Rather, tap into the wisdom in the long-understood, inherent quality of the quintessential

240

mother - one who practices altruism and emotional stability - thereby procuring the ultimate vision of power for all.

Tabloid Trump

The New York Post ran a headline recently (featuring a photograph of Donald Trump). It read: "I'm with the Perv." The headline was referencing Trump's namby-pamby endorsement of Roy Moore. Trump won't actively campaign for Moore but stated: "We need the Republican seat." Once again, Donald is thinking only of self-interest (securing his agenda) - and perhaps self-preservation (fear of reigniting the controversy as to his own alleged sexual misconduct - should he align too closely with Moore).

I'm quite sure if Trump were to show up in Alabama for campaign purposes, some clever T-shirt-seller would come up with the lucrative slogan: "Pervs of a feather flock together." And many would respond: "Bravo!" - appreciating the message of the entrepreneur. (For has not Trump himself been accused of leering at teenage beauty-contestants?)

Have we reached the ultimate low yet? As denizens of the Reprehensible Building, we are no longer at ground level, more like the sub-basement.

They say it is always darkest before the dawn. I long for a new morning in America, along with the vast majority of US citizenry.

Don't Let Up

None of this is normal. When I hear the argument: Over-reaction to Trump's rhetoric and behavior is endemic and not worthy of a country of conciliatory practices, I shudder. Of course, one should respectfully listen to divergent opinions. However, our current president is clearly aberrant in speech and behavior, and this, too, should be noted.

He most often engages in relentless news-making, tweeting provocations, many of which are downright bizarre. He is also obsessed with erasing Obama's legacy on all fronts, both domestic and foreign. The latest examples have to do with to environmental issues and housing issues, often undoing Obama-era regulations on the Fridays before holidays (12/22, 12/29), one assumes to avoid news coverage or scrutiny of same. At once sneaky and bombastic, Trump displays fear-inducing nihilism - quite deliberately perhaps. Rachel Maddow's statement: "Watch what they do, not what they say" has obvious merit.

The president's penchant for dominating daily news-cycles appears to be driven by his personal need. Yet, the sheer volume of helter-skelter information serves to confuse the public in its attempt to overwhelm the legitimacy of the press and indeed all that occurred before the Trump presidency.

There have been times when I wished for a moratorium of coverage on the president's attention-seeking histrionics. Surely, he would implode if he did not get his daily fix of "look at me" response. I know, wishful thinking... This out-of-control person is not likely to cease of his own accord, despite attention or inattention. He is too far gone.

I come back to my experience as a classroom teacher, specifically those occasions when faced with an unruly child. One such individual, if unchecked, can destroy an otherwise safe and productive learning environment. The aggressive and needy behavior of an emotionally-troubled student is often heart-breaking to witness. Yet, to countenance abnormality in particularly conciliatory ways is likely counterproductive both to the power-monger, for that is what the disrupter seeks above all else, and to those innocents within his scope of operation.

The child in the classroom who would destroy for his own need must be stopped. The man-child in the White House, too, must be stopped or at least characterized as an aberration, for none of this is normal: not the inelegant speech, the lies, the subterfuge involved in changing regulations over holiday recesses, not the obsession with erasing Obama's legacy, not the attempt to re-characterize the 2016 presidential election, not the antithetical accusations against those who question Trump's motives and behaviors.

Not normal. The press must conduct itself in grown-up, respectful ways so as not to mirror the chaos of Donald's Trump's frankly hysterical mode of governance. Unfortunately, this intellectual, adult response tends to add a legitimate, normal spin to what is essentially abnormal. No way around this dilemma. However, we the public, must remain incredulous as to the reality of the anarchist-in-charge. We cannot make excuses for pathology, nor become complacent in response to malignant and reprehensible behavior.

One teacher may be ultimately responsible for the climate of a classroom (as the only adult in the room). However, each and every American voter is responsible for the climate of this country. We must flex our intellectual muscles; we must witness all manner of developments to the best of our abilities; we must display courage in trying times; we must believe in our essential humanity. We cannot let up.

Overload

We are suffering from overload. Had Trump engaged in only one behavior of an egregious nature, it would be remembered, and he would be sanctioned effectively. Instead, we witness accusations of money laundering deals; we hear overtly racist speech; we learn of sexual-misconduct allegations; we suspect collusion with a foreign government; we note disrespect of allies; we watch nuclear gamesmanship played out with childish insults; we see a chaotic presidency comprised of a revolving-door staff, sycophants and inept, crude spin-doctors.

We observe a plutocratic Cabinet that serves primarily its own kind. We watch the decimation of the EPA. We acknowledge the undermining of the public-school system. We suspect a new tax bill will, in the long run, serve to enrich Trump's cronies only. We fear losing Medicare and Social Security down the road. We witness the denigration of the press and gag orders imposed upon a would-be testifier in a Russia-meddling investigation. And much more...

And all the while the drum-beat of an alternative reality punctuates our days. Trump says he is for the working man. His tax-plan proves otherwise with its support of private-plane owners, for example. Trump once stated that he liked uneducated people. Yet, he would deny citizenship to those of deprived backgrounds. Trump once stated that he "loved the blacks," yet he would welcome immigrants from majority-white Norway rather than any nation of Africa. And on and on...

I have come to the conclusion that our current leader is incapable of empathy, cogent thought and reality-based behavior. He lives in the alternative universe of "all for me," an amoral "Trump world," a world that constantly generates new scandals serving to confuse, overwhelm and exhaust those outside his chaotic egocentrism. He will smother us all if we let him.

Power Concedes Nothing Without Demand

"Power concedes nothing without demand. It never has and never will," said the visionary, Frederick Douglass. This thought provided a warning for Douglass' time and today amounts to an imperative for ours.

Perhaps you will recall that Trump referred to Frederick Douglass as a living person during a speech early last year. In the way of terrific irony, in a sense Frederick Douglass does live, or his wisdom will soon live in the actions of citizenry. The tide is turning, my fellow, living human-beings. I suggest we ride the wave of our outrage in large ways and small, relentlessly.

We need to see ourselves as a single, powerful presence. Today's binary reality? Good versus evil. We can no longer identify solely as black or white, privileged or poor, man or woman. We must identify as aspiring human-beings or as "one nation under God." Trump's "shithole" comment should, indeed must, provoke the demand to the enablers, especially Congress and Cabinet: Stand up!

Trump's nihilism/racism needs be eradicated, for it is a raging infection, lying dormant (and otherwise) throughout our history. Those who remain complicit spread disease. They must be quarantined by way of the ballot box, in written opinion, through physical demonstrations, by any lawful means necessary.

"Time is up," a rallying cry for patriots, must be invoked from Martin Luther King's mountaintop; the truth of the fearless must relinquish the small fearful, here and now.

245

The Ignoramus Factor

Donald Trump touted the meteoric rise of the stock market as his doing. What will he say now that we're in "correction territory" - that is, now that the market has fallen ten per cent, this in less than a week?

The pundits speak of fears of rising interest rates and a robust economy as primary factors in the market's decline. Seems counter-intuitive, but what do I know? Well, I know what I don't know, unlike the "Blowhard-in-Chief."

Markets become jittery for all sorts of reasons. Is it not possible that the ignoramus-factor, personified in Donald Trump, has finally surfaced in the minds of investors? For a while, the fast and furious shenanigans of Trump were laughed off as so much nonsense. But overload has occurred. Dial up (or tweet up) a scandal daily is the modus operandi of the current administration (what's left of it).

Deflection and side-shows only work in the relatively short run. There is a reason cheesy television-shows have shelf-lives. Also, reason mandated that traveling circuses of yesteryear move from town to town. Scam artists and the general flim-flam associated with such entities quickly cease to amuse.

The current game in town is fast devolving. And the greed that created this game is being replaced by fear as the light dawns - as collaborators and enablers ponder the outcome of an "Ignoramus-in-Chief." And when fear takes hold, anything can happen. Unfortunately, "anything" does not include anything palatable, at least for the foreseeable future.

There exists nothing left to tout beyond a $1.50 pay-raise for the minions - or a $1000 bonus amounting to little more than $20 per

246

week. Well, one can buy roughly five Entenmann's cakes at that price. I'm recalling here Marie Antoinette's quip: "Let them eat cake." We all know what happened as a result of such arrogance. Not that I am advocating bloody revolution; rather, I foresee a revolution of thinking among our vast populace and a resultant new dawn for America.

One might almost feel sorry for those most contaminated by this base president, for they, like the rest of us, were essentially used for the fleeting pleasure of an intellectually and morally bankrupt person. Those who supported mendacity and idiocy are destined to watch reruns of their foolish contortions and the relinquishing of their moral autonomy. Such an experience will amount to the reality of Dante's circles of hell.

Tangential Musing: Marginalia

On the recommendation of a friend, I checked out three S.J. Perelman books from the library. The author's name was vaguely familiar, and I was in the mood for good writing liberally laced with what my friend termed "uproarious wit." In this time of witless government, who doesn't deserve a laugh or two?

Now, old S.J. has been dead for some time, and though once a shining light at *The New Yorker*, he has been replaced by newbies.

It's the name of the game. Times change, after all. S.J. Perelman was part of the cadre that included James Thurber, and *The New Yorker* circa 1950 valued the guffaw. Today? Not as much, but we live in largely humorless times, an era that is not conducive to belly-laughs. (Sorry. This aside is off-topic. Back to the library books.)

The three Perelman books chosen had not been checked out in decades; however, they had obviously been well-read during a certain (in both senses of the word) period of history. Old, somewhat dusty, with spines mangled, they are physically unprepossessing things. No matter, I thought initially. That is, until I perused what I thought would be my first read, *Vinegar Puss*.

Right at the outset of S.J.P.'s collection, a series of essays/stories, a yahoo had seen fit to write her innermost thoughts in the margins. Believe me, this was not a case of marginalia providing context or mildly interesting side-bars. The perpetrator in question was (is?) as dull as Perelman was sharp. A real ignoramus. She represented the antithesis of Perelman's erudition with particularly lackluster inanities.

I say "she" because the handwriting of this graffiti-artist wannabe, was of the florid nature: rounded, upright penmanship often associated with very young women. All that was missing were the little hearts, placed over the "i"s in words such as "idiotic" that pubescent girls sometimes employ at the onset of maturation.

I understand the impetus of that affectation, having been a young thing once. But revisiting those ignorant, less than halcyon, days at aged 68 verged on the excruciating. I often declare: Youth is not wasted on the young; rather, youth bespeaks a wasteland of egocentric tripe. (Not really. The young sometimes speak truth, and even at their worst, they often represent cynicism's opposite.)

Having said that, Morgan B. Stanley (I decided to name the scribbler of the margins) was particularly annoying. Her first stab at wisdom: "He really likes women. Will do anything to be with them!" portended a bout of nausea or a peptic ulcer. I knew at that moment I could not, for my health's sake, continue reading the volume, so chose the second offering, happily devoid of adolescent markings. Titled, *Eastward, Ha,* it proved a delight. Laughs aplenty as Perelman described his journeys through Europe and beyond. I defy anyone to read about S.J.'s elevator escapade in Paris, for example, and emerge from the second-hand experience guffaw-less. He is a master.

Not really in the mood for *Acres and Pains,* I once again hauled out *Vinegar Puss* - thinking that perhaps I had given in to sour-puss behavior myself by setting the book aside. I also remembered that old Morgan had written in pencil. I could simply erase her "look at me" additions. Why I hadn't done so to begin with, rather than encouraging my spleen to do the fandango, I don't know exactly. Perhaps it was a case of what the shrinks call projection. Greatly exhausted by reaction to our not even slightly esteemed president, I chose to implode over another half-wit or me-oriented entity.

However, in all fairness, mindless Morgan's entries were more than just a little exasperating, especially in juxtaposition to Perelman's self-deprecating intellect. Having erased M.S.'s offending items and firmly expunged most from my mind, I hoped, a couple of zircons still survive in my memory, more's the pity: "He loved a gorilla!" and a subtraction problem jotted down as well: 63-31=33. Now I ask you, is such idiocy to be countenanced? Should we erase all adolescent thinking, metaphorically and otherwise, for sanity's (or humanity's) sake?

Penultimate End Note

Anyone, who has lost a particularly dear loved-one, may endure the experience of feeling apart from the larger world. In fact, in bewilderment and grief, it may seem to the one thus afflicted, the world could not possibly go on as if nothing of import had happened. Yet, the world does go on - inexorably. And eventually, the mourner regains a sense of connection and even equanimity. This is the way of enormous life-challenges.

I see an analogy in the making here. The essential upheaval of established political and social norms, evident in public life over the past two years especially, might easily be likened to the experience of grief - of losing a linchpin that helps to define an understanding. Just as a mourner may experience feelings of alienation and disbelief, so do many American citizens at this moment in time. I speak of those of us who no longer recognize what once was a cherished landscape largely comprised of shared belief and idealistic thought.

Well, I'll speak for myself here. The United States is no longer the country I believed it to be. Leadership is steeped in cynicism and mendacity, taking on an almost hallucinogenic cast, unrecognizable in its current form as a once-perceived, imperfect but striving government.

One could go on and on about the "dumbing down" of America, of infantile behavior, of news broadcasts, given the material they must cover, that seem like extended, adolescent reality-shows. Intellect appears to be a thing of the past. Emotional reaction is pervasive. Like "Alice Through the Looking Glass," we appear to have entered another dimension. We, who have lived long enough to remember, at the very least, quasi-idealistic statesmen, regard the present situation as a particular aberration, a nightmare, something alien.

Yet, I have to believe that a more benevolent reality will be restored. Even amid the turmoil and unease that many withstand, I watch the heroic optimism of regular people who carry on altruistically with great character. They raise their children. They plan for the future.

They go to work each day believing in their purposes. Just as the grief-stricken eventually secure places in an on-going world, so do every-day American citizens, for we are the backbone, the working reality of this country. I believe in us. I believe we will demand a reckoning for all that is not fair nor good.

Ultimately, I count on our nation's intrinsic worth, its citizenry. May we attain a recognizable, productive and admirable future, sooner rather than later. May we avoid the fates of many great, but now fallen, nations - those undone by miscalculation and hubris.

The Place of the Fearful

When future generations regard our time
They will note cowardice and white-collar crime

They will decry a false winning
- born of boundless emotion
They will encounter the dearth of all that is wholesome

They will denounce as infamous the childish game-player
He of tweeting ways...
- the bombastic impresario of vulgar, base days

They will describe complicity; the venal non-statesmen
small-minded cohorts of a smallish thieves' den
 - and soon to be known as "blinkered horses"
Men beholden to bloated, surreptitious forces

They will call our time the place of the fearful
thoughtless, self-immolating, eventually tearful

Those adherents to mendacity (self-inflicted and otherwise)
 must then seek forgiveness
- for practiced ignorance - for ignominious lies

May those who follow have reason to revere
Come one day
- courageous, mature intellect
- historians who warned - artists who revealed - conscientious reporters
All of the chroniclers of fulsome decay

May our children deem our president's role
to be blessedly finite
- with our reckoning - our ultimate denial of the fearful, dark soul

They will rejoice in relief when we summon the light
May they forgive us our fragility with intentions to make right

May we and they rise to a much better place
- the ultimate ascendancy
A transformational grace.

Throw the Bums Out

Tired of the alternative reality-show? Turn the channel.

Put on your bouncer-clothes: Throw the bums out.

VOTE!

Only 60% of eligible Americans vote...

SHOW UP!!

Repetition and Explanations

It is true that I have time and again noted the immature behavior of President Trump. Perhaps the repetition of this theme has proved wearing for the reader. Yet, every day new examples of Trump's arrested development emerge, a relentless barrage of behavior I find incredulous in a 72-year-old man - not to mention as the primary trait of the "leader of the free world." Were I not continually amazed and appalled, a new and egregious normal would be locked-in. Put another way, relinquishing incredulity would amount to denying the need for an especially appropriate alarm. Thus, the clarion bell rang incessantly, some might say relentlessly, though I maintain necessarily.

Tangentially, the Trump-camp most recently has taken to labeling critics of the president as "haters." This is a ruse, another pointing of the finger in the hope of deflection, very Trumpian, in fact. I cannot bring myself to hate the man, an individual who steadfastly refuses to bear even minimum responsibility for his actions, for in the end, I believe he will be more pitied than censored. I repeat myself once again: We are witnessing a personal and national tragedy. Donald Trump is the embodiment of a larger denial of probity - as well as a denial of personal responsibility as to the tenor of our discourse and thought-processes existent among the electorate. When rational behavior and thought exit, fear takes hold thus putting our very democracy at risk.

Antithetical reality, seeing hatred in those who point out the (nascent?) hatred in Trump's demeaning verbiage, illustrates a danger

253

we cannot ignore. And though the constant refrain of criticism of Donald Trump has a drawback - giving the president the on-going attention he obviously craves - I see little in the way of an appropriate alternative. We cannot bear witness silently, hoping others will sort out the conundrum of a beleaguered nation. We all are responsible for whatever ensues.

Update:

Antithetical reality is alive and well in the aftermath of the Parkland, Florida school massacre. According to the NRA: "The mainstream media love mass shootings. They don't care about our school children. They want to make us less free." President Trump suggested arming teachers. It seems that any number of contortions are preferable to common-sense gun-laws in the minds of those currently in power.

The Parkland Patriots

They are astoundingly articulate in the midst of terror and unspeakable emotional-trauma. They speak with knowing fervor as they demand clear thinking. Idealistic, believing in the better nature of fellow citizens, they seek honesty, a moral high-ground, an appropriate response to evil and to those who abet evil. No longer innocent children merely beset by adolescent challenges, they somehow gather strength with the conviction that they will make a difference. They will be the impetus for change despite a selfish, self-dealing, governmental climate.

She rails against the hollow platitudes of "thoughts and prayers." She asks: "Who is making the laws, the NRA or Congress?" They vow to speak up for as long as it takes, imploring the "adults" to find a way to justice and peace. The next generation is rising. They are now

254

experienced, and they will bear witness in ways that craven politicians dare not counter.

Yet, he, being perspicacious beyond his years, will not engage in opinion that can be misconstrued as "crazy, lefty" talk. He understands too well how words can be used as weapons to effect no change, to further the status quo of cowardly inaction. He asks the adults to come together, to join the brigade of youthful optimism.

They eschew the careful words of partisan leaders: the selfish, power mongering, old and jaded non-statesmen - those who play puerile, ignoble games. They will stand for country first. They will protect citizenry from self-inflicted wounds with their righteous energy, with hope for redemption. They are "The Parkland Patriots."

Listen to them.

The Lamest Show on Earth

Enter the ringmaster: Vlad, the Sneaky, ever on the lookout for minions to whip into shape. Known for subterfuge of the oiliest kind: promises of Rump Tower to equal or, better yet, best the colorful spires of St. Basil's, subterranean moles, beauty-queen sirens, fat and sassy oligarchs.

Enter the clown: Trump aka Loozo, the Sour. Gaseous entity of the turned-down mouth. Known for feats of incongruity of the most vacuous yet vicious kind: billionaire bankruptcy (multiple times), incessant stupidity simultaneously bleating and cruel, magnet for sloths of gargantuan appetite - eventually given a solo ring complete with off-ramp, for the spin-offs are breath-taking and frequent. Loozo himself will eventually rotate like a whirling-dervish and/or the wicked witch of Oz fame - soon to be a puddle, an orange Slurpee overlooked by the annals of time. (An ironic outcome for the brander of the ages.)

Enter the contortionists: Janus-faced women (you know who you are) those courtiers of specious power, who understand full well they are stooges, but stonewall and lie for the game of it, an embarrassment to their gender, especially. Male counterparts meanwhile plunder and pontificate employing crude parlance - the preferred argot of Loozo, the bombastic. They are definitely duped, these acolytes of Trump. (You don't know who you are, more's the pity.)

Enter the (no longer) lions of Senate, House, and Cabinet: now morphed into alley-cats fighting among themselves for vestiges of the spoils, the quick garbage-infusions of campaign money, beholden to fat cats of industry callously named "united citizens." The consummate loozers of all are the alley-cats, those frequenters of the spacious clown-planes, for the lid is about to be blown off the 1% confidence-trick, even though said scam was years in the making.

Fortunately, the few remaining lions, now toothless, are poised to visit the dental implant place. The clear choice is now visible for all to see. Thanks for that, Loozo!

Enter the audience: once confused by the razzle-dazzle, but awakening in part, due to the lion cubs of Parkland, the turning-point kids of idealistic, articulate ways: "Never again!" "We will not be bamboozled!"

The lamest show on earth is doomed. The tents of the circus, gossamer-like, never substantial, are blowing in the wind of the resurrection of spring.

Time to pull up the stakes, time for the alley-cats to relocate to a wild west planet of their choosing, preferably Mars where they can engage in "shoot-em-up" activity to their heart's delight. The tents of mendacity and greed are coming down. Those structures never evinced integrity, and thus they were doomed from the start.

Held Hostage by the Minority

Donald Trump's approval ratings are said to be the lowest in modern history, so now we have a situation where minority rules. This is not the way a democracy is supposed to work. When a sitting president's base is all important to legislators, when belief is based on games for holding onto seats, with the purpose of maintaining power only, when integrity bows to convoluted strategy, we, the people, are experiencing a hostage situation. Hostage situations are fraught with danger. Usually, negotiators are called upon to steady the nerves of hostage-takers and victims alike. However, unforeseen scenarios may unfold, situations based on emotion run rampant and firmly entrenched positions hardened to the point of ultimate stasis. Put another way, when minority rules, equilibrium is sacrificed for the reality of omnipresent conflict and strife. Then fear takes hold, for combatants engage in a futile civil war that belies a heretofore, supposed exemplar of world nations. All lose.

One could, and perhaps should, rail against a president who wishes to be king, an entity self-enamored to the point of single-minded monetary or sexual power-conquest, ego-boosting activity - and nothing else. Yet, such a character emerges only within the void of complicity. He could not operate with impunity were not secondary leadership playing the equally dangerous and spurious game of seizing the prize. Congress has relinquished its honor, its mandate to serve the people. The ruling-class plays by its own self-enhancing rules instead.

A majority of Americans desire sensible gun legislation, equitable health care, fair immigration (DACA), fewer wars and on and on. And Congress accomplishes nothing. Namby-pamby legislators choose their misleading words carefully, support gerrymandering to increase their bases, appease big-money donors and, generally speaking, refuse to countenance the views of their constituents.

What are concerned constituents to do? Embrace democracy!

Vote! Forty percent of Americans fail to exercise this essential tool of democracy; ironically, this number nearly matches the data of Trump's approval rating.

Speak up! Fortunately, protest continues with examples such as "Me, Too," "March for Our Lives," etc.

Self-educate! Citizens ought to read and view commentary from the left and the right, so as to break through a team-mentality that threatens to annihilate all cogent thought.

Freedom of the press is the linchpin of democracy - despite what the president would have us believe.

As the distractions continue with Trump attempting to deflect from his willfully egregious behavior, as he surrounds himself with henchmen who will abet the notion of his supreme rule, it is incumbent on citizenry to take charge with demands for a reenactment of the credo: "E pluribus Unum."

The time was yesterday, for the current situation is one of a fast-devolving erosion of democracy, an erosion long in the making. However, as all we have is today, we must seize the moment or live to rue our own complicity. We must become responsible stewards of democracy now, each and every one of us, lest history judge us as craven fools. The luxury of complacency is no longer viable.

March for Our Lives: Glory Surpasses Cynicism

Thousands, hundreds of thousands

black, white, brown, etc.
- all-inclusive

young, fervent
male, female
privileged, struggling
gay, straight
- non-affiliated

unified to proclaim:
life defies death
love defies hate
hope defies cynicism

parity, peace

MLK's progeny
at nine years
touts the next generation

with power steeped in joy

Who would not want to believe?

An eleven-year-old carefully reminds:
"We African-American girls have been
killed all along with no headlines following."
- and a "privileged" Parkland student
acknowledges her own discovery of the despicable disparity
heretofore evident

Who would not welcome the beginning of understanding?

Who would be unmoved?

by six minutes and 17 seconds of silence

- the obscene timeline - ending 17 lives

by "Happy Birthday" sung as tribute to a child

on the cusp of adulthood - slain, his promise forever lost

by righteous anger supported with mighty intellect, bravery

and promised fortitude

Who cannot hope?

When cynicism followed:
"These children are being coached by adults. This is not true."
- or words to that effect

When one adult attempted to undermine the students' message by proclaiming:
"They would better serve their classmates by learning CPR."
- or words to that effect,
America groaned.

Then knew.

Hope will embolden

Knowledge will out

Truth will reign

Glory surpasses cynicism

Snark Succumbs to Parkland

The tide is beginning to turn. The pendulum is poised to swing in the opposing direction. Choose your metaphor. The point? With one deft tweet, David Hogg, representative of the next generation, put paid to the immature queen of denigration, Laura Ingraham, without responding in kind; it is important to note. Hogg merely asked "friends" to cease supporting her brand of insensitivity and ugliness. And they did! At last count, four companies have pulled advertising slots from Ingraham's show on Fox News. Soon after, "in the spirit of Holy Week" Ms. Ingraham apologized for her mean spiritedness. In the spirit of Holy Week, I offer no comment on this, her self-proclaimed largesse....

One hopes, the American public grows increasingly weary of the childish rancor most often exhibited by Trump and his supporters.

261

Inane tactics, in the vein of name-calling, raised voices, sniping at perceived underdogs, etc. define the weaponry of an essentially fearful and impotent group. Like the tantrums of toddlers, such behavior proves arresting for a finite amount of time only. Eventually, the adults take over once more. Eventually, grown-up language and mature deportment become the norm again. The incivility show, devoid of intellect, runs out of hot air or, more to the point, ceases to amuse, as it becomes increasingly clear that we are not living in amusing times.

And a 17-year-old led the way today! Bravo, Mr. David Hogg. I look forward to the leadership of your generation. I also note that you are a product of a well-funded public school. That, too, should give pause and a reason to fight for that important bulwark of our democracy, the well-funded (and otherwise supported) public school, in an equitable society, available to all.

As we wait for the nightmare of Trump's dangerous and unseemly presidency to end, let us not reward him with attention paid to inane tweets nor engage in on-going arguments as to his suitability for office. We understand by now that he is inept, crass ("Slimeball Comey") and full of self-aggrandizement. No further proof is needed.

Let us concentrate on the subterfuge instead: the surreptitious destruction of the EPA, the evisceration of the State Department, incoherent foreign policy, the disrespect of land-treasure by a corrupt Department of the Interior, the enhancement of an already lop-sided distribution of wealth, to name just a few examples of the on-going erosion of our democracy.

Let us make known our goals: 1. fair elections (prohibiting gerrymandering, undoing "Citizens United," curtailing outside-influence) 2. equitable tax reform to benefit not just the wealthy, but all classes - admitting that "trickle-down economics" euphemistically describes a reality: "crumbs for the powerless." (Please note the ramifications of the following statistic: 85% of global wealth is owned by 1%.) 3. a sustainable and fair health-care system, one that values patients over drug companies 4. consideration of term limits for Congress in order to support leadership over gamesmanship, etc., etc.

We cannot tout our democracy to the world when norms of democratic behavior are eroding. We claim to be a nation "of the people, by the people, for the people." In these harrowing times, we must vigorously respond to those who seek to undermine this, our credo. We must support the free press, voters' rights and the rule of law as it pertains to all. Not only for ourselves, but for the very essence of the democratic experiment that is the United States of America. The promise is not preordained, after all. Democracy is a premise that demands continual, careful oversight, always and certainly at this pivotal moment, though one cannot assume that Trump alone is responsible for the devolution of our governance. We, the people, have been asleep for far too long.

We must view the current situation as a crossroads, an opportunity to make America truly great. We must aim higher, we must speak of truth and vote - or rue our complacency, our lazy acceptance, our complicity - this a form of cowardice - that which will undermine the promise of our nation, if practiced indefinitely. Though we are understandably weary, we must not sleep, not now.

Waking Nightmare

Convoluted Trump world

Absurdity heaped on absurdity

He didn't pay Stormy Daniels until he did.

"No collusion! No obstruction!"

- amid changing stories and threats of blatant, investigative annihilation

claiming "bias"

 - an antithetical construct.

Fake! Fake! Fake!

Yell loudly and repeatedly!

Sow dissent!

- But embolden truth-seekers, an unintended outcome.

"Rocket-Man" then "Honorable Leader"

Momentary pontifications predicated on selfish need.

Denigration and mindless pivots

 - for this, a hallucinogenic mention of the Nobel Peace Prize, no less!

Play to fear, the anti-intellectual place.

Post-truth

Deflect, deflect, deflect.

Live in the pin-ball reality of Trump? Never!

Exhausted

Yet, I dare not sleep

The waking nightmare demands unwavering vigilance, principled reality.

A consciousness.

A conscience.

Anatomy of a Tantrum

When young children realize they are autonomous beings, when they begin to discover individual desires beyond primal necessities, mechanisms for procuring said desires emerge. The gurgling baby of sweet disposition gives way to the recalcitrant toddler, lover of the word, "No!" or "I want." To be sure, the "terrible twos" comprises a necessary phase of human development. Obviously, parents are meant to understand this flexing of the id-muscle. Yet, to fail to temper extreme, self-centered behavior is to raise, at worst, a megalomaniac.

Occasionally, out-of-control behavior in the form of tantrums occur. The anatomy of a tantrum has to do with key components: decibel level, verbal repetition and manic, physical gestures. To witness a full-blown tantrum is to witness a faux psychotic-episode: ugly, disorienting - resulting in an untenable discomfort for those within range. What to do? Many choose appeasement which serves to reward

265

unacceptable behavior. Others, those of fortitude and a long-range view, wait out the storm and then follow up with rational discussion, by far the better strategy.

Unfortunately, we witness near-daily tantrums in the form of tweets and speech from our president. Decibel level is evident in capitalized tweet-pronouncements completed with exclamation points. Verbal repetition is evident, too: How often we have heard "NO COLLUSION," "WITCH HUNT," etc. Recall the physicality of Trump's facial expressions and hand-gestures employed, especially present in campaign speeches. It's all there, folks. Beyond metaphor, the Trump tantrum has proved relentless, ugly and disorienting throughout.

The Office of the Presidency requires a particular deference (think of your two-year-old throwing a fit in church). Yet, to appease this man, to accept such behavior as befitting the office, is to create a precedent of monster-building. Enough!

Republican members of Congress: Do your job! It is in your power to deal with this conundrum. To mollify this president with concessions, allowing a devolution of the Justice Department, to reward antithetical messaging, to ignore the denigration of the free press, to sit on the side-lines, as if the tantrum is not escalating dangerously is to join the cadre of now-despised appeasers of other remembered eras. It is not too late to end the tantrum. Stand up! If you do not see fit to remove Trump "from church," at the very least call out the ignoble behavior. Certainly, you should not be bolstering his desperate measures. History will judge your response.

Baby-Gate

Initially, an epic nightmare... In my dream, a demented "Baby Huey" ran for President of the United States. The original Baby Huey, a big lug of a duck, was essentially benign. His shtick entailed trying desperately to make friends, despite his gargantuan (and off-putting) size. He didn't brag about shooting people and getting away with it. He just bumbled about causing mayhem, usually by accident. His counterpart, in my dream, was anything but benign. Of German ancestry, he conducted himself as the worst brat possible. Get it? Bratwurst? Sorry about that... Don't get me wrong, his ancestry is tangential, really. Every ethnicity produces a clunker (or worse) on occasion.

In time, this Baby Huey character morphed into a Daffy Duck-type entity (especially after he won the election). Mostly, he spent time twittering: "You're despicable!" - or words to that effect. This epithet was shouted to the glee of those who thought he was "telling it like it is" and repeated relentlessly so as to hypnotize said followers. And it worked for a while - even though insulting folks was basically all that WB (Worst Brat) did.

Meanwhile, behind the scenes, Craven Miller attempted to corrupt the ethos of our immigrant-based country, and Betsy Da Boss worked to destroy public education. Others in the president's inner circle were content to bolster WB's hissy-fits shamelessly and for no good reason, I might add. Kellyanne Wayofthecon was in it for the game. Sarah Huckster Sanders proved to be a ludicrous shill. Eventually though, she began to sicken even herself with evasive tactics that were easily parodied. Others in the posse, who initially seemed reasonable, were sullied beyond recognition, example: "Smelly Kelly." Too bad! And sad, to boot.

267

As time went on the worst brat regressed into extreme infancy. He cried, "Wah, Wah!" repeatedly when an investigation began to close in on his presumed, nefarious behavior. But behind the scenes, he was working hard to "brand" his defense. He thought he could deflect and/or turn the tables on investigators by accusing them of spying illegally on his campaign: "Wah, Wah, Spy-gate, Spy-gate!" You see, WB thought, if he just cried hard enough, the public would throw up their hands in exhaustion, the result of many a tantrum, unfortunately...

However, what with nothing good getting done along with scary domestic and foreign conundrums multiplying, with an obvious "flying by the seat of his pants" administration not working in full force (on-again, off-again, on again summits, wildly inconsistent rhetoric and so forth) coupled with some rats who jumped off a sinking ship of state, well, the puerile presidency was fast losing its mojo.

Soon, my nightmare became a palatable dream. That is, the mantra "Spy-gate" was replaced by "Baby-gate," for Trump was contained and eventually disciplined by the greatest nanny of them all (in the best sense), American justice.

(I value decorum. However, sometimes expressed outrage is warranted. This is one of those times.)

Branding by Trump

Trump tweeted: "The Democrats are meddling in the mid-term) elections." And some more palaver about investigating the FBI and Hillary Clinton. We need to remember that winning is all to Trump. He adheres to a Roy Cohn philosophy of saying and doing whatever it takes to remain on top. Tell thousands of lies (literally). Create an antithetical reality: Up is down. Accuse others of behaving as he behaves. Yell. Repeat mantras until they become firmly entrenched in the consciousness of the electorate. Conjure up zingy concepts such as the "deep state." Lead from adolescent fear of becoming a loser - eventually dismissed as a has-been, irrelevant, in last place and despised.

To those who still wish to believe in this man-child of dubious action and rhetoric: Consider those of Trump's billionaire-soaked, money-guzzling Cabinet. Recall the "P-word." Question his past business-practices. Note his impulsive responses to world issues. Admit his questionable credentials and his inability to learn from others, from history. The man-child will always be running for president of his sixth-grade class. Intellectually bereft, morally unfit, this puerile manipulator has and will continue to soil the idealistic premises of this nation as long as he remains in the public eye.

Refuse to mirror the ugly imagery of Trump. Refuse to be branded like unwitting cattle.

Deep Sh** (An Apt, though Vulgar, Title)

"Deep state"? How about "deep sh**"? Those that buy into a vast conspiracy-theory of a deep state have been manipulated very effectively. Diabolical playbook: Convince folks that the pillars of government, checks and balances, are corrupt. Assure them that one man, and one man only, will save them from penury as well as real and imagined catastrophe. Hype an antithetical reality in order to confuse. Tell them they are smart, "in the know," to promote compliance.

How's this for a conspiracy theory? A small number of hoarders, nee businessmen are amassing great wealth and power. The members of this cadre include Trump, Putin, Kim Jong Un, etc., authoritarian all. A great, world-wide fiefdom is in the making. Witness the precursor-developments: vast income inequality, education geared to producing worker-bees rather than thinkers, mind-numbing, reality-show entertainment usurping various news outlets. Civility? Gone.

Thus, team-sports-mentality replaces unity. Competition is all. Regression topples enlightenment. Survival of the fittest, a caveman concept, is revered. A game has ensued - and a rigged one at that. The money-grubbers have taken control of the ball, for now. (85% of the world's wealth is owned by 1% of the populace.)

And that's no bull.

Game Over

Trudeau hurt his little feelings. So, in a fit of pique, Toddler Trump refused to honor the G-7 communique. Game over as far as the petulant president is concerned. If statesmen still exist, they must find a way to curtail the practitioner of "all for me." Moreover, pundits of all persuasions must cease looking for a grand political-plan. There is no plan save "Me, Me, Me." Trump, not the entire US, should be banned from the practice of diplomacy (as one would ban a bully from the schoolyard, a huckster from a boardroom).

Sideline the grossly incompetent one before he creates an isolated nation, an authoritarian's dream. Odd that, the use of the word authoritarian... Far from being an authority on anything, nor a father-figure to his countrymen, self-absorbed Trump is incapable of seeing beyond his own pathetic need. His world is small. He is small.

We (news anchors, government officials and ordinary citizens) must be large of heart, mind and soul in response - lest we forfeit our democracy - that which, contrary to Donald Trump's view, is not a mere game, but a belief that denies crass competition by way of a large and lofty vision.

Then, with clear conscience, we shall once again say: "Proud to be American."

Lead US Not Into Temptation: Immoral and Divided We Fall

With the years of mendacity, outright deceit and criminal fraud piling up, I was tempted to wash my hands of the whole Trump debacle in sheer exhaustion: quit reading newspapers, watching commentary,

271

etc. Living in an age of anxiety, amid constant animosity and worse, becomes ever more debilitating, stealthily destroying the best part of our souls.

Then rank cruelty foisted on children... One cannot selfishly ignore ever-increasing immorality.

Trump is counting on the populace to weary, his on-going tantrum sustained well beyond the tolerance of many. Yet, exhausted though the public may be, we must not be tempted to give up our sense of what is right, our dreams for what could be, our belief in the United States. Abraham Lincoln bears quoting once again: "America will never be destroyed from outside. If we falter and lose our freedoms, it will be because we destroyed ourselves."

Insult-Chess

Make no mistake. Donald Trump is playing a form of chess. Contrary to my prior stated opinion, there is a game-plan, albeit a crude, simplistic game plan. The notion behind Trump's subterfuge, while lacking cogent intellect, works precisely because it purports irrationality. Knowing full well the grandeur of the Office of the Presidency demands an audience, Trump and his cronies spew lies and nonsensical statements faster than a whirling-dervish spins. The result is constant reaction to that which does not deserve on-going acknowledgment. While the pundits along with everyday citizens react with outrage, the full measure of Trump's incompetency and the practice of his authoritarian ways are too often lost in the storm.

Literally, Trump knows the devil is in the details. Most reacted to Melania's "I don't care" jacket with predictable emotion: outrage as to the message and the stupidity of such a sartorial choice. Once again, the ground shifted; eyes were averted from the important news of an impetuous and cruel policy regarding immigration.

Welcome to Trump's fun house where up is down, fat is thin, reality is skewed. Eventually, amid such hallucinatory trickery, normally observant minds become unfocused. The sheer repetition of Trump's deflection-ploy has proved effective. This should come as no surprise. We witness not a three ring-circus but a circus of seemingly infinite distraction.

Of course, none of this would be possible without the complicity of supposed statesmen. If you must rail against Trump, do so. However, a better response would involve a demand that those others - those we have elected to serve the country - actually perform the function of providing checks and balances. One man can do a lot of damage, but not without the aid of power-seeking, self-absorbed players, those who lack essential decency. Vote judiciously come the mid-term.

The Man is the Policy

Recently, I witnessed an interview of a Trump supporter. He stated unequivocally that he had no use for Trump as a person but believed in his policies. Naturally, I wondered just how said supporter squared such variant opinions. Would he consult a doctor of known immoral tendencies? Would he countenance a boorish, unkind teacher educating his children? Would he enjoy the company of boastful, mendacious co-workers? I'd be very surprised to hear affirmative answers to the aforementioned questions. It seems the notion: "It's not personal; it's just business/politics" resonates with some voters. Yet, politics is personal, very personal, as all are personally affected by policy and by the character, or lack thereof, of leaders in all fields.

In fact, intellect (necessary for producing cogent policy) does not exist in a vacuum but evolves by way of character and/or emotional soundness. Those democracy-based leaders of yesterday, those we revere, evinced particular traits: courage, humility, compassion along with open-mindedness and, ultimately, rigorous intellect. Abraham Lincoln comes to mind. Autocratic leaders of the past, those of infamous remembrance, practiced cruelty, ego-centrism, impetuosity, single-mindedness - traits ill-suited to developing
intellect. Joseph Stalin emerges.

My point (aside from panning Trump's boasting of his supposed intelligence) is simply: Character matters. Those who represent us should reflect and/or mirror us as to acceptable conduct and belief. Politicians are servants of the people, not grandiose gods given free rein as to their personal and political behavior. The pedestal should be relegated only to those deserving leaders of practiced morality and sound intellect.

Policy created will ultimately reflect the essential man. Please recall Lincoln's magnanimity and Stalin's "reign of terror." If a man is inherently flawed, it stands to reason that his ensuing policy will be flawed as well. Conversely, an intellectually sound leader will create sound policy. In short, the man is the policy.

A Man Without...

Fantasy time.

With Trump's recent capitulation of the United Sates to Russia's Putin, let us now consider our president as a man without a country. In other words, let's assume he has forfeited his citizenship, and therefore we must deport him. Would his ancestors' country take him? Doubtful, given his treatment of Angela Merkel. Is there any country on earth that would welcome the beleaguered one? Get this: He is even unpopular among Russian citizenry with an approval rating south of 20 percent. Still, it's worth a try for the sole purpose of forcing an empathy-pill on one who has never experienced immigration or any other hardship or challenge.

This is the problem: Our president truly is Trump-baby. All of his needs have been met on demand. He is a man without the sufficient experience necessary for developing heart or rationality. Therefore, questions of morality are beyond his ken. Simply put, Trump really believes the entire world revolves around him. Such an outlook fosters his lived fantasy-reality, a place of cunning reaction only. Incapable of seeing experience beyond his own, Trump lives the life of an animal, forever hunting, lest he be hunted. Oh, how he loves competition, the game, the hunt.

Back to the fantasy. Let's develop a reality-show called, "Trump Seeks a Country." It would be interesting to watch his attempts to secure a home.

Yet, even with all of the destruction Donald J. Trump has precipitated, part of me feels sorry for this man; it is painfully obvious he is a man without.

Don't Play the Game

The View's time with guest, Judge Pirro, illustrates the effectiveness the antithetical game Trump-supporters inevitably employ. The playbook is as follows: 1. always counter concerns raised with accusations of similar behavior as to the other side. 2. Raise the emotional stakes of the discussion with provable untruths preferably relayed via a raised voice. 3. Be as outrageous as possible so as to precipitate anger on the part of the interviewer. 4. At this point, your goal has been achieved. The narrative has shifted from issues to displays of emotion.

My advice? Interviewers must refuse to play the game, instead, labeling the interviewee's initiation of said antithetical strategy each and every time said strategy is put forth.

Of course, Trump essentially invented the antithetical ploy. To cover up his own lies, he created "Lyin' Ted." To deflect from Trump University payments and alleged fraud, "Crooked Hillary" was quickly invented. More recently, he has stated that Obama emboldened Putin. Literally thousands of examples of Trump's subterfuge and/or his alternative reality exist. The sheer number enhances the distraction factor allowing for protracted, pointless, ultimately destructive, game-playing rather than problem-solving via the intellect. This game amounts to reactions of the moment, denying cogent plans for our country.

The game is all to Trump. Lest we all become Trump-like, it cannot be so for us.

Absurdity and the Waning Days

It comes down to this: Trump is ranting and railing about a "deep state" and a threat to national security because some unnamed source reported what has been patently observable all along. The president is unfit to govern. Was anyone surprised by the notion that Trump's minders made it their business to curtail his most egregious impulses? After all, we've watched the president attempt to walk back fits of pique multiple times, and the worst of policy impulses have somehow been tempered (full-blown trade war, indefinite separation of immigrant families and so forth).

As Donald Trump bemoans his supposed persecution, I pose several questions. How is it that books that essentially paint the same picture of an incompetent, self-serving, amoral Trump emerge with great regularity? Have we ever witnessed such concern before? Can you remember anything remotely similar in reaction to Obama, Bush? Of course not. Commensurate, scathing rebukes were unimaginable in the Bush, Obama eras. Trump's mendacity (thousands of proven lies) and his relentless, childish, name-calling-tweets give credence to the notion of Trump's inability to govern cogently.

In a desperate attempt to hold onto his roughly 40% base, Trump stated: "Don't believe what you see." This particularly troubling statement will not be heeded by a vast majority, for many more than not are unwilling to join Donald Trump in hallucinatory thought. The way I see it, Trump has two options at this point in time: He could resign from the Office of the Presidency with some semblance of dignity, or he could be dragged kicking and screaming to his ultimate destiny. Given the record of Trump's past behavior, he may well choose the latter option. Very sad - for him - and for us.

He Trumpets a Nation of Lost Values

The leader of the free world is a hedonist of the first order. Those in the Senate who tolerate his anti-intellectual "me-first" agenda sell their souls for presumed power. They are game-players at heart, beholden only to winning. So, we, the lowly public, all too often throw up our hands in dismay or assume we are impotent in this current environment. We are not. We are also not blameless for the undoubted mess many of us abhor.

By revering those of wealth and celebrity, by buying into a skewed definition of what it means to be a successful person, we have sold our souls to the religion of wealth. When we tacitly support the outlandish salaries procured by hedge-fund managers, for example, or those whose primary existence involves making money for others (entertainers, sports figures, stock-jockeys and the like) without questioning the meager (by comparison) salaries of scientists, physicians - doers and teachers of all persuasions - we have shown our cards. We are shallow, easily distracted by shiny objects - even donning the roles of apprentices for celebrity at times. In short, we have forgotten that success has to do with hard work, intellect and benevolence.

My gastroenterologist earns meager fees for the potentially life-saving procedures he renders. He spent much of his early adult life eschewing the notion of merely making money in order to train for his profession. He will never be rich by today's standards. He will never be famous, though he is not seeking celebrity. Another unsung hero - except to those who benefit from his care. Were he now an immigrant working his way up in pursuit of his dream to heal others and with occasional benefits offered by the government, Trump and his cronies would see fit to write him off as a leech. He would be deemed unworthy because of his lack of money. And then? One fewer idealist to heal our bodies and our souls.

It stands to reason that Trump, who inherited wealth and is defined by his attempt to amass more wealth - a shallow, anti-intellectual, enamored by flashy celebrity - would live by a perverted, amoral vision of success. Yet, he is but a symptom of a broader phenomenon. As long as society accepts the mediocre minds and antics of celebrity-whores as somehow acceptable, as long as society reveres, above all, the guy who has the most money, as long as society views living as one big game of outdoing others, we are doomed to leaders like Trump and many others in Congress I could easily name. Yes, we all are to blame - perhaps for not voting regularly, perhaps for not educating ourselves properly as to issues and the stances of candidates, perhaps by falling into the trap of bogus hero-worship. It is time to reassess our values as to heroism – to consider the not so quaint notions of unselfishness, compassion, and service.

Lest you assume I am advocating some sort of socialist-government, I call only for fairness. It is fair that those of great wealth pay appropriate taxes. Clearly, the "trickle-down" theory of economics has failed when companies that do well choose to line their own coffers while denying increased hiring and/or increased wages for workers. When private-jet-owners merit special consideration, multi-million-dollar corporate-jet write-offs, we are witnessing a scam.

Tragedy

I have had occasion to witness the aftermath of alcoholic blackout - the morning after an inebriated state where vile statements were made. In the light of day, the alcoholic vehemently denied his words of the night before, truly believing he was incapable of such. Though I felt I could not say so at the time, I found his amnesia to be "awfully convenient" as to his not bearing responsibility for the hurt he had caused nor, for that matter, facing his demons. It seemed to me that nothing would change unless the truth were known to him. Terrible for me - perhaps even more terrible for him in the long run.

Brett Kavanaugh has everything to lose. He knows this. A lifetime of preparing for the ultimate prize (Supreme Court Justice appointment) hangs in the balance. More important, the very notion of his current and past identities, as lived in important family relationships, is

279

suspect - certainly to observers, but perhaps, on some level, even to Judge Kavanaugh's nearest and dearest. It is vitally important that the truth of the incident of 36 years ago is understood. When the American Bar Association, previously supportive of the nominee, calls for investigation, it behooves all (legislators, citizenry) to take note. One cannot help but wonder why Kavanaugh time and again refused to call for this opportunity to clear his name.

We have witnessed the tragedy of a woman who has lived with the memory of abuse for decades. We have witnessed the tragedy of a man who apparently believes he has been wrongly accused. We watched the emotional yet calm testimony of Ford. We watched the emotional and angry testimony of Kavanaugh. It seemed apparent that Kavanaugh opted to behave as Trump had previously suggested: Suddenly the whole incident was made up by Democrats to derail a process. We were meant to discount the words of Ford based on conspiracy-theory with no evidence to support such a claim.

I wonder if Judge Kavanaugh has moments of doubt as to his youthful behavior. Has he seen fit to question his memory or lack thereof? Perhaps demons of adolescence were ultimately overcome. Perhaps such vile behavior is inconceivable to him, but only in his current state of adulthood. His pain is obvious, and his pain will not be assuaged until the matter is fully investigated. We need to know the truth. Judge Kavanaugh certainly needs the truth to emerge. To deny a full accounting will lead to continued destruction and tragedy for all concerned.

Reality-Show Entertainment

Trump has attained his fondest desire, 24/7 coverage of all things Trump or, as he would put it, the ratings for news-coverage is at an all-time high. Particularly lately, he has managed to garner attention with every decision he's made, turning the American public into junkies of a governmental reality-show.

With the unseemly and cruel spectacle of the latest Kavanaugh hearing, we reached a new low. One had to witness this pivotal moment to understand the enormity of spectacle - what governance in this country has become. In witnessing the event, one became unwittingly part of the Trump scheme of eternal ugliness, strife and rancor. I suspect that he enjoyed every minute of it. After all, Trump has proven himself to be the antithesis of civility, decorum and practiced intellect.

There was a time when this country projected fairness and stability. There was a time when anxiety, as to the viability of our constitution and basic values, was not evident. There once was a time of at least tenuous unity. Though, in truth, we have been inching toward this place of salacious and emotional reaction over the course of several decades or so.

This sorry state of affairs coincides with the rise of TV reality-shows and other "entertainments" that feature folks behaving badly: talk shows that feature teen-age mothers and their cheating boyfriends, fighting housewives, out of control children, etc. That's entertainment? Hardly. That is spectacle: the modern version of circus side-shows (the former venues of so called "freaks") - spectacles that trivialize human angst and dehumanize individuals. Such entertainment flies in the face of basic decency. It is base in its negation of empathy. In fact, it precludes all thoughtful human response. Is this what we have become?

Evidently. Witnessing the testimony of Dr. Blasey Ford during the Kavanaugh hearing was intrusion at best. While Ford acquitted herself well, with most finding her story "credible," empathy required one to note the terrible ordeal she obviously endured by coming forward. And yet, I witnessed little empathy among Republican senators during or after the hearing.

Judge Kavanaugh did not acquit himself well, choosing angry emotion as a defense. He shouted, he insulted sitting senators, he sneered, he engaged in obfuscation at best, lies at worst, as to his drinking habits and the meanings of phrases in a yearbook. As many have noted, his hearing-performance alone should have disqualified him from the Supreme Court bench. He simply did not behave in a judicious manner, but rather was combative, aggressively emotional and painfully defensive. Still, there are many in the Republican field who intend to rush to confirmation. And, by the way, many of these folks, too, displayed vociferous anger in their defense of Kavanaugh. More spectacle.

Is current American-governance merely a crude, two-bit reality-show? Surely, we have not succumbed to this.

Vote!

An Admonition

This work, written over the span of Trump's rise and presumed fall, provides reaction to specific events. In hindsight, there exist entries I now vastly prefer over others. Yet, it seems to me that all have merit with regard to presenting a history of emotional as well as intellectual response to governance. After all, politics engenders both human-reactions in its inexorable desire to win hearts and minds of the electorate. In fact, of late, emotion has played an ever-increasing role.

Still, though I am tempted to somehow highlight what I view as the best of my thoughts, to do so would infringe on reader assessment - the freedom of readers to react in their own ways to arguments as they are couched. I also note that I have attempted, as best as I could, to create an honesty in the telling of my on-going response, largely by including all entries. This book presents one woman's observations in the time of Trump - observations not necessarily infallible, but perhaps valuable in their telling, perhaps indicative of a larger perception of concern.

Disappointment

Contrast the speeches (prior to voting on the confirmation of Judge Kavanaugh to the Supreme Court) of Senators Murkowski and Collins and note differences of intellect and tone. Murkowski expressed a process of agony couched in intellectual rigor. Collins put forth a bit of outrage, as to partisan political maneuvering, and arguments that were occasionally specious.

For example, Collins equated the Clinton Whitewater-investigation with the Trump Russia-probe to counter an argument that Trump should not be nominating candidates while under investigation. It seems to me that possible business-fraud should not be equated with national security concerns. Additionally, conceivably erroneous precedent should not preclude change. Murkowski, concerned about the left's efforts to mobilize against any and all Trump choices, concluded, quite rightly, that such a concern was not the point in the end. The real issue had to do with Kavanaugh's portion of the Ford/Kavanaugh hearing - his conspiracy-theory-laced rhetoric, his less than judicious display of intellect - a performance that deemed him to be unfit for the position of Supreme Court Justice.

Murkowski believed the testimony of Ford to be credible. Collins stated that while she believed Ford was assaulted, she could not deny Kavanaugh the presumption of innocence. We were left to assume either that Collins believed Ford was confused as to the identity of her assailant, or that because corroborating evidence was lacking, Kavanaugh should be believed. I submit that corroborating evidence is difficult to attain in a locked-room situation, and that the FBI's hands were tied as to whom they might speak during a supposed week-long investigation that, in fact, lasted four days or so. This is not how one promotes public trust in our institutions of government.

Susan Collins railed against the months of Democratic "obstruction" prior to Kavanaugh's hearing. She spoke of millions of dollars raised. She, along with Grassley and others, began to sound a bit like Trump in vociferous arguments put forth as to obstructionism. Yet, I have a memory of one Mitch McConnell who once stated arrogantly something on the order of: "We will not consider (even for a hearing) any Supreme Court nominee, Republican or Democrat, put forth by President Obama." Egregious precedent, to be sure. Hyperbolic hypocrisy, indeed, as far as current Republican response to partisanship is concerned.

A reminder: Kavanaugh was not on trial in a criminal case. The hearing was conducted in order to ascertain his fitness for the Supreme Court. His hearing-performance sealed his fate as to his lack of appropriate temperament. Now we are left to compare two senators, Murkowski and Collins. I have concluded that only one displayed the necessary tone and intellectual rigor conducive to governing well, and that individual was not Susan Collins.

Dear Mitch: A Necessary Rant

Dear Mitch,

My salutation does not reflect a closeness to you nor does it indicate a warmth as to your behavior. I use your given name as a diminutive, only. Like "the Donald," you are but a boy in man's clothes - forever playing "King of the Mountain" in hopes of garnering accolades as a powerful male. Adult men get beyond the stage of mere gamesmanship. Examples include the unsung heroes of medicine, science, education and so forth, the doers rather than the players, in other words.

285

Your arrogance is without equal. The sheer audacity of your recent statements as to Democratic obstructionism indicates that you possess not one iota of self-reflection. Were you not the individual who stated: "We will not confirm (or even entertain a hearing for) any Supreme Court nominee, Republican or Democrat, put forth by President Obama?" Such a statement projects a breath-taking, puerile willfulness - a willfulness born of self-regard over concern for those you supposedly serve.

You once referred to the Republican wing as the party of Lincoln. Of late, nothing could be further from the truth. Lincoln was an intellectual. Lincoln was self-reflective. Lincoln sought to unify rather than divide. You and your ilk represent the antithesis of the ever-developing man who was Lincoln. You live in a boys' world of faux grandeur and culture. You seek an impossible immortality with your bellicose words, while Lincoln accepted his place as a mere mortal - one who questioned, one who attempted, in the end, to find a just peace.

Though I detest your behavior, I feel pity for you, the faux leader. Lord Acton once stated: "Power has the tendency to corrupt, and absolute power corrupts absolutely." Please consider his admonition. Additionally, I suggest that you stop playing "King of the Mountain," read of individuals and nations that succumbed to the tantalizing drug of power and ultimately reassess your position as a man - for our benefit as well as your own.

Should self-reflection and resultant change prove to be an impossible task, perhaps you should retire and feed your love of strategy by playing bridge - where you can finesse to your heart's content without doing irreparable harm to our democracy.

The Power of Shtick

Countless times, I have asked myself why Trump's base continues to hold. After all, our current president has engaged in mendacity to the extreme, thousands of proven lies, and counting, along with unseemly behavior at nearly every turn, indicators of possible tax evasion, a never before seen number of resignations/firings and/or unprecedented West Wing chaos - behavior that should have unraveled a presidency, or would have up until now. I have concluded that these are dangerous times, upended times.

Theodore Roosevelt is known for the adage: "Speak softly and carry a big stick." Our current president's adage? "Bellow loudly while wielding a big shtick" - incessantly, relentlessly. The shtick is Trump's nuclear weapon, really his only weapon, and it has proven to be an effective weapon thus far - with approximately 40% of the American populace residing in Trump's little corner of the world, and a party that turns a blind eye.

How does this shtick work? Ask Rush Limbaugh or any number of showmen who straddle the worlds of entertainment and politics. I suspect that Trump has borrowed a number of pages from Limbaugh's playbook, in fact. Examples: Both men are enamored with name-calling and/or faintly humorous put-downs of adversaries. Both enjoy the resonant sound of their own bellowing voices. Both love "uneducated" people, those who do not question their shtick. Trump actually stated thus in an early rally. Limbaugh, more sophisticated, chose the moniker, "ditto-heads" to describe his following. With the confluence of entertainment and politics, we have a situation of life mirroring art or at least responding in kind to artful (manipulative) showmanship.

Those who partake of Trump extravaganzas exhibit a rally-mentality by engaging in call-and-response activity. The showman is adept at eliciting reactions that serve to both massage his ego and stir up the crowd. In these situations, more often than not, Trump accuses his adversaries of behaviors that mirror his own. Antithetical reality has worked well for Trump, in other words. Moreover, promoting antithetical reality appears to be a contagious ploy. Witness Mitch McConnell referring to those who dared protest the most recent Supreme Court nomination process as proof of mob-mentality in the Democratic Party.

I anticipated the next step of ridicule of "earnest" Democrats, but Trump went further. From his point of view, or at least the point of view he wishes to impart: "The Democrats have lost their minds. They're dangerous." Antithetical reality then appears to be escalating in more ways than one. Some might argue that it is Trump who has lost his mind and is dangerous. And this is the point: Tit-for-tat ensues to the detriment of all. More chaos, more undermining of a basic unity necessary for democratic governance. The current circus in town seeks to reduce the thinking-public to cheerleaders at a pep-rally, or worse, pugilists in a prize-fight arena.

Of course, both scenarios have to do with the notion of entertainment, the relinquishing of personal responsibility for our governance - this for an easy, emotional "fix." Trump has learned that shtick needs to be exponentially outrageous in order to maintain entertainment value and resultant attention. (Kanye West, anyone?) Should such behavior continue or expand, we, as a nation, will cease to think cogently. Therein lies the danger of losing our autonomy and, ultimately, our freedoms. It is perhaps ironic to note that a large swath of the public fear losing all, with regard to confronting an appropriate anxiety as to state of our union, and such fear has resulted in rote-responses often seen in autocratic situations.

288

I maintain that when we choose to partake of the "big shtick," we are actually giving away our freedoms, for in that state of anesthesia, we have succumbed to the increasingly prevalent drug provided by the showman, the essential nihilist. We are no longer ourselves in these scenarios; we are mere extensions of Trump. And, it seems to me, this is all Donald J. Trump ever wanted from the very beginning.

The Sin of Expediency

Often overlooked, the sin of expediency can be attributed to most of us. In our own self-interest, we often look the other way or fail to speak up in the face of bullying behavior. Should the bully be harassing others and not engaging in particularly cruel behavior, we make the decision not to intervene, telling ourselves the fall-out is not worth it, or posing the question: Why exacerbate matters? Therein lies the excuse for forgetting that today's victim deserves support, that bad behavior needs to be confronted for the sake of humanity. Martin Niemoller's warning is particularly apt and bears repeating:

"First, they came for the socialists, and I did not speak out -
Because I was not a socialist.

Then they came for the trade unionists, and I did not speak out -
Because I was not a trade unionist.

Then they came for the Jews, and I did not speak out -
Because I was not a Jew.

Then they came for me - and there was no one left to speak for me."

I can easily recall two times when I chose expediency over courage. I am ashamed of my cowardice and regret both instances. The first occurred in a social situation where a friend was particularly rude to another friend. Perhaps it was wise not to intervene right then and there. However, after the fact, I should have spoken of the rudeness, the hurtful behavior. I did not need to tacitly accept bullying by remaining silent. Much later, I, too, became the target of similar treatment by the same individual. I had no one but myself to blame for not speaking out earlier and then. Eventually, the outcome of craven expediency was made evident: a fractured friendship and a sense that both victim and bully were diminished by the process.

The second memory has to do with a particularly toxic boss of my experience. Time and again this person undermined the workplace with snide comments, egregious tirades - thoroughly demoralizing behavior. Soon it became known that I would relinquish my position. Perhaps prior to that decision, it would have been unwise to speak up publicly, for my work-life would have exponentially worsened, such was the power the boss wielded coupled with perceived, practiced vindictiveness. However, I could have put up with unpleasantness for the last months, in hopes of making a difference for my colleagues. I clearly remember imagining myself rising in a meeting to confront the boss, assuming that I would be standing alone to face the inevitable backlash. But perhaps others would have followed my lead. If not, I had little to lose - not the job, anyway, and my courage might have made a difference for others. As it happened, the boss ruled for five or so additional, damaging years before being ousted.

Expediency has always been evident in political circles, though currently it is practiced more brazenly and unabashedly. Some Trump supporters readily admit to personal distaste for the man, but support him nevertheless in order to secure a particular, political agenda. Many congressmen have weighed their options, as to up-coming elections, and then supported Trump despite going against their own core beliefs in some instances. In fact, those who excoriated Trump during the primaries suddenly found their way to praising him - coveting outcomes such as stacking the Supreme Court with conservatives. One congressman, as stated earlier, has even taken on Trump's mendacious, manipulative talking-points, that which he once derided.

Expediency is very much a human-response meant to maintain self-comfort. Yet, when practiced to the extreme, expediency enters the realm of immorality - becoming, in essence, a sin. In the long run, the practice becomes self-immolating, too, as Pastor Martin Niemoller ("First, they came for...") understood only too well.

Down and Dirty

Rivals of Donald Trump would be wise to avoid entering a down and dirty contest with him. Trump is a master at this tactic; frankly, this is all he knows. Presumably you know better and infinitely more. Face it; you are not Donald Trump, and you should be ever grateful that this is the case.

More to the point, when one enters the arena of nasty, political mud-fights, one has played right into the Donald's hands. He doesn't want to talk about ideas because he has no well-thought-out plans. He flies by the seat of his pants; he makes it all up on the go; he considers his current audience, only, when he is pontificating nonsense. He is in it for the attention - that I can tell you.

Presumably you are seeking office with a larger purpose in mind, a moral purpose having to do with service to your country. I suggest that you tout said emotional and intellectual purpose in lieu of playing a game that Trump will always win in the end. It's a shame that Elizabeth Warren resorted to countering "Pocahontas." She has ideas; she is more than a combatant in a childish insult-fest. Had Trump actually paid out a million dollars to her chosen charity - a charity in the name of indigenous people - the ploy might have been worth it. But we all know that Trump never backs down from a position. Also, it has been said that he is rarely keen on "paying out." The whole fiasco of DNA-testing was a loser from the very beginning, in essence, because Elizabeth Warren lowered her standards. Will she recover? It's hard to say.

At the very least, rising Democrats ought to view Warren's particular decision as a cautionary-tale. In other words, don't play Trump's game lest you be perceived as merely a lesser Trump. Eric Holder is wrong when he advocates metaphorically "kicking" those of Trump's ilk. Michelle Obama was right: "When they go low, we go higher." At the very least, Democrats should not forget who they are or hope to be.

A Manifesto for Democratic Messaging

1. Succinctly define the ploy and essential absurdity of antithetical reality as practiced by Trump. There is no need to belabor the point - a few apt examples of Trump's playbook and/or his strategy based on self-absorbed need will suffice. His words have no meaning, couched as they are in the purpose of simply maintaining his position.

2. Consider the use of strategy in your own party. That is, admit that you, too, have been mesmerized by strategy as it relates to the procurement of votes and power.

The Democratic Party ought to utilize planning, not merely to win elections, and erroneously assuming that great ideas of serving all of the people will follow. Energy needs to be spent on strategy (and messaging thereof) as to specific ways of improving governance amid issues of concern. What specifically will you do to ensure fair elections? What programs will be developed to support gender equality? How will you create a fair tax system? How will you react to climate change - with regard to real legislation that will consider fossil-fuel job-loss and the creation of "green" jobs? Most important, to whom will you turn for help in developing your strategies?

3. Create sub-committees that partake of the great minds of science, technology, economics, and so forth, as you develop your agenda. Get out of the bubble of your own political cadre. You are not the answer; rather, you are the conduit for answers. Remembering the old adage, "Actions speak louder than words," provide studied substance rather than emotional entertainment.

And if you think all of the above is merely "snowflake-idealism," you have missed my point. The current choice is simple: idealism or cynicism, status quo or growth, in other words, democracy v. stasis and, ultimately, autocratic rule. History is littered with the relics of cultures felled by hubris and attendant immorality.

Though I find the word, exceptionalism, somewhat smug in perceived tone, in lieu of a different word, I submit that said exceptionalism - if indeed it still exists (and I believe it does) arises with its premise of the seemingly impossible endeavor of seeking perfection in a country of many peoples, of striving voices clamoring to be heard - a belief in a country that touts the experiment over worn-out ideas, a country that is willing to share power.

It all comes down to the "king of the mountain" v. the mountain itself - this experiment of democracy that flourishes with the continuous flux of intellectual ideas connected with an inherent morality. This morality sees the promise of humanity as a whole - rather than the transient, cynical use of humanity.

In short, it seems to me the Democratic Party will prevail if, and only if, it finds its idealistic voice and exercises the humanistic hope that defines appropriate leadership.

Fear Only the Loss of the Collective

Like a maelstrom, the ego-driven, power-mad entity seeks to destroy

everything beyond himself

A tornado born of a peculiar confluence of destructive, fomenting forces

- amid an erratic break-down of morality, decency, truth

We are witnessing the individual in place of the collective
 - a would-be autocrat poised to destroy the very notion of democracy

From whence this need to destroy?
For power-ecstasies? For validation?

Relentless is the maelstrom
- while it lasts

And all things pass...
The tornado wears itself out - the destroyer is inevitably destroyed

Yet, the carnage left behind... The innocents lost
The ideals squandered

All in the name of an absurd madness

- the appeals to hatred - initially through name-calling, derision

Later through senseless bullying, and the inability to reason
- to countenance anything beyond self

To hold onto individualism - at all costs
Never perceiving the future, attendant and sure self-annihilation

Why does destruction resonate beyond the perpetrator?

Why are others drawn to support or to turn a blind eye?

Why do they not see?
In the destruction of the collective,
the eventual destruction of themselves?

Destruction comes from within - when divisions are stoked

- when fear of the other sets in - when egoism replaces the idea of
oneness,

a country of promise

Fear not the caravan of women and children

Fear not the person of a misunderstood or denied religious-faith

Fear the loss of empathy

Fear the loss of reason

Fear the loss of democracy

- unraveled by individualism in extremis

And see your part in all this

An American Funeral

George H.W. Bush passed, and the nation paused to honor a man of integrity, humility and service. At once a public and very private experience transpired, the quintessential American funeral. Amid the pomp and circumstance befitting a leader of stature, came the realization that George H.W. Bush potentially represented us all.

And I must admit that as I mused on the solemnity of a great man's passing, I wished that all souls understood the preciousness of all lives or that the world saw fit to pause for each and every individual. I believe the late president would agree with this notion, for had he not paused for the deaths of his (WWII) co-pilots? In a sense he lived in that place of connection. Profound empathy was the result of that pause - as was a perceived mission to know truth and love, to partake of life joyfully.

In essence, the funeral of George H.W. Bush celebrated fellowship - the greatest and most befitting honor of all. Amid the pomp and circumstance, the solemn hymns and psalms, in the place of a soaring testament to a belief in all goodness, spoke a love born of empathy. For a time, we were of the Bush family. Familiar were the memories, the humor, the tears shed despite a valiant attempt for essential dignity

- this not a failure but providing the gift of vulnerability - recognized by all who have lost a parent. In that moment we were as one, profoundly human, rising above the chillier notions of decorum or self-importance. In that moment we mirrored the best qualities of George H. W. Bush. I imagined him smiling in response.

EQ

One does not need a genius-IQ to understand that our country is teetering on the brink of profound disaster. One can no longer rebut with arguments in the nature of: "They're all crooks," thereby relinquishing any responsibility for the Frankenstein that lives in the White House.

One does not need to be a Peter Salovey (President of Yale and well-known scholar of emotional-intelligence) to know intuitively that a virtually non-existent EQ (emotional intelligence quotient) leads to a virtually non-existent IQ. In other words, those with severe emotional hang-ups also exhibit neural hang-ups as regards intellectual processing; circuits of reason and creative thought are blocked when emotional obsessions take hold.

One does not need to be an eminent psychologist to take note of Trump's "look at me" obsession - to ascertain that he lives in toddler-ville seeking the constant attention and the adulation of quasi Mums or Dads. Trump is incapable of listening to others, incapable of empathy, incapable of seeing beyond himself. Hence, his erratic behavior, his ever-escalating tantrum that manifests as the attention-span of an infant. Personal need is everything to Trump.

One did not need to reach this point: coddling a president who fired would-be colleagues on the whim of perceived disloyalty (Comey, Sessions), accepting a president who forced those of intellect and experience to flee their posts, citing an unwillingness to serve an unprincipled governance (example, Mattis), a president who clings to a soon-to-be decreasing base as the lies become more frequent and the danger inherent in Trump's small world-view becomes increasingly evident.

Witness the disrespect of our allies, note the nascent disruption of a world-wide economy, watch our foes chortle with glee, (tellingly) referring to our president merely as Donald (the easily manipulated boy). More important, acknowledge those of little power who will suffer the consequences of one who represents the antithesis of empathy and/or intellect based on morality and emotional intelligence.

Eschew the notion that our country is now the laughing-stock of the world, as such an idea misses the point in these dire times. We are more than a grandiose symbol of might and power. At least we used to be.

And could be again. It is not yet too late.

Addendum: Evil is defined by unchecked selfishness. Evil is stupid as well, for no man is immortal nor an island. The collective is all, and the collective always triumphs ultimately.

A Bridge

I sit in judgment
- the required place of the voter-spectator

Aware of lies, cruelties

Unwittingly a player in a fantasy-game

Winner takes all...
The end justifies all amoral means

The movie plays out - a simplistic antidote to life - where villainy is despised

We watch our villain with horror while we eschew all complexity as to why and how such leadership came to pass

Surprised were we
Surprised was he
It never should have come to pass...

The public man, ironically the showman of the ages,
adheres to the notion:
"All the world's a stage, and all the men merely players."

And many in the audience see a comedy of errors but not an underlying tragedy

- What of the private man?
Is he lost in the play or in play?

I cannot judge the private man. I do not know.

I long for a bridge to reality - a place where reason
 - honest attempts to understand –
replace the faux, machismo tactics of the cheesy, good v. evil script

I fear we have succumbed to the easy alternatives of mind-numbing games
and the escapist's film.

Turkey in my Craw

The humorless Trump-roast persists
Daily...

Five new lies to report as well as the latest outrages
 (to deflect from prior outrages)

Red meat for the informed...

Always, the turkey responds: "Fake news!"

Dark meat for a rapacious audience
(along with fodder for the ensuing Trump-roast)

In the battle for the deli department

there is no winner - at least not yet....

The turkey is relentless
And to be fair, Trump-roasters are indefatigable, too
(Thank goodness)

Though I consider vegetarianism, for my health's sake,
the turkey's in my craw

- And unlike the singer of "Jimmy Crack Corn" (and Melania Trump in her infamous jacket)

I still care.

Will the master be jettisoned? Soon?

As the Audience Turns

A insults Trump.

Trump insults A...

X insults Trump. Trump insults X. Y insults Trump. Trump insults Y. Z insults Trump. Trump insults Z...

Viewer: "WTF has usurped the WWF (re: relentlessly pointless entertainment) BORING!!"

The Centipede and Donald J. Trump

Lily, the cat, and I visited the vet as we do frequently in order to have her necessary subcutaneous-fluids administered. Invariably, light conversations ensue - the following about the instinctual "intelligence" of bugs. Said vet, upon admission of a loathing for "super-speedy" and wily centipedes, described an incident that should have been filmed, such was its comedic value.

Picture this: 1. Revolting centipede travels blithely across a kitchen floor. 2. Vet spots and attempts to catch and mash into oblivion. 3. Vet too slow. 4. Centipede finds refuge under a piece of furniture. 5. With flashlight in hand, vet discovers centipede tucked away in an "impossible to get to" place. 6. Vet pretends to leave the room by faking receding footfalls. *7.* Centipede pokes his head out from under piece of furniture, spots vet and ducks back once more. 8. Vet marvels at the centipede's remarkable, instinctual intelligence. 9. Vet decides to ignore centipede. 10. A few days later, centipede decides to decamp of his own volition through an open backdoor.

End of story.

A Particularly Apt Metaphor:

Trump is a centipede. Wily, ruled by instinctual intelligence only, he's managed to make fools of appropriately thinking people. Ignore his twitter feed lest you, too, become just another 100-legged insect. Focus on his actions instead. Gather up and explain the import of edicts and illegal ploys accomplished. Like the centipede, Trump will eventually exit out the backdoor.

Not end of story. The bug will be gone, cause for celebration, but we'll be left to pick up the pieces: fractured norms and shaken institutions.

Stupid or Smug - Which is Worse?

Now that we live in an age of entertainment-news, which is worse, stupid or smug?

Believe me, I tried to view all cable news options, to find an outlet that fairly reported on the news of the day, even within the entertainment-context. It came down to stupid v. smug. On one channel I could watch emotionally-wrought individuals bellow nonsense rarely couched in discernible fact. On another network, I viewed less emotion, but this was not all to the good. Too often, pundits evinced a tired smugness, certain of their superior understanding of the "poor, duped" followers of Trump, certain that they were on the moral side of politics. Disheartening....

The practice of stupidity may indicate an honest misunderstanding; though, one suspects said misunderstanding often has at its root a desire for self-interest above all else. Practicing smugness, unwittingly or not, exacerbates division among citizenry in cruel fashion and even overrides material of provable truth. Both stupidity and smugness engender the emotional response of the viewer primarily, and this bodes not well for thoughtful choice as to those we elect to important offices.

Emotion defined the 2016 election and continues to clog our airwaves today. So, we react with disdain for all players in the political field in our own ways. We look for "inauthentic" miens, or conversely, we condemn boorish behavior. Unwittingly impotent, we take to judging contenders in junior-high-school jargon. Where is the meat of political substance in all this? Lost in stupid or smug. Lost in entertainment that has no business driving the news-cycle.

Do you not long for the days of Walter Cronkite? No, we can't go back to white, male dominance of news-purveying; it's true. However, Cronkite's every-man demeanor, his essential dryness in the purpose of conveying fact, cannot be faulted. We did not expect Cronkite to entertain us, nor did we seek his validation. Equally important, Walter Cronkite did not view himself as a star. But that was when objectivity was a watch-word, not just for news anchors, but perhaps throughout the experience of the electorate?

The Unwitting Promotion of an Ugly Game

Inherent are the pros and cons of the ubiquitous news-coverage made available through television, radio and the internet. Certainly the "real-time" minutiae of politics and governance are provided for the electorate, details often omitted during the days of mostly "evening news" coverage. Yet, the quality of today's fare, too often of reality-show caliber, engenders a mere curiosity as to "What happens next?" - rather than a sophisticated understanding of substantive concerns. In essence, the minutiae become the story and/or substance is clouded with the experience of common entertainment. More important, big ideas fall prey to an unrelenting focus on political strategy.

Case in point: the constant reference to Trump's base, roughly 40% of the populace. Aside from inordinate attention paid to a distinct minority, such coverage unwittingly enhances cruel manipulation. A faux importance (in the minds of Trump-supporters) takes hold, certainly as regards Trump's true feeling for them. It is clear that Trump cares little about the experience of the angry and ignored, particularly as to policy (tax policy, for instance, that benefits the uber-wealthy most of all). Also, the president's overt derision of his base: "I love my base, the uneducated" (by which he means the easily manipulated), though made clear, somehow becomes a derision paradoxically lost in the fray of the subterfuge of strategy.

Trump is not the only culprit in the business of dispensing cruelty. The attention paid to the base, as it relates to electoral outcomes, promotes the false notion that Trump supporters are heard, that policy, meant to address concerns and work for equitable outcomes, will ensue - this amid a shutdown that hurts, not one whit, the self-satisfied wealthy, but rather those who live paycheck to paycheck. (And an emboldened Trump then had the audacity to gleefully state: "Most are willing to forgo a paycheck to pay for my wall" - or words to that effect.) Trump lives by cruel strategy. No substance is revealed with regard to long-term plans engendering upward mobility or a level playing-field for all Americans. Yes, he loves his base, but only as an audience for his personal rage, and as the manipulated in his quest for personal power.

When the visual media, especially, relentlessly report on "the power of Trump's base," they abet Trump's Machiavellian strategy. Once again, it is cruel to create false hope among the base. Some might argue that it is base to dwell on the base with regard to imagined political outcomes. It is also cruel not to understand the denial of substance; enhancing the reality-show quality of current governance results in the ultimate cruelty of incompetence.

Many television journalists, especially commentators and "analysts," too often act as referees in a senseless, strategic game. And so, I say to particular practitioners of the media: "In the era of Trump, you, too, have been duped." Also, I suggest that news-purveyors consider the following analogy: A competent parent does not entertain the absurd arguments of a recalcitrant toddler. "No more!" suffices. Perhaps the thoughtful journalist's practice of such an adult stance will catch on. Perhaps even the Senate will follow suit, eventually. I'd like to think that substance and statesmanship will again serve our nation.

One Last Rant

Please spare me the specious argument having to do with the supposed "unfair" and "corrosive" hatred of Trump. I have heard various renditions of the following from acquaintances (and politicians during television interviews): "Those folks just hate Trump, and such a stance is wrong." Am I to overlook the hypocrisy evident in such a statement? Are Trump supporters blind when it comes to Trump's mode of operating? Is puerile name-calling, especially when combined with comment on others' physical appearances - and even physical malady - not hateful?

Let me be very clear: I do not hate Donald Trump, though I consider much of his behavior to be eminently despicable. There is a difference, you see. I do not wish Donald J. Trump ill. Rather, I wish him enlightenment with regard to his mendacious and ultimately self-destructive path. I am also cognizant of the self-harm the practice of pure hatred engenders. I do not wish to live in that emotional wasteland. However, a citizen's right and, more important, a citizen's duty, require me to react unequivocally to practiced amorality and incompetence.

Bearing Witness provides ample criticism of Trump's behavior; it's true. Yet, I have (for the most part) deliberately avoided puerile name-calling and mostly any reference to Trump's physical appearance. On one occasion I referred to his hair as a "Cheez-it 'do" within the context of a fictional story. I admit here and now that such a ploy, meant to provide cheap humor, was beneath me. Mea culpa, sincerely. I reserve the right to employ metaphors having to do with infants, however.

I submit that the calling out of Trump critics as "haters" is a studied, political ploy. (It must be written down in a playbook somewhere - so often has it been tried.) Such a ploy illustrates another instance of antithetical reality, the promulgation of untruth. Hypocrisy and/or lying to oneself is not only intellectually unsound, it promulgates confusion and destructive emotion, a precursor, ironically, to unthinking hatred.

So, please do not waste your time by calling me a "hater." I'm not having it. In return, I shall scrupulously consider all rhetorical ploys of my own making with regard to verisimilitude and honest usefulness.

Who Needs Ann Coulter?

The simple answer to such a question is no one, for Ms. Coulter's stock in trade is destruction: first, foremost, always. Her metaphorical stiletto-heels wound and ultimately crush those within her ken - without exception. There are no allies in the worship of destruction, only erstwhile connections groomed for ultimate humiliation or worse.

Witness the evisceration of Donald Trump - played like the mouse-toy that he is. In Coulter's consciousness, at least publicly, other individuals are merely mouse-toys, and she is the cat-woman, sans a cat's nuanced sensibilities.

The more complex answer to the question: "Who needs Ann Coulter?" has to do with those who relish her cruel put-downs and smug rejoinders, those who rejoice in another's evisceration - this stemming from suppressed rage (sometimes justified or, at least, understood) as to a chaotic, often unjust, world.

Yet, rage begets rage. Destruction knows no boundaries. Whoever delights in the downfall of others, fails to register the target on his own back. Destruction simply morphs when relished - eventually affecting all of those who partake. The only immunity to destruction is absolute denial of its validity. In other words, admitting that the victimization of one person is the prelude to the victimization of all.

To deny Ann Coulter's game, to refuse to abet her essential narcissism, is to inoculate against hate. Realizing that narcissism is but a cover for self-loathing and the fear of proximity to others, one ought not express rage nor harbor hatred toward or in the name of Ann Coulter; rather, cease to listen, avoid the trap, the destructive talons.

Quick Review: Seven Deadly Sins

Religious teachings have much to do with living well, avoiding behavior that proves detrimental to self and others. The seven deadly sins encapsulate the essence of immorality. They are as follows: pride, greed, lust, envy, gluttony, wrath, sloth. Unfortunately, Donald Trump is wed to all seven. Examples follow: Pride ("I know more than the generals.") Greed (Trump's mode of operation involves the relentless amassing of wealth, power, attention). Lust (reported, multiple, gratuitous affairs). Envy (the impetus for greed, evident in attacks on others who are perceived as potentially or actually successful). Gluttony (over-spending). Wrath (ubiquitous in Trump's speech, constant belittlement of opponents, especially evident in puerile name-calling). Sloth (Trump eschews the hard work necessary for study (reading, thinking] in favor of "entertainment news.").

Trump's one hundred percent compliance with established sins ought to matter.

Immorality in Motion

Sin frequently

Sin openly

Eschew intellect

Celebrate emotion

Deny others

Feed self

Revere rage

Disparage mercy

Don victim-hood

Maim opponents

Bury truth

Destroy

No Work, No Pay

How's this for an idea? Until government officials produce the effects of hard work rather than the drivel of game-playing, we see to it that their paychecks are withheld. I know, pie in the sky, wishful thinking. But seriously, in the real world, employees are expected to work with tangible results ensuing. The latest examples of political bridge-playing (political finessing) and "I win" attitudes - ignoring the mountain in a puerile endeavor to proclaim "I'm king of the mountain" - are but cynical replays of other shut-downs, other missed opportunities to honestly serve all of the citizens of this country, behavior all-too-prevalent in the last decade, especially.

I've said it before, and, unfortunately, I will no doubt will be saying it again many times: The country-club set, those who have managed to wrangle power, are clueless as to the experience of average Americans. Moreover, they are addicted to the inevitable perks of "being important." Yet, the grandeur of democracy lies not in hallowed halls inhabited by grand-standers - grifters who are constantly looking to win the next election or bolster a dubious power. (You know who you are. More to the point, we now know who you are.) Rather, the grandeur of democracy is reflected in a citizenry of hard-working people those who understand that work often offers its own reward, idealistic folk who are able to see beyond themselves. These people do not seek accolades, applause or the constant attention reminiscent of childhood need.

Though we may not be able to garner paychecks, I think that Republicans, especially, should be forewarned as to the change that is sure to follow the debacle of current governance. Sooner rather than later, those who have been overlooked, taken for granted and marginalized will see to it that the "old guard" is replaced. Get yourselves ready for political support for those who understand the plight of minorities, women - the less moneyed.

Power-mongers often over-play their hands as we have witnessed. When selfish behavior is brazenly exhibited, it is clear to all that hubris reigns. (The emperor really has no clothes; moreover, he doesn't care.) Cue the idealists: "Enough is enough!" they'll say. They will begin to believe in the possibility of freedom from the cruelly mislabeled "Citizens United" subterfuge. They will begin to believe in themselves. I do believe that change is coming for 2020 and beyond.

Fellow citizens, please make this happen. Contrary to perceived, current governance, "This land is your land..." Don't relinquish your say as to what happens next, your power.

The Undeserving Rich

George Bernard Shaw's *Pygmalion,* first presented to the public just prior to the Great War at a time of enormous economic disparity in Britain (think Downton Abbey), uncovered the grand hypocrisy of a class-society and the unabashed worship of powerful positions stemming from wealth. Interestingly enough, it is Shaw's creation of the character of Alfred Doolittle, the uneducated, honest scoundrel, who speaks to this madness of "morality" based on acquisition:

"I'm one of the undeserving poor; that's what I am. Think of what that means to a man. It means that he's up against middle-class morality all the time. If there's anything going, and I put in for a bit of it, it's always the same story: 'You're undeserving, so you can't have it.' But my needs is as great as the most deserving widow's that ever got money out of six different charities in one week for the death of the same husband. I don't need less than a deserving man: I need more. I don't eat less hearty than him; and I drink a lot more. I want a bit of amusement, cause I'm a thinking man. I want cheerfulness and a song and a band when I feel low. Well, they charge me just the same for everything as they charge the deserving. What is middle-class morality? Just an excuse for never giving me anything."

Most recently, a condominium on Central Park South in Manhattan sold for 240 million dollars to one hedge fund manager - whose contribution to society has to do with the amassing of great wealth. His New York property will be used only sporadically, as essentially said billionaire is in the business of collecting abodes. Perhaps this latest acquisition could be compared to the bygone grand estates of

Britain, the fictional Downton Abbey, and the other myriad great-houses such as Castle Howard. In any event, the Central Park South apartment will likely remain darkened for much of each year, along with various other properties ubiquitous on the East Side but also in other cities around the country, indeed, around world, as the moneyed class engages in conspicuous consumption for the fun of it.

I think that it is fair to say that the "aristocracies" of all ages have rarely asked themselves: "Am I deserving of my good fortune?" Nor does the middle-class, for the most part, question the amassing of astounding wealth. Rather, the titans are revered, not for enhancing the experience of a larger society, but for merely accomplishing a personal feat.

And yet, we have seen this movie before. We've witnessed, historically speaking, the Great Depression following a Gilded Age; we've seen the demise of the great estates of Britain. We remember callousness in the statement: "Let them eat cake." Nothing good comes of vast economic-inequality. We know this, or we should. Even the titans eventually suffer.

Several current Democratic contenders for the 2020 presidential election espouse increased taxes on the ultra-wealthy, those making $10 million dollars per year (per year!) while four in ten Americans do not possess $400 in savings for a rainy day. Why is such a plan seen as unworkable or unfair? I remember the prosperity of this country under Eisenhower when the rich were taxed fairly. Higher education was afforded GIs, a vast highway system was installed, a solid middle-class was created. Metaphorically, the whole country was lifted to meet its promise.

Donald Trump recently stated: "Don't believe what you see." Really? Sorry, Donald, no dice. I see hubris, corruption, ultimate folly. I see the evil of selfishness on full display. Yet, I remain hopeful that legions of others will remember past debacles and will see a way forward.

(By the way, the character of Alfred Doolittle has the jump on Donald Trump, for Doolittle was an honest man... and a thinking man, to boot.)

Finding Equanimity

We currently speak of immutable change evidenced by migrations, social upheaval and, underlining all of this, climate change. And it's also true we are but specks in the big picture, though we live as though we are the center of it all. (The individual can't seem to get away from a finite consciousness.) Yet, awareness tells us that migrations and social upheaval have existed throughout history. (I recently was made aware of the idea that migration rather than conflicting religions precipitated the troubles in Northern Ireland, for instance.) However, climate change ups the ante to cataclysmic proportion eventually: the demise of our planet as we know it.

We are always witnessing the beginning of demise personally and now globally; however, it seems to me that the short term is especially relevant, even as we ponder the long term. Ever-increasing inequality bespeaks a desperation among wealth-holders; too often, hoarding is employed as a hedge against inevitable loss.

If we are to break through a finite, self-generated understanding of experience, perhaps our best option lies in developing more awareness of the present experience of others - fueling compassion, empathy -

and in those small moments of connection, we may see fit to replace ultimate loss with useful memory and associations of equanimity, if not peace.

Power

When I was 12, just beginning to question the ways of the world, and mightily disgruntled with the poor quality of school lunches, it suddenly occurred to me that students vastly out-numbered the adults in our sphere. There was no way that "the powers that be" could easily counter an uprising, should we stage one - and stick together, a big proviso. Of course, nothing much came of such a thought-process. I suspect that underlying my bravado was a very real fear as to what would follow.

However, it did occur to me that a small "fighting-back," as to school lunches, might effect some change. Here was my plan: When asked (as we were each morning) whether or not we would be partaking of the offering for the next day, all students would reply in the affirmative. When the next day arrived, none would eat the school lunch but would enjoy home-brought fare instead. And this is where the memory ends. I know that we went through with the plan. However, I don't remember the broader outcome, just lunch-ladies standing about with nothing to do. I suspect the adults simply chose to ignore our rebellion as something finite, which it was, of course.

Obviously, we cope with issues of power throughout our lives, and the Frederick Douglass quote, "Power cedes nothing without demand," bears repeating. A failure to stand up, certainly in the face of injustice, most would argue, illustrates a cowardice and profound ethical-negation. Though we are like twelve-year-old children in a sense, often finding ourselves cowed by the enormity of those who

314

control our workplaces, and more to the point, our country, we ought not cede our adult power through ignorance, narcissism, general weakness - or any of the other limitations of childhood.

The powerful adult sees her place in the scheme of things: seeks to overcome her own ignorance, fosters (in herself) an awareness of others beyond her immediate circle - eventually gaining strength by way of principled thought, and appropriate action. Put another way, the powerful individual lives in the realm of ethical responsibility - remembering the questioning that began on the cusp of maturation, remembering the optimistic certainty inherent in standing up for what is "fair" and "right," two words inevitably and frequently used by idealistic, uncompromising youngsters - and called once again to the fore by inspired, autonomous grownups.

This is the power that resists its faux counterpart: tyranny.

Addendum: Excerpt from another manuscript, *Sharing My Women's Stories*

"Indifference, perhaps the most insidious of all cruelties, spawns an equitable society's own demise. In the end, the love of power upends the power of love, and all of those involved is such a fallacy of thought (sadly enough, often unwittingly) suffer an ultimate corruption. And we who witness, but fail to speak up, bear responsibility for the continuance of the degradation of our best selves."

The Insidious Banality of Trump

With the insidious banality of Trump, the risk of his fondest wish, an alternative reality, becomes possible. When the outrageous becomes banal due to relentless expression, fatigue sets in. There is only so much garbage one can process before waste wins.

Witness the rhythm of Trump's expression: outlandish vulgarity and proven lies manically spewed during rallies (and in tweets) using a bellicose voice, this followed by the texture of his delivery in White House settings - the use of a dropped voice, a matter-of-fact, nearly emotionless, soothing voice - that which reveals the hypnotist at work. The back and forth of the hypnotist's medal on chain is an apt analogy for the diametrically opposed voices of Trump.

The prior paragraph describes the public Trump. One imagines a truly terrified, private Trump - when his own self-hypnosis abates, when reality looms - perhaps only momentarily. Reality represents danger to Trump, something to be avoided at all costs. Something he trusts the public will deny at all costs as well, for Trump, in delusion, will rearrange the world to his liking for as long as he is allowed to do so.

It is up to those he would hypnotize, with his waste heaped upon waste, to awaken - to end the madness, not with surreptitious planning, but with truth proclaimed in sunlight fearlessly and vociferously. To do otherwise is to enter into a fateful temptation - where reality is apt to end not with "a bang, but a whimper" - insidiously and fearfully becoming the ignominious alternative-reality of autocratic lore.

"Enemy of the people!" Bosh! Rather, the fourth estate enables reality for the people: consciousness and voice.

A Bogus Father-Figure: Above the Law, Above the People

The Mueller Report, more correctly renamed the Barr Report at this point in time, hints at the notion of presidential immunity from charges of obstruction. Absurdly, we are to assume that the very position of president precludes an obstruction challenge (as in firing Comey because of "the Russia thing.") Also, we are to swallow: "A

316

sitting president may not be indicted for alleged crimes." Really? Was Donald Trump correct when he gleefully stated something on the order of: "I could shoot someone on Fifth Avenue and get away with it?" We are witnessing the arrogance and the anti-intellectualism of rank power.

During childhood, when questioning my mother's authority, I was occasionally stymied by the following edict: "Because I'm the mother, and I said." One accepts such a power-play in context; parental power is deemed acceptable when one is inexperienced and learning to cope with a complicated world. Yet, to bow down to unchecked power in politics is to relinquish adulthood, to become childlike or worse: mere pawns in an insidious game of manipulation.

Absurdity heaped upon absurdity: Our essentially puerile president, he of the "Me, Only, Movement," enjoys the adult role associated with power while many secondary "adults" of governance cede their positions of authority, core beliefs and ultimately their maturity.

Absurdity heaped on absurdity: President Trump has often admitted his attempts to obstruct, publicly without a hint of self-consciousness, and once stated: "It is more important that I am believed than what I say is true." Thus, brazen bravado counters suspicions of subterfuge and ill intent; in other words, paradoxically - knowingly or not - Trump "honestly" manipulates. Put simply, a devious con makes way for a regressive kingdom; our democracy is presently undermined by the would-be boy-prince, abetted by other power-hungry courtiers.

The United States ought to stand by and for us. Conversely, we ought to relinquish the need for bogus father-figures, anointed "kings" and/or children in disguise. We, the people, must deny edicts, lies and destructive game-playing. Our intrinsically moral and intellectual adult-power, if acknowledged, might right the wrongs and/or prevail

317

- for the sake of subsequent generations - for the sake of our country's basic premise: "of the people, for the people."

The Mueller Report should be released to the appropriate committee of Congress in its entirety. Public admissions of obstruction in no way indicate that obstruction has not occurred. Quite the opposite.

The Playbook of Anti-Intellectualism

I witnessed Senator Kennedy of Louisiana, the latest partaker of the anti-intellectualism playbook, state that it was clear many were disappointed with the results of the Mueller Report (what they've seen of it - very little). He went on to refer to the old saw: "We're only young once, but may remain immature indefinitely." Thus, he insinuated that those who dare to question Barr's summary are merely puerile individuals emotionally prone to a "sour grapes" reaction. There is no intellectual substance to this argument, based as it is on assumption. Some individuals prefer to come to a conclusion based on substantive evidence of the actual report, denied thus far - to Congress (including Mr. Kennedy) as well as the public. To essentially resort to name-calling ("immature") is to support the demeaning language so often employed by President Trump. Such rhetoric is meant to stir emotions; it is the antithesis of objective, intellectual argument.

We've seen this movie before. When protesters gathered to decry the early-day policies of Trump, they were often deemed "sore losers" by Fox News, by sundry politicians and, of course, by Trump. "Hillary lost. Get over it!" became a rallying cry. Yet, it seemed that no one was more focused on Hillary Clinton than Trump himself. He remains so to this day.

The Democrats lost. Republicans were solely in power for two years. However, rather than bearing responsibility for legislation not passed, Trump, in particular, chooses to place blame on others, specifically Obama. Some have noted that Trump has been known to resort to outright lies, for example: "Obama started wide-spread separation of families at the border." The truth is the Obama administration separated families only when adults were accused of felonies. Crossing the border illegally is a misdemeanor, and it was Trump who separated families on this basis.

As long as members of Congress persist in anti-intellectual stances, appealing to emotion rather than remaining laser-focused on facts as they emerge, as long as members of Congress view their roles as protectors of party over principle, confusion reigns and ultimate truth becomes less of a certainty. None of us have seen the Mueller Report, written by a special counsel with the premise of objectivity based on law. Until more of the report is viewed more widely, none can speak with any intellectual depth as to conclusions. We simply do not know. Mr. Kennedy's ruse of name-calling and appeal to emotion is but one small, yet insidious, example of behavior that is beneath the dignity of democratic governance.

Another Strategy in the Playbook: Exhaust the Public

Though it may be naive to hope for a speedy resolution to issues relating to the Mueller Report, one cannot help but note a protracted process, perhaps unnecessary, as players now appear to be resorting to "running the clock," to invoke basketball-parlance.

Barr attempted to end the game with brief, "bottom-line" pronouncements, knowing full well that his amended "Cliff Notes" version would not stand. However, his opinion was out there and left out there for a purpose. The vacuum of no substance, as to Mueller's findings, was quickly filled with emotionalism, a continued entrenchment of public opinion on the right and on the left. With little information to contemplate, the "teams" continue to dribble the ball of speculation.

But the basketball-metaphor is misleading in a sense. Running the clock near the end of a game of basketball heightens suspense, and any particular basketball match-up is blessedly finite. The investigation of Russian interference, necessarily careful and protracted in its unfolding, now sits in abeyance while the game of stone-walling and obfuscation plays out.

At this point in time, three weeks out, only Barr has spoken. He holds the court, and he will continue to do so for as long as possible. Why have we heard not one word from the Mueller team - their own brief and carefully constructed summaries? I maintain that any on-going suspense has been carefully countered with measured ennui; in other words, vague promises to "release soon" enable the implementation of a well-thought-out strategy meant to exhaust the public.

Unfortunately, exhausting the public is not a new strategy in the playbook of politicians. Gridlock has been the order of the day for over a decade. Speaking as a former worker who met deadlines with day-to-day productivity, I see the current game of strategy over substance in our governance as abhorrent. In fact, I see it as immoral.

When Unseemly Approaches Unlawful

Attorney General Barr's press conference of April, 18, 2019 could easily be characterized as unseemly. Couched in carefully rendered legalese, Barr's pronouncements, as the self-appointed arbiter of Mueller's report, failed to acknowledge Mueller's own words as to

Trump's alleged obstruction, a denied full-exoneration of the president with provided examples of Trump's obstructive behavior. For reasons we do not yet understand, Mueller provided no definitive conclusion. Leaving this up to Congress? In any event, Barr chose the mantle of the final arbiter of truth and chose to do so before the report was released to Congress or the public. This behavior is clearly unseemly. Perhaps it is, in and of itself, obstructive as well.

As so much of Trump's alleged obstructive-behavior was publicly viewed, Barr pivoted to the notion of Trump's intent. Ludicrously, Barr spoke of "frustration" on the part of the president, as if emotion excused such statements as, "Russia, if you're listening, I hope you find Hillary's 30,000 emails." Openly courting malfeasance does not negate malfeasance, quite the contrary. Furthermore, frustration does not entitle the president to behave in an undermining-of-our-country-fashion. Such behavior is clearly unseemly. Unlawful? Mueller's Report was meant to answer that question, though up until now, the special counsel's own words have been eclipsed. We witness the unseemly and possibly something even more egregious.

I'm no Lawyer nor Legislator, But...

"All are equal under the law."

According to the Office of Legal Counsel, a sitting president may not be indicted for criminal behavior.

There exists a statute of limitations (five years) with regard to indicting Donald Trump for his alleged obstruction of the Mueller investigation.

Were Donald Trump to win re-election, the statute of limitations might be surpassed well before the end of his second term. In that case, Trump would skirt possible criminal-liability.

"All are equal under the law except presidents" - unless some accommodation is made with regard to the statute of limitations.

Mueller has produced viable evidence as to obstruction; however, he may not indict. It seems to me the statute of limitations should be extended to cover the time of the president's protection from prosecution (his time in office) - especially given the memorialization of witness-testimony. Otherwise, "All are equal under the law" morphs into an undeniable falsehood.

Donny One-Note

The White House daily spews its "hit parade" of tired songs: "No Collusion," "Witch-Hunt," "Fake News" and "Build the Wall!" There have been no ditties added to the play-list for the duration of this presidency, just riffs on said exhausted themes. Perhaps this is the point. Inane tunes often become lodged in the brain forming persistent "ear-worms" of little substance, the repetition mesmerizing, eventually deadening neurons that could be put to better use.

I do not necessarily fault those who succumb to the pointless barrage, for like the dripping of water on a hard surface, relentless repetition serves as a kind of torture producing the inevitable erosion of freedom of thought - denying individuality and wearing down the will to question or seek nuance. Caught in a weird time-warp of one-note sameness, folks come to wait for the inevitable chime of the clock. And nothing seems to change for the good, at least not yet.

I do fault those in the thick of things: Donny One-Note, perpetually and literally wed to one note on the musical scale ("mi" - translated ME!) and, even more so, a fearful, sycophantic back-up chorus, acolytes of selfishness, ego-driven non-intellects - those who roll over or seek a dubious distinction for themselves.

We need to replace mundane, low-brow quasi-tunes with a symphony comprised of wide empathy and honest intellectualism; better yet, let us not settle for less than a celestial choir of transcendent, moral souls. Despite the crude, amoral behavior exhibited over the past few years, the premise of this nation is one of idealism and rectitude. The people produce the leaders; a rediscovery of our latent morality has never been more urgent.

Simply put, reverence for locked-in tunes prohibits essential, broad-based freedom and a resultant redemption.

Hope

Hope implies not "pie in the sky" fantasy nor an unsophisticated belief in the obvious merits of positive thinking. Hope implies resiliency, steadfast intellect, a reigning-in of self-destructive fear.

Hope speaks to possibilities not yet envisioned, the impetus for a creative, meritorious outcome.

Needs be, we deconstruct the past and practice vigilance in the present. However, we must never relinquish hope and our future.

End Note: Pollyanna Speaks

Most people are basically good. I do believe this. However, the world is a complex place as are emotions in response to that which is difficult or demoralizing. Thus, we are a misguided lot - too often. And yet we speak of ultimate fairness, of belief in the creation of a "more perfect union." Though cynicism, fear and anger may batter our country and thereby influence our understanding of existent government, our on-going experiment of democracy is, at its core, an exercise born of promise.

"We, the people" - all of the people - have unalienable rights. We are equal under the law according to our credo. We pledge allegiance to "one nation, under God, indivisible - with liberty and justice for all." It would seem we are audaciously idealistic and serenely hopeful at our best.

And yet, the nation finds itself politically divided to the point of vitriol and hopeless non-cooperation. We witness daily name-calling, belittling language that denies rational discourse. We even partake of the notion of conflicting realities, a misnomer, but more than that, an intellectual journey into potential chaos. Mendacity as well as the attempt to curtail public discourse via the free press undermine the notion of demonstrable reality. When reality is questioned, democracy is at risk.

Reviewing my diary of sorts, *Bearing Witness*, enabled me to note thematic threads that ran through the work: the importance of civility, the notion of emotional intelligence as a precursor to developing intellect, the importance of intellect over mere emotion, the idea that words may serve to destroy or unify, the belief in the development of established virtues.

I quote below from an essay, "The Trouble with Elitism" - a piece I wrote well before the election of Donald Trump, for it is apt now. (Note: "elitism" as discussed here has to do with the privilege of wealth and the too-often, subsequent abuse of power.)

"Elitists often exist apart from the comprehensive reality of a larger world. They are segregated from broad experience and, as a result, are essentially unaware. While elitists may create, they do so in the context of narrow, pragmatic experience, believing that they are all-knowing. When elitists gain inordinate power, humanity is lost. When broad intellectual and artistic expression is maligned, vulgarity and base behavior emerge. As entitlement of a few evolves, ideals of democracy wane, for the ruling-class comes to believe that the masses need 'nurturing through strong leadership' - a convenient cover for the hoarding of treasure and, more important, the limiting of opportunity."

And, in counterpoint, I remind myself of the aphorisms of world philosophies:

Christianity: "Love does not dishonor others; it is not self-serving."

Islam: "No man is a true believer unless he desires for his brother that which he desires for himself."

Judaism: "Love your neighbor as yourself."

Buddhism: "If we fail to look after others, who will look after us?"

Reminding myself, as well, that "this too shall pass away," for I believe that "we the people" shall ultimately relinquish cynicism by choosing optimism, the premise inherent in the ideal of "a more perfect union." I have concluded that to be less than idealistic is to be complicit. I know I am not alone with these thoughts. I write as the representative of many.

P.S. (I Hope This Proves True)

He walked away. It was all he could do.

To those who seek revenge: Let not Beelzebub reign with anger manifested as hate.

Do you not see that he is broken?

We need not continue a contest of thoughtless will.

Let the games cease, the rancor die.

Justice lies in new beginnings.

Provide no attention now to our modern-day Lear - save to learn from his profligate life (stemming from who knows what) - a tragedy.

Let us pause for a moment.

About the Author

Jane Marshall taught English in New Haven, Connecticut public schools for 27 years and was a fellow of the Yale-New Haven Teachers Institute. Published works associated with the Institute include: "Collegiality, Creativity and Continued Learning," "Poetry and Paintings: A Comparative Study" and "American Detectives: On TV and in Books." She received an "Excellence in Teaching" award and was the recipient of the English-Speaking Union's scholarship for summer study at the University of London. That experience and subsequent time spent in England and Scotland fostered a personal objectivity with regard to her own country. She lives in Connecticut with her mainstay, Bill, and their wonder-cat, Lily.

www.ingramcontent.com/pod-product-compliance
Lightning Source LLC
Chambersburg PA
CBHW070409290526
45791CB00005B/1690